# NOTES FROM THE INTERIOR

# *Notes from the Interior*

## Settling in at Heffley Lake

### *by*

## Elizabeth Templeman

OOLICHAN BOOKS

LANTZVILLE, BRITISH COLUMBIA, CANADA

2003

National Library of Canada Cataloguing in Publication Data

Templeman, Elizabeth

Notes from the interior : settling in at Heffley Lake / Elizabeth Templeman.

ISBN 0-88982-220-4

I. Title.

PS8589.E385N67    2003    C813'.6      C2003-910631-4

PR9199.4.T45N67    2003

The Canada Council | Le Conseil des Arts
for the Arts | du Canada

We gratefully acknowledge the support of the Canada Council for the Arts for our publishing program.

BRITISH
COLUMBIA
ARTS COUNCIL
Supported by the Province of British Columbia

Grateful acknowledgement is also made to the BC Ministry of Tourism, Small Business and Culture for their financial support.

Canada

We acknowledge the financial support of the Government of Canada through the Book Publishing Industry Development Program for our publishing activities.

Published by
Oolichan Books
P.O. Box 10, Lantzville
British Columbia, Canada
V0R 2H0

Printed in Canada

## Dedication

*To my mother, Anna Marie Pellicani Miller,*
*with affection and admiration.*

# Acknowledgements

I'm fortunate to have good friends who have been generous in supporting my writing in a multitude of ways. Among them, I am especially grateful to: Philip Garrison, for encouragement and fellowship; Stan Bennett and Susie Safford, for gamely agreeing to read and comment on early drafts; and to GR, for advice.

Thanks to Rob White for allowing me to include his writing. Back cover photographs were taken by Christine Litchfield, Nicole Templeman, and Monty Templeman. Front cover photo by Nicole Templeman. The author photo was taken by Bob Clark.

I am grateful to my editor, Hiro Boga, for her encouragement, and for her attentive and affable manner, and her discerning eye.

Thanks to Monty, above all, and to Nicole, Andrew, and James, for allowing their stories to be told, and for suffering the preoccupation and agitation of a wife and mother who writes— more gratitude than words could convey. Where *ever* would I be without you?

The people mentioned, and no doubt many I have failed to mention, all contributed to the strengths of what follows. Its weaknesses are mine. The accounts included are my rendering: They emanate from my faulty memory, my eyes and ears, and my perspective. There are so many versions of each truth.

# Foreword

In 1782, a man named J. Hector St. John Crevecoeur published *Letters from an American Farmer*. His full name was Michel-Guillaume-Jean de Crevecoeur, but the man called himself "A Farmer in Pennsylvania."

In this volume, published first in London, Crevecoeur set about "describing Certain Provincial Situations, Manners, and Customs, Not Generally Known; and conveying Some Idea of The Late and Present Interior Circumstances of the British Colonies in North America."

Crevecoeur's descriptions of the ideas and manners of the new world were conveyed through letters to Abbé Raynal in England, a friend to the Pennsylvania farmer. "Trifling lucubrations"—insignificant studies produced by lamplight—the writer called his letters.

But Crevecoeur was a sensitive observer, a man with a passionate regard for the natural world, and for the social worlds of community and family. Speaking of the new world settlers of eastern America, he says, "It is not easy for those who seldom saw a tree, to conceive how it is to be felled, cut up, and split into rails and posts." Any settler will tell you so.

As a settler in the interior of British Columbia in the 1980's, I felt disconnected from my past and unconnected to my new surroundings. This area, situated midway between Calgary,

Prince George, and Vancouver—significant points of reference I had barely heard of five years before—looked and even smelled different. The culture was different, too. The social conventions felt as strange to me as this interior landscape did—so very far from the private, tightly lidded landscapes of my New England background.

Trying to assimilate, here in the valley that runs from Heffley Creek to Heffley Lake and on to Tod Mountain, my husband and I were under scrutiny, even as we were aided and supported in our efforts to build a home and a life here. Perhaps it is an aspect of western culture, but it's also a spirit of settlement, I think.

Crevecoeur revered the spirit of the Americans he lived among, two hundred years ago. Yet his words resonated from here in the middle of western Canada, as the twentieth century tipped to a close:

> A great prosperity is not the lot of every man, but there are many and various gradations. . . . After all, is it not better to be possessed of . . . a few sheep pastures; to live free and independent under the mildest governments, in a healthy climate, in a land of charity and benevolence; than to be wretched as so many are . . . possessing nothing but their industry: tossed from one rough wave to another . . . or fettered with the links of the most irksome dependence?

On matters of the home, Crevecoeur refrained from comment, claiming them "unworthy of perusal" and "domestic mysteries adapted only to the locality of the small sanctuary wherein my family resides . . . the narrow circles within which I constantly revolve." As for me, I won't refrain from comment upon those domestic mysteries and all the dizzy wonder of those narrow circles. Because they are so fleeting, I feel compelled to study them; and because so inextricably associated with the culture and landscape around me, I couldn't deflect them even if I wished.

In a sense, it seems that we are all settlers, forever settling, always, everywhere we live. The very idea of settling implies layers of satisfaction, familiarity, reconciling, resolving, making peace. This is where I began.

In the end, what I set out to do in the essays, notes, and smaller bits that follow, was to raise all the questions that I would like to have been able to ask of my grandparents, who made the so much more amazing journey from Italy to the United States at the turn of the last century. How have we gotten here, and why here? Why just then? What kept us here? Why this way, and not another? And who can know how it matters where we live, and when?

There were a good many such questions to ponder, such as: How do we, here and now, think on such things as death, and birth, and marriage? Then there were smaller questions— mundane, yes, but in a sense the concerns which define us: What of grocery shopping, Christmas trinkets, sibling squabbles?

Contemplating the answers has taken me along circuitous paths, which I did not resist. "Trifling lubrications," indeed, but what else would satisfy niggling curiosities about human endeavour?

Elizabeth Templeman
Heffley Lake, B.C.
November 2002

# Contents

*Notes from the Interior*

It didn't matter that the story had begun, because . . . the Great Stories are the ones you have heard and want to hear again. The ones you can enter anywhere and inhabit comfortably . . . They are as familiar as the house you live in . . .

—Arundhati Roy, *The God of Small Things*

To the soul, memory is more important than planning, art more compelling than reason, and love more fulfilling than understanding.

—Thomas Moore, *Care of the Soul*

# Part I

⟶

*Getting Here*

⟶

I spent 1972 to 1980 meandering—from Maine to New York to Ontario to Montana, back to Maine, then out to British Columbia. Though they were years of homelessness, where everything but relationships felt temporary, they were significant years. Looking back, I'd say they were my years of passage, and of maturation.

to meander: to follow a winding or intricate course; to wander aimlessly or casually without urgent destination

—*Merriam-Webster Collegiate Dictionary*

# *Choices*

All morning I've been listening to my children outside playing. They have a friend over to visit, and the three of them are getting along uncommonly well. Their clear voices carry through the west windows so keenly that I expect them to tumble through at any moment, an anticipation that keeps me on edge.

The game that so rivets their attention has been unfolding for nearly two hours. It hasn't begun yet, though. The elaborate planning stage is what I've overheard. It goes something like this: When Nicole asks Sonja to go to the store, if Sonja agrees, then Andrew should run down to the sheep pen and get the store opened; if Sonja says her baby is napping, then Nicole will go get the baby, which would be Andrew, who will have run to the side of the house and made crying sounds. If, on the other hand, Sonja's gone to the store before Nicole gets to her house, then Andrew should be getting pine cones ready for sale.

And undoubtedly, I've gotten some angle wrong. Certainly I've oversimplified. The chain of conditions has been forged then retooled then re-examined for every possible contingency.

I can't much help thinking about their play, which intrigues me. I listen to strings of "no, no, no. You do *this* when she does that. . . . Yeah-but, if she does *that*, then. . . ." I can't

17

imagine how they hold all the accepted choices intact. But they do. They negotiate and wheedle and stand firm and renege in as intricate a set of interactions as I've witnessed in a long time. It's obvious that Andrew, the youngest, has the wildest ideas (an aspect of his character), gets more ideas tossed out (a result of his age), and shouts the loudest to have some impact upon the scheme of things (a combination of vocal chords and tenacity). The oldest child, Sonja, has more leverage, probably due to age as much as temperament. The middle one, imaginative and reserved, takes the role of mediator. But none of the three seems impatient to get on with the game being devised. Which leads me to think that perhaps it's all an exercise in choices—that they aren't so bothered about not getting into the game because setting out the options and making the choices and then examining the possible consequences and implications of those consequences *is* the game. It's like playing life, in a way.

I don't remember setting up games such as this one. But some inkling, something just beyond a memory, suggests that I did. Perhaps it's the familiarity of their banter. And too, there's something about the abrupt way in which I leap to a choice which seems to have been learned. After, I tend to stand by my choice, as though it was the only way for me to go. It becomes such a matter of pride, and of satisfaction—just as it does for the children who play outside.

❧

One place I remember learning to make choices was the public library. The thick granite walls of the Knox County Public Library rose above a slope of grass, meticulously tended. The grandest building of my early years—except for our parish church—its silvery granite blocks formed rectangles and curves, punctuated by high recessed windows.

18

Inside it was brown. Smooth dark wood creaked and echoed. In here, I knew my place: the children's area. But I could wander anywhere, subject to no forbidding frowns or subtle disapproval. Freedom, serenity, and indulgence pervaded this place like the odour of varnish and old books. While I know that others were surely there, that often I went there with friends, my memory is of being pleasantly secluded.

The world was me, and books—as far as I could see, and further. My choices would be a private matter, and even the satisfaction or disappointment they resulted in was private. My selection opened into a world where I could stay until the last page closed me out. I remember finding my way, as if by instinct, to the "twin books," where I happened on the discovery of vastly different ways and times of living. Who could say what was waiting between the covers of *The Twins of the American Revolution,* or *The Twins of 1812?*

I remember other special favourites: slim blue, cloth-bound stories of a girl whose name won't come back to me—some dignified name, Emily, perhaps, or Belinda. This Belinda was definitely *not* of Italian descent like me: not Catholic, dark or slightly plump, the fourth of five children in a family fraught with tensions. *She* was slender, bright and sweet, and she moved with enviable ease through adventures of airplanes, and hospitals, (although maybe memory mixes her with Madeline, so familiar with her appendicitis and rows of beds).

Sometimes I wandered through the rows of thicker books, choosing one whose promise might remain slightly out of reach, pleasingly elusive. Once it was *Jane Eyre*—a red, cloth bound and palm-sized thriller of the scary possibilities for a young girl wandering the town. Another time the biography of Ben Franklin—impressive, but frustratingly mute on the matter of how to grow up a great thinker.

I read my way through whatever I chose, checked out, and

carried home. But the worlds within those books have all dissolved into blurred images. All that remain clear are my memories of choosing them.

☙

Another arena for choice was the neighbourhood store my parents owned. The Market Basket seemed an exhilarating jumble of smells, colours, and tastes. Though I learned much later how this place led to dark family disruptions, during my childhood it represented a safe haven, a surface of comfortable civility. Whatever else seethed beneath, I had more immediate preoccupations.

Outside, the narrow wooden rectangular exterior of our store—years before painted a hopeful red—had blistered and flaked off to reveal grey. Inside, it smelled of pizza sauce, and the nutmeg from fresh-made donuts. In the back, dill pickles floated in their wooden barrel.

I remember my brother, just to the right of the entrance, nearly hidden behind a high counter, creating pizzas and Italian sandwiches. His sandwiches were masterpieces: each one a still-life—the blackness of olives resting on wedges of red tomatoes, green pepper strips lacing the rectangles of meat and cheese, everything glistening with olive oil.

Most of the time I would be busy behind the candy counter. A double-decker of wood-framed glass, the counter ran back along half the length of the store, separated from the pizza counter by a narrow, well-worn aisle. I arranged the bars on the top shelf, the penny candies on the lower. Chocolates had to be back from the warm summer sunlight that spilled in the front door. I filled all the ornate glass dishes, taking care to maintain an appearance of freshness, and of plenty. I took pleasure and pride in the arrangement and composition of the whole image, forever experimenting with contrasts—

red licorice next to black, foil wrap by cellophane, boxes beside bars.

Standing there, I could feel coolness seeping from the ice cream freezers along the front wall. On them, I would stack the boxes of candies being refilled. I don't know why I remember the Nelson chocolate cremes—cloyingly sweet, never a favourite—but their box, when finally empty, held coconut that had jarred loose from the candies. I'd pour it into a small brown bag and bring it home for my mother to bake with.

All those candies crowd my memory: root-beer barrels, red hot fire-balls, malted milk balls ("mop balls," we called them). I know now, wishing I didn't, that their glossy chocolate coating owed its smoothness to a close relative of floor wax. There were coconut "bacon slices," and buttons—those genteel pastel dots stuck onto strips of paper. There were miniature peanut butter cups (two for a penny) in black waxed paper dishes, and miniature Tootsie Rolls as well. Fragrant sweet waxes formed lips and red-painted fingernails which we'd wear for hours. Sometimes there would be jellied licorice babies, or cardboard boxes of brittle candy cigarettes, tips a faintly glowing pink.

Above those rows of dishes of candies peered the faces of the neighbourhood kids. I presided over their choices. Snapping open the flattened brown penny candy bag, I would anticipate and wonder at the selection of the child gazing through the glass. Proud of my accountability, I would take the pennies or nickel, depositing them in the cash drawer. Then, I would fold the top of that bag down over whatever choices it contained.

For my help, I would most always be given five cents to spend. I don't ever remember any of us taking freely from the store's goods, so it never seemed strange to spend my nickel there. Nor would it have occurred to me to spend it anywhere else. I chose my candies out front, like every other kid. It was a matter of propriety: A certain distance is necessary for making choices.

Even now, I am much more predictable than impulsive. Insisting that this constitutes an exercise of choice, I will again and again select the same things. Certainty of satisfaction entices me more than a hope for something better. Back then, nearly every day I would select a root beer barrel, malt balls, something of licorice, a sweet wax thing, and a fire ball to linger over. The combination of shapes and textures and how they tumbled together in the bag mattered to me. Important too, was a combination which would out-last, or at least contend with, that of my friends or sisters. But most important of all was the predictable satisfaction, start to finish.

So I practiced daily, living with my choices. I clung to them, both believing that they were good, and wanting others to know that I did. The social ritual was only interrupted and complicated once yearly, for Lent. During Lent we Catholic kids gave up candy, it being our only tangible decadence. I never did understand how our enjoying penny candies, or not, bore any relationship to that anguished figure nailed to the cross. But I hoped that it did, and did not give in to temptation. Instead, we'd hoard our nickels for the inflated rubber balls, dusty in their bin. Or maybe a bag of potato sticks.

❧

These days, students will come to my office in the throes of decision making. They want affirmation, or neutral ground, or sometimes, resistance—I'm hardly ever sure which. They believe, I think, that sometime down the road a master plan will be revealed: deviations noted, failure gauged. We instructors foster that illusion with all of our grading and assessment.

They're worried about changing a major or transferring to another college, dropping a course or leaving a friend. I hear them out, acknowledge their anxiety, offer ineffective words of encouragement. I try to provide a broader perspective, and finally just send them along. The choices they make and the mysterious ways they respond to the tugs of reason and intuition will become the directions that their lives take.

I remember being where they are, where choices loom, and where making those choices feels so conscious and reflective and hard.

᪥

My family drove me to University. And I immediately pushed them away, anxious to confront all aspects of the place on my own. Startled by the loneliness, I missed those I'd pushed away, and all I'd left behind. Cornell University, Ithaca, New York— each of the concentric circles of location intrigued me, but remained abstract for several disorienting weeks.

I was sure of my bearings only within my dormitory, Donlon Hall. Modern, ugly and three-cornered, it provided me with a small bed, a room with a generic view, and more strange faces than I ever imagined could be contained in one building. When I emerged from Donlon, eager for what would surely be kinder settings, I was lost in a three-sided mystery, never quite sure which of the trio of identical exits would lead me in the direction I needed to go.

My first semester's course selection stands out now, as it very likely did *not* then—tucked in amid the confusion and anxiety, alienation and even hunger. But the calendar was thick with promise. As I chose—six of hundreds of offerings—I knew that in ways beyond fathoming, I was making choices that would alter what job I'd have, how I would think, and even who I'd become. I can remember only some of my choices and even fewer of my reasons for them: Russian Literature and British History, Calculus for Biologists (a love of biology, confounded by a dread of blood), and Greek Classics (a diplomatic gesture since the advisor assigned to me taught this).

Balanced between fear of encountering my limitations and anticipation of discovering new ideas, I took that familiar leap of faith—toward stubborn certainty. I remember being so satisfied to have meshed my quirks of interest and inclination with all the unyielding requirements and the intricacies of timetabling. It was my first experience of braiding times and rules and preferences in the configuration so familiar to me now. I even enjoyed the other new challenge: decoding the abbreviations for buildings, rooms, credits, hours and days, to sketch the skeleton of the months to follow.

᳤

At about fifteen, I learned to cross-country ski. I fell in love with the combination of kick and glide, with the rhythm of resistance and release. I've never learned to ski well, but have skied often, and with great pleasure. It's a steady forward motion, and the sureness of that motion depends on how the catch of pole-plant combines with the friction of kick. A tentative movement, a second thought, will cost energy, effort, and grace. It's all in planting that pole, pushing that foot off the snow, and surging forward.

Each day of our lives we wind our way through choices. And each choice, in the moment of negotiation, seems to magnify the time and circumstances framing it. Yet I end up thinking that maybe our fluidity and grace—a certain sure-footedness—matters more than the path we choose, or even the destination we arrive at. In the final analysis, the act of getting there may be the essence of the game.

# Montana Nights

When I teach young people to write, I know that I talk often about context, continuity, and coherence. Sometimes, in sleepless hours before dawn, I see things a different way. As rains wash the mud from a field stone, its shape emerges: Identity is in the freeing of contexts, the rupturing of continuity. I grew to know myself in the years when my life was turned askew—years of working nights, sleeping days, seeing as many dawns as noon-day suns. Wedged between the smooth, prescribed years of formal university education, and the patterned life of family and career, were the rougher experiences against which I took shape.

During these years my goal was to make ends meet: to pass the time, quite incidentally in Montana, while keeping myself intact. I would do any paying job that fell my way—substitute teaching and math tutoring, waitressing and hostessing, sometimes even labouring in the area's potato fields. It was an on-call existence, and if it lacked focus, it certainly provided diversity.

One particular stretch stands out in my mind. I'd just arrived in Whitefish, Montana, where I'd end up spending the next three years. I was cocktail waitressing at the Hanging Tree Lounge—slinging drinks called "ditches," to locals who were insatiable and nearly indistinguishable. They were men, mostly.

The few women there seemed tough, sometimes terrifying, and always impressive. In my memory the faces of those guys form a mural which represents the countless bars on countless main streets of western Montana towns. But some of those faces stand out with surprising clarity.

I can still see the judge, a fat cigar clenched between his teeth, hunkered over the poker table. A squat man, no taller than I, he stands just two places to the left of the dealer. He once tipped me a five dollar chip, and once fined me twenty-one dollars for speeding. I'd have to say he came out ahead.

Other faces emerge. Just inside the door, drinking rounds of cold beer, one cluster of boys recovers from a scorching day of concrete work. They, at least, bore some relationship to people I had known before. They were, in fact, sweet and funny. I grew to care for them as avidly as I held off the ceaselessly blasting country music, the thick stale smoke, and the grizzled leering faces of men who could so casually unsettle a twenty-one-year-old eastern girl who didn't even know yet how to drink.

I lived out those days between that cocktail lounge and the Cadillac Hotel it adjoined. In the conservative small towns of coastal Maine from which I had come, bars and dining rooms were never Hanging Tree Lounges. By living there, in Montana, I was ripping away from my roots, tearing away the tender tangled root-hairs, and shaking free all of that enriching soil.

The family who ran the hotel and lounge was, like the building itself, an amorphous, ramshackle aggregation. In the weeks it took me to learn where it began and ended, I became a part of that family. Irish Catholic, they were unlike my own in all ways, or maybe in just a few. Certainly their living in a hotel was one tangible difference. The grandmother—left speechless by a stroke—still lived, while mine had died years back. Michaela and Heaven Love were the grandchildren (whose resemblance to my niece, being raised on a commune in New Hampshire, eased my homesickness). They seemed to blow in with the cold dry winds, those two runny-nosed and ragged little girls, their lean and tired-looking mother, and the lanky, shiftless man who trailed behind. Within minutes they could fill two or three rooms with the aura of spontaneous and casual permanence that most of us take years to acquire.

Along the long corridors of the Cadillac Hotel, sisters and uncles occupied various other rooms: a dashing brother with a vague but cherished connection to Hollywood, and a maiden aunt, sweet and gracious, indispensable for a time, then gone again. There were tensions, and tears, and long arguments behind closed doors. Holding everything together, the owners Paddy and Laurie were at the centre of the family and the establishment, as well as of my memories.

This was not my lifestyle, but it surely was the surroundings in which those days unfolded. Waking when the dry heat and hissing radiators aroused me, I would walk the streets by day, trying to push away the unfamiliarity. But it wouldn't budge. I read, and went for lonely runs, and nudged away the discomfort which fell back upon me like dust settling.

Evenings brought relief as well as dread of the routine: serving dinner, then drinks, and finally, sitting out the graveyard shift at the front desk. I spent the late night hours poring through *Newsweek* magazines, and writing letters to reassure people how fine I was, how eccentric and interesting this all was.

I remember exchanging letters with a sister, seven years older than I, whose marriage was splitting apart. She wrote to me for approval, or maybe for advice. I swung between fear of a sharing that felt too great for me to shoulder, and pride that she considered me old enough to share with.

My front desk shift started at midnight. For the first hour, the street-front lobby hummed with the noise of its old TV, and with its tattered collection of viewers. I waited impatiently for the TV to be turned off, and for those old men—who lived behind other doors just down the hallway from mine, who shared a communal bathroom with me, and whom I resented for all that—to shuffle down our hallway, and disappear behind their doors for the night. For the next six hours, I'd hope against hope that no one would come in off the street. I waited out each moment, poised in the expectation that something would intrude upon the eerie silence over which I presided.

One of those old men had become, it seems, quite certain that the maid was secretly radiating his room. To prove his point, and maybe to get himself protected in the bargain, he sent his pillow to the FBI for testing. They notified the local police, who found two loaded pistols in the bureau in his room.

I lived in that hotel for three months. But across the fifteen intervening years, I recall the vivid contours of that time. Longing for contexts more familiar, I discovered myself adapting to the contorted surroundings of the Hanging Tree Lounge. In those long Montana nights I came to know the twists and turns of my own life.

# Making a Difference

We all try, I think, to make a difference with our lives, to leave our mark on this world. As a child, I imagined myself saving souls, writing books, building bridges. I would think about Lucy Farnsworth, the fabulously rich but physically dwarfed daughter of our local famous family, and how she died of starvation on a bed stuffed with bills. That was how the story went, anyway. Whatever the reality may have been, the truth is that she made a difference to me and my young girlfriend. We would gape and stare into her bedroom, held back by a red velvet rope, the home by now converted into a showcase attached to the art museum named for and endowed by her family. We were spellbound by her inexplicable act of starving herself to death, as well as her deformity and the renown lent her by generations as curious as we.

My friend and I would move directly past the other rooms, past polished knick-knacks from the daily life of rich folks now dead, pausing only to visit the stuffed horses and the carriage stopped fast behind them. Despite admonishing glances of perfumed matrons behind desks, we would stride purposefully toward the other velvet roped marvel of my early years, that splendid painting by Andrew Wyeth, *Her Room*. I can hardly recall the details of that painting: a window-ledge, a distant view of ocean, a vase. But I certainly do recall the wonder that overcame me as I stood there studying it.

For me that bedroom of Lucy Farnsworth and that painting of Andrew Wyeth both made a difference—moving me and leaving their impressions with me—however unlike they were in all other regards.

Some fifteen years later, in 1980, I spent a few months as a surveyor's helper. One year married, graduated and certified to teach, I had arrived in British Columbia to find twenty-seven local teachers laid-off. So there I was trudging along through the thick undergrowth of what would soon become the community of Logan Lake, BC. Splintery wooden stakes under one arm, metal legs of the transit stand under the other, I trailed along behind our neighbour surveyor, who had finagled this job for me.

Physically strong, energetic and cheerful, eager to figure things out, I was great for the job but for one critical short-coming: a dismal inability to orient myself spatially. Though quick to catch on to the trigonometrical calculations required, I was days learning how to hold the balance rod, or manipulate the plumb line. I would hike enthusiastically over hillsides, ferreting out iron markers, only to grasp the meter stick at an angle so ridiculous as to render me totally useless to the meticulous man shouting to me from behind his transit lens a quarter mile away. The more he shouted, the more anxiously I clung to the rod, fighting the tug of gravity needed to balance it properly.

But learn I did, at last. The understanding flooded my brain on one of those long, dusty drives home, a private sense of mastery routing the humiliation of those first days. I became a good surveyor's helper, adept at level and transit operations, at calculations, at any number of menial, tedious tasks so necessary to the survey of roadways.

It was a wonder to me, this community to be, this brand new town built to support the copper mines which plundered the hills in the distance.

In New England, every little community rests upon three centuries of history and myth. Families we'd known for only one generation were newcomers. The one-storey ranch-style houses popping up here and there, during the sixties, we considered to be curiosities, strange as three-legged chickens.

But here, along roads emerging between our rows of numbered stakes, brought into being by our rows of pencilled calculations, signposts bravely sprouted, bearing family names. They looked so funny out there, scattered amid willow and wild rose. Amongst monstrous backhoes and towers of gravel, they seemed to exert some tenuous hold on that scarred landscape.

A few weeks later—an astonishingly short time to an easterner—the dusty hard-hatted workers witnessed the trucks groaning up to deliver, in two halves, the first of the mobile homes. I remember the young owners driving down a gravelled track of the soon-to-be roadways. They piled out of their beater pick-up to watch the arrival, unloading, and snapping together of their new home. In that instant neighbourhood about to materialize in the settling dust, they reminded me of my husband and myself.

That same night we celebrated our first anniversary amidst boxes and the gentle breezes of unclosed soffits. It was our inaugural night on our new land, spent in the plywood shack we'd erected to live in while we built the permanent dwelling which was to become our home.

What started me off on the notion of consequence was not the difference my husband made, year after year, shaping our acreage into our home. Nor was it the snapping together of those two gaping halves into the double-wide of that other young couple. No, I was thinking of a difference brought about by me alone, maybe the most significant, enduring difference I'll ever make. Like Lucy Farnsworth's room, like Andrew

Wyeth's painting of some other woman's room, the difference I made will both articulate and outlast the circumstances that occasioned it.

While I was surveying I left a slight hill in a road, a feature independent of the whole surrounding landscape. An error in my calculations caused it to come about. Out of my scrawled columns of figures, certain digits—once they were felt-tipped onto stakes—had summoned truck after truck to spill its load, gradually raising the road-bed from coarse gravel to pavement, and then machine after machine to rake and roll it down to the level indicated by my markings. My stubborn pride was what left that hill permanent. Unwilling to relinquish the grudging respect I'd won from the men I worked with, I never admitted to having confused centimetres with decimetres. I remember how peculiar that slight, sudden hill looked, years later, when I had occasion to drive through that subdivision. I also recall the thrill of recognizing it.

I think that small town already is dying—that the copper has been scraped out of the hills, and the miners laid-off, and the young families of those instant neighbourhoods moved on. Who knows where they've gone, or what they're doing? My own rising piece of road may not get driven on much these days, but that doesn't change the way I feel about it. In the universe there remains a bump in the road, and it's my doing.

# Roguing

She always called me Kid, which drove me crazy. I was twenty-two; I had graduated from university and was living on my own, three thousand miles from home, holding down two jobs: And she called me Kid. Later, I'd worked long hours in the heat of July, back aching and fingers stained brown, with no complaint, earning, finally earning, her respect. Still, she called me Kid. The name stuck, and I had to get used to it. (I half expect that, if she met me on the streets of Montana today—forty-five, greying and frazzled—she'd call me Kid.)

We were roguers, Ida and I. Roguing is something done in potato fields, and particularly, in fields of seed potatoes: Until the hour I talked my way into that job—claiming to be experienced in agricultural jobs (four whole weeks picking tomatoes in southern Ontario), strong and willing—I hadn't a clue what that meant: to rogue. Had never considered culling "inferior" plants from the healthy ones, nor imagined diseases like black leg, purple heart, mosaic, each bearing its own symptoms: a texture of leaf, a curl away from the sun, a certain hue of green; a subtle deformity of colour, size, shape.

I never did learn if that handsome young Dutch couple who owned the farm suspected my ignorance. But without a scrap of a doubt, every one of the women working in the fields knew. They knew just by looking at me.

One of those women, Donna—a blond, heavy-set mother

33

of teenaged kids—shrugged and disappeared into the field. I swear the others rolled their eyes as they turned from me. Not one of them was within ten years of me, and some, like Ida, had been working these fields summer after summer, for two generations of farmers and more years than I'd lived. Ida nodded in my direction and said, "Well, come on, Kid, let's get going."

I followed her, trying for the appropriate combination of humility and assurance, fighting awkwardness at every step. Ida stepped lightly, a woman with a job to do, no time to waste. From behind her I was surprised at her petite figure. She couldn't have weighed a pound over ninety. Her long-sleeved shirt was tucked into blue jeans, both showing signs of ironing. She wore a brimmed straw hat that morning, and every other day. No matter how hot and dusty, or how soaked by irrigation spray, Ida always looked trim and tidy.

Over the next month we got to be friends. I liked to make Ida laugh with stories of my adventures substitute teaching at the high school, or living with four other waitresses in a trailer. Ida told me stories too, about making wreaths in a warehouse in the fall, about raising her two daughters with her husband who had died a few years ago, about reupholstering her couch and making pickles.

Just once she told me how her sister, who lived just down the street from her, was "not quite right in the head." Years back, when Ida's mother and sister had both worked for the same family farm, the sister had stepped on the prongs of a rake, causing the rake handle to fly up and hit her in the head. So that's why, said Ida, the family was so good to her, always giving her work. "And that's why you should never lay tools down on the ground, Kid."

The work had a steady, satisfying rhythm. Each roguer would pace through a row, scanning the plants to the right and the left, stopping now and then to uproot one, dig its spuds, then continue through the row, keeping alert to one's progress in relation to the roguers on either side. If I kept my eyes sharp, my mind was free to roam. If repetition lulled me, the cold spray of irrigation would revive me.

As we covered section after section of the field, the sun would advance, first taking the chill off the morning, then shining hotly overhead, then settling slowly toward the western plain, its rosy tones marking the end of our work, mingling with growing hunger and a bone-deep weariness.

Lunch was a mid-day luxury. We would debate about when to quit, whether to stop now, or do another round. We had no water to wash and no place to take shelter, so we ate our sandwiches with dirt under our nails and grime in our skin, sitting on the ground. The truck was our home base and we could lean against it, or lie under it for relief from rain or relentless sun. Sometimes we ate quietly, but usually with joking and gossip. Precisely thirty minutes after we'd stopped, Ida would sigh and pull herself up, and, with regret, we'd all follow.

One time I remember we were working the north field, a narrow strip of land with rows nearly double the usual length. We were nearly an hour late stopping for lunch, slowed down by having to haul diseased plants clear off the field to an incinerator. The sky was overcast and my back ached from hauling bags heavy with infected spuds. The truck was at the east end of the field, adjacent to the road. We'd no more than settled on the ground with our sacks of lunch when Ida jumped up, agitated. "Come on, let's get back to work. What if Teddy drives by and sees us still resting at this hour!" No amount of reasoning would persuade her otherwise, so back into the field we went. I was hungry and tired, and angry at such foolish submissiveness. We barely spoke for two days.

But I also remember another day when, after a late night waitressing, the distorting white light of noon confused me. I

35

had by this time grown confident in my skills of detection, was quickly able to detect blight even as the maturing of the plants brought symptoms of new diseases to watch for.

So when I noticed how the leaves of a plant had a pronounced curl, a tinge of lime, I pulled it expertly. Then the next plant. And the next. My shoulders were tired before I noticed how far back I had fallen; then, how large the chunk of field I had stripped; and then . . . how *all* the plants before me were showing these symptoms.

"Oh, Kid! What are you doing?" I heard, the tone at first vexed, then sympathetic, then fearful. She recognized before I did, that the turning of the mature leaves toward the shifting light had confused me. Ida didn't mention it again, but for days I could feel her watching out for me. We returned to the same field twice more that summer. Each time, the other roguers would wonder at the sudden bald spot. Ida never said a word, and neither did I. Donna said that lightning caused it, no doubt.

On Fridays we would emerge from our last row feeling giddy. This was payday. We'd pile into the groaning truck that Donna used to move us from field to field, and drive right up to the farmhouse. Teddy and his wife would be waiting for us.

They would hand out our pay for the week in white envelopes, sealed and with our names written across the back. Though I made considerably more money waitressing, the heft of that sealed envelope of cash brought me a satisfaction that was unrivalled. Teddy, usually so shy, would joke with us as he handed each of us our envelopes. Sometimes his wife would have glasses of lemonade ready for us.

I liked those two. They were close to me in age. But I could sense that my easy familiarity with the family made the women I rogued with uncomfortable. And I had my loyalty. So we never became friends, though sometimes they would slip a frozen steak into my pack, or a jar of jam. And when I left

Montana to be married, Teddy and Cynthia presented me with an early wedding gift—an electric griddle. It seemed such a domestic thing to own, back then, but I get that griddle out nearly every week now to make pancakes for my husband and kids.

We never mentioned what was in our own envelope on payday—never compared, nor even opened our envelopes until we'd left for home. Like everything else we did, that ritual was prescribed years before I wandered onto that place asking for some outdoor work. I didn't question it, and stopped wondering what each woman made—whether Donna made extra for driving the truck, or Mary for moving irrigation pipes before we started in the morning, or Ida, for recording hours. I did notice that each summer my hourly wage increased, and that, after one brutal month when we'd managed to maintain the certification standards during an epidemic of black leg, there was a bonus equalling a full week's pay.

Once, on our drive home, I asked Ida if she did okay on her wages roguing and making wreathes. It was a bold question, but by then our relationship could tolerate such brashness. I could see how well-kept her home appeared (small, but attractive and neat, like Ida), I knew she had put her two girls through university, but I wondered how she'd manage in the future. She answered, or didn't, in her own way. "You know what I did last spring? I redecorated my whole kitchen," she told me. "Just for the heck of it, Kid. It's yellow now, so bright and cheerful.

"And do you know what the man told me when he pulled up the old melamine? He said he'd never taken out a counter in such beautiful condition. He said it was as perfectly kept as the ones he installs. Imagine that, Kid. But I always wanted a pretty yellow kitchen."

37

# Studies in Silence

In the year 1981 I was living in the dusty little town of Merritt, BC, teaching a variety of basic skills to a variety of Native students, who, by the way, called themselves Indians. While I taught them the rudiments of writing and mathematics, they taught me who they were.

One thing I learned about was silence. Ever since, I've regarded silence as a distinguishing feature of Native culture. One of the curious effects on me is this impulse to speak about the silence—to explain it and to tell stories about it.

One student I learned from, a boy of seventeen, arrived the first day pulling a red hockey bag. "I don't spell good. I got practice at two-thirty," he informed me, taking a seat at the back table. Two weeks later the hockey bag had disappeared. In its place sat a shiny new pair of boots and a worn rodeo glove which smelled of pine pitch.

During the second month of class he won a purse at a local rodeo. With his winnings, he decided to take his teacher and his older sister out for dinner. We went to an Italian restaurant where he ordered me a glass of wine and himself a beer. "D'ya want a glass for your beer?" the waitress grumbled in his direction. Not missing a beat, my friend replied, "Naw. Just bring it in a paper bag." We had finished our spaghetti long before I appreciated the full subtlety of that exchange.

This boy once shared his fear that a mirror can take away your spirit. His grandmother, he believed, had died because the mirror on her bedroom wall, little by little, took her spirit away. "Never have a mirror in your bedroom," he warned me, "and don't wear the colour red." He didn't explain the latter bit of advice, but I avoid red to this day.

He also told me that spotting high flying birds is a sign of clear-headedness and living right. Sometimes, driving home at the end of a hard day, I'll catch a glimpse of a red-tailed hawk swooping over the hills, or a golden eagle circling far above the road, and I'll feel—for that brief moment—all the day's tension drain away.

One time, about a year after our spaghetti dinner, this same kid came to visit me at home. That night my husband and I overheard him making a call to his girl friend. He'd asked if he could place this long distance call, then waited till we went to bed. Our home then—the basement of our home now—had only bedroom, bathroom, and main area serving as everything else. We were in the bedroom, trying hard to be asleep.

Through the pine panelled wall we heard dialling. And we heard breathing. We waited for the relief of conversation, but it was the oddest thing: The entire call consisted of a few murmurs punctuating a huge amount of silence. The exchange with the operator to get the charges reversed seemed animated in contrast.

That student kept in touch with us for a couple of years— until he had ceased being a student and a kid, becoming more of a friend, and on his way to becoming a man. All the time I knew him, he seemed so successful in bridging the gulf between Indian ways and small town Canadian ways. He taught me lots and impressed me in many ways, but that peculiar telephone call to his girl comes to mind when I think of him now.

Another story emerges from the same time and place. It's about the mother of another of my students from that same classroom where I first taught. This student was a woman, the same age as I was, and we got to be friends. She had split from her husband, and was raising three little girls. What she lacked in formal education, I lacked in real life experience, so we were a pretty good match.

Her busy home was a welcome relief from the quiet apartment where I boarded with an older lady, weekdays. My friend was also Indian, though she always looked Italian to me. She had a number of sisters, and one brother who had shot himself years back. Their mother lived just down the road from my friend, though I remember the mother mostly from the diner or the pub. She seemed always to be in town. She was rotund, with short grey hair, and a smile that you could get lost in. She never spoke. Never ate or drank. She just sat there, watching and smiling.

Once, in the year after I had left that job for another position closer to home, I was in Merritt visiting my friend. Her house was full of sisters and kids. We were sharing stories and preparing food. My friend's youngest daughter was shelling peas with her grandmother. The little girl, four at the time, stood at her grandma's knee, chattering aimlessly. The girl was scrawny, with thatches of blond hair, big, light brown eyes, and was dressed, on this day, in a ruffled dress.

"Have a pea, Grandma. They're good!" she said, eating a fistful, smiling and talking, all at the same time.

"Gramma got no teeth, Honey," her grandmother replied.

"You don't *need* teeth, Gram. Look!" "Gunck," we heard, as she swallowed to demonstrate. "Gunck. Gunck. Gunck."

We laughed, this silent old woman and I, till the tears streamed down our faces.

This is such a silly, inconsequential little story, but it's stayed with me all these years. I laugh just thinking about that little blond-haired Indian girl with a belly full of whole, raw, green peas, and her grandmother with such generous humour and so very few words.

# Becoming a Mother

I see her as I write this. She's there watching—sitting up on a stool, legs crossed, elbow on knee, chin in the palm of one hand, fingers of the other quietly drumming the lunch counter. She's bemused, waiting with interest to see what I will write. She is The Angel of the House. And I am grateful to Virginia Woolf for having introduced us. For so many years, never knowing who the Angel was, I have felt her baleful eye upon me. I knew she was watching. And that she disapproved of much of what I do. She still gets furious when I head out the back door, flashlight in hand—leaving behind children in pajamas and dinner ill-conceived and unprepared—to shake off the tensions of my day with an evening run.

One of my second language composition students, tangled in the web of English verb tenses, wrote "Since last September I have been coming to Canada." Well, since January of 1985, I have been becoming a mother. That was the time my body exploded into pregnancy—at about four months and just past the slightly-sick and mostly-disbelieving first trimester. The trouble is that, like my student, whenever I start thinking that I've finally arrived, I come up against yet another mile-post.

◦

Engendering children is at once the most natural, and the most levelling, of experiences. Intricate, fraught with risk, this experience which so firmly situates us within our biological selves also confounds us.

I remember feeling astonished, perturbed, sometimes even solaced by the intrusions upon my privacy. Once a bulging belly declared my state of pregnancy, women accosted me on street corners and in grocery stores. Exhausted after work, I leaned against my cart in the check-out line of Safeway, savouring the two minutes of necessary inertia. Falling upon my shoulders like blows, the words "When are you due?" would yank me out of my private thoughts, my restful oblivion.

I remember this incident from my hospital stay, a moment of sheer burlesque. A nurse curtained us off together for the first time: my husband, yellow gowned, me, and our baby, bundled in my arms. We were becoming a family. Sitting beside her dad, I nursed our bright-eyed daughter, first knowing that sensation of prickly pain, and then the sweet release of milk to the urgent nuzzling of a downy head.

Suddenly, with a burst of light and hiss of metal curtain hooks, the curtain flew back. The spell was lost. A small dark man appearing at our side seemed as startled as we were. He was exchanging our window curtain, he apologized, pulling the stepladder in behind him. Please excuse him, he asked, and we did. Suddenly self-conscious, my husband and I fidgeted and made small-talk. The child held her place, impervious.

During the days I spent in the hospital I came to know a lovely, fine-featured woman in the bed next to mine. She had given birth to a robust and red-cheeked boy. She was, it turned out, a Philippino mail-order bride, ordered by a local man, a logger with few social graces but ample finances. The morning after she gave birth I watched her pull herself out of bed and set to restoring herself before her husband arrived, lest he see her in such an exhausted and bedraggled state.

When he did come, she was polished and manicured, fresh and lacily robed. This man must have thought that the rest of us, so visibly marred by the labour of childbirth, were of another species. After he left, she shuffled heavily down the nursery to feed her son, and then crumpled into a pale heap of lace, closed her newly hung curtains, and slept.

୧

Pregnancy and childbirth, and the hospitalized recovery from these two events: They form a steady continuum of discomforts, great and small. The return home ruptures that continuity. There you are met by the tangible reminder of who you *had* been, and the less tangible but more formidable aura of The Angel of the House. You turn from one to the other. Incapable of reaching either, you start becoming a mother.

One day a collection of friends and neighbours sat around the broad kitchen table of the woman who took care of my daughter while I worked. We were drinking home brewed beer in iced mugs while she told us a story that made us laugh. But I knew the story was also meant to give me confidence.

On this one winter morning the woman had taken her kids—two, four, and sixteen months—on an outing. She'd bustled around for an hour—collecting and toiletting, bundling and mittening kids, gathering skates and socks, thermos of cocoa and sacks of peanut butter crackers, spare socks and diapers. Out the door, up the backyard hill, across the street and to the neighbourhood rink they trekked. There, she lined her three children up on the bench. She first laced her own skates, then tottered to the oldest child, lacing hers, and setting that child out on the ice. She moved on to the middle child. Laced up, he too slid away. But by now the youngest was nowhere to be seen. She'd inched her way off the bench, and wandered a few feet away. There she stood, firmly stuck by the lips to the water spigot. The mother hoisted her up—dripping blood and tears—repacked all the gear and collected the older children, unlacing and re-booting them for the long walk back home.

Of this other story, I remember neither the teller nor the characters. But I know it happened. Or I think it did. I know for certain that it *could* have happened. The woman of this story was new to motherhood—still staggering and reeling from the emotional upheaval and physical exhaustion of it. She'd only been home with her infant for a couple of weeks, and hadn't yet ventured away for so long as ten minutes. A well-meaning friend advised, and then insisted: She must get out. "It's time . . . just *do* it!" said the friend.

Dazed and distracted, the young mother gave in to the advice, preposterous though it seemed. She left her baby and home, pushing herself through the motions of a walk downtown and a snack in a cafe, where she ran across the friend whose advice she'd followed. With dismay verging on horror, that friend discovered that the mother had left her child unattended.

The tone of this story leaves me sure that everything turned out fine. I've remembered it for years, and retold it often. I'm grateful for the sense of community which it asserts. Although I don't know the woman to whom it happened, and she probably doesn't know me either, we are sisters in this process of becoming mothers.

◈

All through pregnancy, childbirth, and childrearing, a woman's centre of gravity shifts. I remember the sensation of lightness just after birth, giving way to the aching shuffling awkwardness of recovery. And then the unwieldy weight of car-seats, diaper bags and breasts full with milk.

As soon as my first child was a month old, I dragged us both back to Maine, proud to show her to my family, to show myself as a mother. On our second day there, coaxed by my sisters and brother, I abandoned my baby to my own mother's care. We were going off for a few leisurely hours exploring some of the back roads that thread their way through the small towns along coastal Maine. Until that day, other than the three or four hours of sleep I'd snatched between feeds each night, my daughter and I had not been separated.

Hours later, my brother and sisters and I were wandering through a barn-like antique shop in one of those small towns. Now and then I would lose myself to the moment: enjoying a laugh, examining a cane chair or ceramic vase. But mostly, I remember the sheer effort to appear relaxed. I'd been a mother for ten long weeks, and was desperate to exhibit a casual competence. When my sister pointed to the milk dripping on my shoes, I learned all over again that there is no retreat from the physical state of mothering, or from the endless exposure of it.

Becoming a mother humbles and wearies us. It can also brace and affirm us. Our babies grow to become the voices by which we know ourselves. One evening I was busy preparing husband and kids for the next evening, a late work night. Arrangements had to be made: who was to pick up whom, who'd run the daily errands, which vehicle was to carry which after-school snacks, when and where each of us was to have dinner.

I was tucking the kids in, and wishing my older one good night. "I won't see you tomorrow after day-care, but I'll come in and kiss you goodnight when you're asleep," I told her.

"Please write that on your list," she replied.

I assured her, "Mommie would never forget to kiss you goodnight!"

Framing me in her own clear light, she responded, "You

*know* how you forget things, Mommie. You just don't have a good remembery. But don't worry, because I do."

٭

These days, the cycles close in on me—cycles of birth to death, of child to mother. I spin dizzily, sometimes longing for the days I gently arched along.

Anna was one of those model mothers for me. She was a few years ahead of me in the experience of first pregnancy, of young marriage and new home building—and admirable in each of those endeavours. Years later they would move away from the home they had built and she had loved caring for, away from the lake and the years of friends. Then, not long after their move, her husband would move away from her.

But I can still see her as she was that day six years ago, emptying a baby bath deftly—the rapid and sure motions of her hands scooping out the bedding plants temporarily rooting there. She scrubbed it out thoroughly, then handed the clean, damp tub to me. It has since bathed my three infants, then retired to a hook on the wall of the rootcellar, from where it is sometimes pressed into service to soak potting soil.

"Mothers give to new mothers. It's OK. You'll pass along what comes to you," she said, packing a box with tiny worn white tee-shirts and corduroy rompers. In ambled her children, appearing so enormous to my eyes. Happy and unkempt, they prodded my tiny infant. The distance between her children and my delicate bundled girl seemed unattainable. But my children are now the age hers were back then—now as big and eager, as unkempt and boldly happy.

Anna died last Wednesday morning. She dropped dead in the bathroom of the school where she was a teacher's aide. I imagine that she was a wonderful teacher's aide, a blessing to some teacher who, I hope, deserved her. I think of her now and then, remembering the sweetness of her voice, the competence of her home-making, and the things she shared with me.

⚬

The day I learned of Anna's death I also learned that my daughter's kindergarten teacher had adopted a baby. She had waited for eleven years, but for us, it all happened too quickly. She would be a lovely mother. Meanwhile, my daughter and I adjusted to yet another kindergarten teacher, our third that year. The adjusting was difficult for my daughter, agony for me. She said nothing for the first two days, and then talked to me about the transition. "Oh well, Mrs. M. is nice . . ." she concluded. "Maybe *all* kindergarten teachers are nice." But I know better.

I remember as though it were yesterday the kindergarten classroom I attended, its walls of thick glass bricks forming obtuse angles around us. Twenty-five boys and girls, we sat in two long rows. I remember the painted wooden cake which would emerge for each birthday. It would sit on the desk of the birthday child, while we all sang. I thought it a wondrous cake.

But just as clearly, I remember the ritualistic humiliation and punishment meted out in that room. Threat loomed heavy—the apprehension in that room was as thick as fog. Children were singled out for obscure transgressions, slapped or made to stand in corners. I remember reacting with shame, pity, and fear—three feelings as despicable to me then as now.

After a while, I knew that the same kids got singled out time and time again. I know now, perhaps even suspected then, that abuse at school even more than poverty at home damaged such kids directly and permanently, and hurt the rest of us in ways more subtle. The very thought of it enrages me still.

Lately, feelings have run uneasy in our family. My daughter wants her own kindergarten teacher back, the one who left her for a child of her own. She mixes that up with wanting back others who have gone: the first cook at her day-care; Jasper, our cat.

My two-year-old son is sad and angry that the woman who's cared for him since infancy has gotten another job, leaving him. He kicks away his sadness and anger, as well as our efforts to ease those feelings. At night, he reaches under his pillow desperately rooting out the two pacifiers he found in his baby drawer. He sucks on one and toys with the other. Every morning, he replaces them beneath his pillow, a kind of ritual. The pacifier he sucks becomes a yellow plastic grin he wears: It gives him a foolish appearance, vulnerable and alien. The very look of him with his two pacifiers—this child who exerts, by day, a fierce independence—evokes disgust in his dad.

My husband's reaction to my son's reaction binds them together. Why do males seem to pull so anxiously away from what runs deepest inside them? I'm exhausted from the days of soothing knotted sensibilities, smoothing away surface distress, pacifying the rebellion against pacifiers. I'm worn out from wiping tears. I long to fold into myself, even for a short time.

The Angel of the House is the attendant spirit of motherhood: the embodiment of serenity and selfless grace, of toil and smug, stalwart perseverance. I crossed two thousand miles and a border to leave behind her accusations, her delight in my shortcomings. For years I blamed my husband, my friends, and two generations of mothers. But now I know her. And unlike Virginia Woolf, I cannot kill her. There's too much at stake. And winning her respect matters to me. So I confront her.

49

It may just be that confronting the Angel and becoming the mother are the same phenomenon.

# Finding the Canadian Side

For just over a decade, I've been living in Canada. I used to apologize for being an American, sensing that it was such an alien, undesired way to be, up here. Now, having given birth to two little Canadians, I consider my American-ness an aspect of who I am. I issue no disclaimers. Before moving up here, I had lived most of my life along the northern border of the U.S., sliding ever westward from Maine to up-state New York to Montana.

I grew up thinking there was little distinction between these two nations, or perhaps simply *not* thinking much at all about such a distinction. Then in the fall when I was nine years old, my parents packed up our Oldsmobile with seldom-used suitcases and set out for Quebec, my youngest sister and I in tow.

I remember the colours of fall, and my mother, her sweater draped across her shoulders, commenting on the foliage. Then across the border the foliage was immediately displaced by the French-ness—that foreignness which, for the next fifteen years, I would associate with this country. The next memory I have is that of being lost in the streets of Montreal, trying to decipher the bewildering French names on the road maps with which my parents struggled. My sister and I gawked at the people in city clothes, walking their city streets, past the black wrought iron gates of their apartments. We never had seen a city. So

the citiness of Montreal got all mixed up for us with its French-
ness and its Canadian-ness.

From that trip I'll never forget the eerie calm between my
parents. Had their truce arisen naturally, one more travel
arrangement, or was it a phase in a long-evolving conflict? My
sister—no more than three or four years old—shared with me
a sense of that special calmness, of being The American Family
on Vacation. Together the four of us shared adjoining motel
rooms, toured wax museums and fortresses, even rode a horse-
drawn carriage through the narrow cobblestoned streets of Old
Quebec. Someday my husband and I might be doing the very
same things, I expect, in those same places, with our children.
    Two distinct images round off my recollection of my
childhood trip into Canada. One is of a lovely French pastry.
Allowed to select for myself I chose, with great consideration,
an elegant lady's slipper that, when I bit into it, horrified me
with a smell of liqueur. I couldn't even swallow that first bite.
(Years later in a little white painted room with a sloping high
ceiling, my husband and I would suffer a long night of
indigestion after frogs' legs in more garlic than our young
palates had yet encountered.)
    The other image comes from the doorway of that majestic
cathedral, Ste. Anne de Beaupre. Two massive columns frame
the main entrance, each covered with testimonies to past
miracles—tiny crutches, heavy orthopaedic shoes, canes and
braces, bandages and even wheelchairs, all strapped up on those
columns. A fervent Catholic, I had been anticipating this visit
and, most of all, the mass we'd attend. But in that cathedral
air so heavy with miracles, I felt as though I might suffocate.
Afraid my family might ridicule my foolish frailty, I slipped
away under the pretext of exploring.

So my first trip to Canada left a jumble of exclusions—speech

I couldn't understand, sweet pastry I couldn't swallow, air I couldn't breathe. On my next trip, in the late summer of 1975, I was visiting Simcoe, Ontario to see the young man I had fallen in love with, and would marry four years later.

I was lost on my own, this time. The road maps heaped unfolded beside me in my newly acquired 1950 Ford Coupe, I was traveling solo for the first time. On this journey we became friends, my first vehicle and I. A new cotton lavender blouse I had bought the day before softened the overalls in which I nearly always hid myself, in those days. I played mind games with myself, ignoring the mileposts marking each ten mile stretch in the endless New York Throughway—Mass. Pike to Buffalo—then guessing optimistically how many I might have missed. Buffalo did finally come, and the border I didn't yet know enough to dread: no firearms; no sir; and no citrus; oh yes, lots of money, more than thirty dollars.

Then I hit the fog. Or it hit me. Bleary, worried about visiting in the home of the family of this man I loved so, I thought about his perky youngest sister, her speech as rapid and as lilting as French to my slow New England ears. The fog was as dense as any I had ever driven in. Never mind all those years on the coast of Maine. It bore down on my car; rolling up off the winding highway, curling over the contours of the old Ford, swirling around the windshield till tears stung my eyes, it drained my pride at having survived the throughway tedium.

Dizzy with disorientation, stiff-necked with weariness, I lurched along for what may have been ten or two hundred miles, gripping the opened door to search out the edge of Highway 9, as one long white slash after another appeared beneath my wheels, then vanished into the mist. Every now and then the fog would break open, whole scenes spinning into place through the sharp damp air. Finally, at the end of a twisting residential roadway, my lover stood in the doorway of his family's home.

For the next fifteen years he and I would cross this country more times than I can count. Today as I draw my index finger along the dusty map on our bookshelf, the names bristle with association: Sicamous to Golden and on through the Rockies to Banff, then Calgary and long flat windy hours to Medicine Hat and Moose Jaw, then Brandon to Winnipeg. Later, miles of fog and lake from Thunder Bay to Sault Ste. Marie, on into the wild regal rock and scrub from Espanola to Sudbury, before dropping down into the sober heart of Ontario.

Those years of driving and watching through the windshield of that old black Ford taught me about this place. We almost always listened to the CBC, the auditory source of my sense of things Canadian. We often drove separate vehicles, Mont's being a 1957 Chevy half-ton. We packed all we'd managed to acquire—mattresses, tent, skis, plant pots, sewing machine, stereo, books and more books, assorted chipped dishes—a customs official's nightmare.

We'd travel poor and drive for twenty-hour days, coffee-stained plastic mugs on the dash. Sunrises stretched for hours out over the majestic prairie horizons. Curled into each other in the front seat, we once napped while huge insects smashed into the windshield in some expansive parking lot outside a Manitoba diner. Mist swirled in through our windows under the immense grey boulders of Northern Ontario.

I know that my love for my husband evolved along with my sense of his country. I see us wedding-bound in 1979, having been separated for seven months, him up at Whitehorse, Yukon, me in Whitefish, Montana, working and saving to begin our married life. With two days to get to a reception at his family's home in Waterford, Ontario, we were travelling with his brother and his brother's girlfriend, the four of us in three vehicles, permitting ourselves but one motel stop, to shower and sleep for six hours. At that motel my husband-to-be perched on the toilet seat, where the light was best, while I cut his hair. Tired, he weaved back and forth as I snipped away with my sewing scissors.

Somewhere else, between rendezvous and synchronization, I found myself travelling with a friend of the brother of my husband—a short, wiry, red-haired man who had a tense high-strung Dalmatian. It took less than ten miles for this man and I to know that we didn't much like each other; the dog darting back and forth in the back seat knew my disdain sooner. This guy shattered my illusion that men are innately good drivers, that they have an intuitive access to spatial orientation. Each time I'd drift off to sleep he'd awaken me, muttering curses, lost and bewildered. Once I awoke to the sickening crunch of his having driven up onto a gas-pump island.

Some other time, my husband and I were camping, an activity new to me. We camped at Lake Huron in Ontario. We even camped in Ottawa, wandering unkempt and happy through the stately streets lined with grand government buildings. We pitched our tent on a quiet campsite along the river, directly opposite the three sites selected for the Boy Scout jamboree which erupted barely an hour after we'd settled in.

The very next night we set up camp in the Laurentians where, even in that summer month, we saw our breaths etched in frost. A bear shuffled, thumping and wheezing, just outside our flimsy tent-skin, leaving me terrified. (Now, all these years later, we share our sloping acreage with a family of cinnamons, as ordinary a sight in late spring as wild strawberries.)

The peaked roof-lines of the wooden homes of the Eastern Townships of Quebec hinted at snows thick and heavy. Narrow strips of farmland, reaching thirstily to the waters of the St. Lawrence, spoke of families grown too large for their holdings.

Mostly these are fond recollections. They come from that time of my life after I left school, before I started work and family, a time when getting displaced in time and space and culture left me with images of gas station diners and miles of wild unpeopled landscape, grain elevators standing like sentinels, the wind bunting tumbleweeds.

❖

On April Fool's Day in 1980 I made the trip which would bring me home, which marked my spirit having edged to this side of that great, stretching line of border.

This time I was rejoining my husband. After we were married in September, I had stayed behind in Maine to do my teaching practicum. I crossed the continent on the American side. He flew to meet me in Chicago. A long day later, we were at a familiar Montana border crossing where I clutched my Landed Immigrant papers, anxious about the crated possessions which weighted down my old Ford.

Nothing more from that trip remains in my memory: not the Rocky Mountain passes, not a single one of the rivers and lakes that lace British Columbia. What I recall next is trudging over the acreage which we later purchased, above Heffley Lake, on which we built our home and raised our family.

We hiked for perhaps two hours, up beneath the copper ledges that rise out over the quarter section from which our property is carved, through wild roses and tangled willow brush, studying the creek beds which yield the water that makes our land liveable. We followed the rancher who sold us the land, who aided and encouraged us in all the ways rural folk do, and who now hires my husband to build for him.

I've since learned to accept that reliance on water—and on neighbours—which has made our version of a Canadian lifestyle possible. But when I try, now, to articulate my own sense of Canada, I know only that it is most definitely a distinct nation. And that I quite like living here.

I know that whether I'm heading north or south, wherever I cross the border—whether it's Jackson, Maine or Buffalo, New York; Eureka, Montana or Night Hawk, Washington—I have to cross some other, more visceral border before I can settle in. For the first morning or two I awaken from sleep, then awaken from some deeper drowsiness, and force myself to align with an American or a Canadian sense of things. I need to remember on which country's ground I will set my feet. It feels like walking out of the movie theatre, as a child, after being so absorbed in whatever movie I had seen that I couldn't be sure which direction would get me home.

What it finally comes down to, for me, is a tangle of thoughts and feelings. When I go back down south of the border, I'm slightly alien there. The boldness startles me, and small gestures and phrases perplex me. I feel somewhat aloof, am too easily abashed. Up here, I often feel driven to impatience, irritated by austerity, heated to my hot-blooded Italian roots.

I don't know what exactly is Canadian, and what is simply my own shape as defined by this land and these people. I wouldn't even wish to imagine life without having drunk mugs of morning coffee tuned to the national pulse as "Morningside" opened its phone lines to Dalton Camp in Halifax, Eric Kierans in Fredericton, and Stephen Lewis in Toronto. Or having pressed my face into the bark of a ponderosa pine to inhale its butterscotch fragrance. Or having watched as the mountains rise from the edge of the Fraser River as it snakes its way toward the west coast. Or having glanced up from my kitchen sink at a room full of beer drinking guys yipping and cursing through Hockey Night in Canada. I guess that what I finally know is my own life, up here in Canada. And maybe that is quite enough.

# Part II

 ❧

*Settling In*

 ❧

The dweller in the West has made his journey not very long ago, not much more than a century ago, or yesterday—he or his English father, his Scottish great-grandfather, his Irish uncle, his European parents, his grandparents from Upper or Lower Canada, his American forebears . . . He does not show a disposition to rest. The same disposition that brought . . . these newcomers westward keeps them or their descendants on the move. They will not so often travel further westward now— there is nothing but the Pacific Ocean to move into. . . . This newcomer and his sons and daughters who live on a periphery and are animated by circumstance and the urge that brought them there and by the fact that there is somewhere a place that remains (as yet) a centre wherever it may be, are moved by these things to go across the country again and again (as soon as they can afford it, or before) to this centre wherever it may be, to do their business or to refresh themselves there with the things that a periphery cannot provide. They then return across this country, content, to their homes. . . . They go vast distances . . . . They are not confined by their distance.

—Ethel Wilson, *Love and Salt Water* (1957)

# The Gifts We Give

Last spring I retrieved from a heavy-lidded old trunk the doll that was my favourite childhood toy. I wanted to give it to my daughter. I was leaving my children with my husband for two weeks, while I began summer school and set up our summertime housing down in Washington State. My daughter was upset about my leaving, about finishing her kindergarten year without me, and about leaving the daycare she'd been attending since she was three. And I'd meant to give her the doll anyway. I'd just been waiting for the right age, the right occasion.

In the musty old trunk my husband and I brought out here from Maine about ten years earlier, we found my Shirley Temple doll, an old "Etch-a-Sketch"—leaking silver powder from its seams—which I'd gotten when I had my tonsils out, a bulky coat, and all of Shirley's possessions, packed in her own small trunk. I had expected the mustiness, the dust, and some surprises long forgotten. I hadn't counted on the rush of eager emotions.

Shirley has a varnished wooden bed, a matching bureau, and a table and chairs. These had been built by my father. The glue is brittle now, and the legs fall out of the chairs. But the drawers still work. And there are quilts for the bed, and a pillow in an embroidered pillowcase. All these gifts delighted me as a child. There's a red crocheted cape, a velvet cape edged in lace, even a sequined tutu to match the one I'd worn for a ballet recital about thirty years ago. There are pleated skirts, white cotton blouses, and tiny knit sweaters with pearl buttons. My mother sewed, knit, and crocheted each of those items of clothing, along with most of the clothes for her four girls, and probably even for her son too. The memories fall into place: dressing, undressing and redressing Shirley would occupy me for hours at a time, for all the years that she was my constant companion. She was all the more special for being my own, not a hand-me-down from older sisters.

Now she is my gift to my daughter. My daughter's pleasure in the gift is ours to watch. Her dad will re-glue the wooden joints, and her grandmother and I will mend and restore those clothes. Shirley has borne her years in the trunk well. Her lovely curls have "worn down" a bit, in my daughter's words, and her tiny white teeth have pushed up into her smile. But my daughter, without even knowing of that child star I was so intrigued by, is in love with this doll. She thinks that Temple comes from our last name.

Thinking about that doll and all those hand-made clothes started me thinking about gifts. I hardly remember my mother doing anything besides working hard: She never sat down with us, even to eat, except for special dinners. She was always tired, and almost always anxious. I wonder how she felt when she sewed those tiny elaborate clothes for our dolls. Maybe it was restful, a kind of indulgence. Or maybe it was another need pulling at her, keeping her awake in the late night hours.

⤞

When I set out to gather these reflections of gift-giving, a friend told me of a book, *The Gift*, by a man named Lewis Hyde, who explores gifts through history, art, and legend. When I found the book in a college library, it had only been checked out twice in all the years it had sat on the shelves there. I felt good opening its pages, and once more giving voice to Lewis Hyde. Hyde writes with passion on gifts of art and intellect: The flow of ideas, he calls it. His study is one such gift, and my friend's putting his book in my hands is another.

The referral of a book requires that one individual know another in just such a way as to connect him or her into its flow of ideas. A book taken up and read often gets passed along to another, in the way that readers will do. It transforms us as it works its way through us, one to another, enriching what we share.

Like children tossing a ball along the bank of a river—the ball aloft, sailing from one up-stretched hand to another—a book referred represents ideas moving from mind to mind. The idea, like the ball, moves forward until it gets dropped or forgotten. It could roll down into the river, to drift back with the current. Or it could lie in the weeds to fade from view.

Gift exchange opens us to interdependence, keeping us connected. Gifts foster group ego, reaffirming both our belonging within the group, and the boundary that defines and protects the group. The flow of gifts provides cohesion, balance, and exhilaration for the community, as well as the subtle power of transformation for the individual. The community may be as intimate as a few close friends, or as extensive as a web of kinship or of professional association. Gifts move in circles, Hyde tells us, "like stars in a constellation."

I remember a painted wooden moon and stars, hanging on the wall of my bedroom when I was a child. Miniature china figurines sat on stairs which ran up the moon's crescent surface. It was made by my grandfather, known to be both handsome and violent, who'd died years before my birth. I never knew to what grandchild he gave the moon and the stars. I pretended he gave it to me.

One woman my husband and I have gotten to know in our ten years living here, is a member of an extended family. They farm for a living, in a valley northeast of us. We buy our chickens from them, also turnips, fresh eggs, and turkeys.

I remember the ornaments this woman made for the Christmas bazaar at her two boys' school. They were all lace and sequins and ribbons, in six or eight different figures that, by now, I can't remember. But I do remember her pride as we looked at them, how her face lit up with a kind of serenity.

You would hardly have guessed that moments before, she'd been plunging her hands in icy cold water to clean out turkeys just slaughtered. Those crafts seemed to give her some release from the drudgery of her work: to keep her spirits above a dreary weight that those who received her gifts could scarcely imagine.

Farming for a living is hard and endless work. This woman and the family she married into have built up their place, grandparents to grandsons. The latter are young yet, around eight and ten; the grandparents are getting old and losing health. The grandmother has a bad back and limps a bit; her husband has had heart surgery and lost the use of his hands to rheumatoid arthritis. So over the years during which we've been learning to farm our own small place, we've seen the weight of their place falling to their son and his wife.

The family seems to enjoy our visits. Every month or two, on our way out there, Mont and I gather stories for them. We like to bring them laughter, with our affection. We drink cups of coffee and eat home-baked cookies and share every silly slapstick story we can think of, about our children and our farming and building ventures; about escaped pigs and busted tools.

On our last visit, in May, the daughter-in-law was working on a tablecloth of a lace flowered pattern. A wedding gift for her sister, she embroidered it in ivory coloured strands, exquisite in design. Eager to show us her sister's dress which she'd already finished, she pulled it from a closet and held it out, delicate and frilly against a background of coffee stained mugs and piles of rubber boots. She weaves such elegant things that seem to have no place in the sober life of gutting chickens, baling hay and planting turnips.

~

The bare bones of our needs and desires are softened by the ritual act of gift exchange. Gifts gentle our existence, fleshing out the skeleton of it with grace and whimsy and goodwill. Most of the gifts that stand out in my memory are of books— read long ago, passed along or wedged between two others on the shelves that form the backdrop of our living room. And I've been graced with many a bottle of wine. One friend sends us cookies she bakes, in addition to bringing bottles of champagne with which we've toasted our years of friendship. Her other, more lasting gift, has been music. First introducing me to Emmy Lou Harris, she's kept me current ever since. Now, from five hundred miles away, the sweet strains of Emmy Lou Harris's voice can bring my friend close to me.

The oak desk I am writing at was a gift, and the slender silver-plated Cross pen I prefer writing with. The pen I use has, in a sense, been twice given, first by my mother for high school graduation, then by my husband years later; I lost the first and he replaced it. My first car—that lovely, bubble-shaped, gleaming black antique Ford—was the gift of my brother, who also gave me my first stereo, and a beige electric Smith Corona typewriter.

The year before our wedding while I was working in Montana, saving money and waiting to be reunited with the man I would marry, I passed the spare minutes and hours of my days designing and sewing the quilt I'd decided to give him as a wedding gift.

It was an ambitious project, a patchwork design on either side, and my very first quilt. The cramped little shack I lived in was filled with that quilt. Triangles and squares of salvaged fabric, lint and bits of threads, drawings and cardboard templates covered the bed, table, narrow floor spaces, even the top of the fridge. Sewing it seemed to hold my life together. The quilt filled my days with colour, and with a concern set apart from all else in my life those days—my three separate jobs and the anxiety of forthcoming change.

We sleep under it still, but after twelve years, it's a bit worn. The colours have faded, and some older pieces of fabric are wearing through. Still, I take a special pleasure in turning it each season, revealing the pattern on the opposite side.

Now, my husband and I tend to give each other more practical things—a sewing machine or a skill-saw, a cast aluminium garden trowel or a book of building codes. Sometimes it's hard to remember whose gift a particular implement has been. Other times we give each other thick, hard bound books that we have no time to read. I once knotted him a hammock of mariner's rope, and another time bought a fly fishing rod and a box of flies. In the years of our life together here, I don't think either of us has ever laid down in that hammock, although children who visit spend hours swinging each other. And my husband has been fishing maybe twice, in the evening after work. It seems like we sometimes give the gifts for a life we wish we had, or maybe for the one we are determined someday to share.

~&~

The spirit of gift-giving, Hyde contends, is latent with risk-taking: The individual giving a gift risks submersion in the group, or community; the individual receiving one risks the communion of gratitude. Like a lit torch, the gift illuminates our steps, as well as obligating us to keep the flame alive.

If the giver attaches indebtedness, or the receiver fails to be grateful, the flame dies out, and the gift becomes a commodity. Hyde distinguishes between labour and work, gift and commodity. Both work and commodity, as well as the notion of indebtedness, all characterize our consumer-based society. We all need to grace our lives with the flow of gifts, the labour of caring. Commodity exchange may seem essential to our lives, but gift exchange sustains us, he claims. It fosters unity and preserves a healthy climate of intellectual sharing. The flow of ideas, he argues, is constrained by assigned value and obliged remittance.

While I was reading Hyde's study of gifts, my eldest aunt died of the complications of a long life lived at full throttle. Her age, eighty-two, did nothing to mitigate my heartache at losing her. I found comfort in the discovery of a tradition, the "threshold gift." Offered in the memory of someone transformed, as by death, threshold gifts celebrate the past, and recognize the new state of existence.

To confront the reality of my aunt's death, I had to find the appropriate gift and recipient. Not surprisingly, I settled on books to be donated to my hometown's public library. Along with other members of my family, I chose volumes which people of our town might read and that we would wish to have associated with our aunt's name. For a family unused to coping with death, this gave us an occasion of peace, and solace, and cohesion.

My brother and my mother collected cheques and made

phone calls. I chose the titles, a task not easy but satisfying. My choices included a volume of Sam Pickering's essays—New England in flavour, tender, light and funny; two novels by Robertson Davies—rich with spirit, with quirks of human frailty and faith which would have been both startling and familiar to my aunt; and three books by Margaret Laurence—because I could imagine her writing my aunt's story. I worried that amid my family, two Canadian titles would assert my identity too strongly. I struggled over the omission of any Italians or Catholics among those writers. Finally, what satisfied me was the sheer unlikelihood of those three drawn together for any purpose: the picture of them elbowing one another with their contradictory styles and notions; the idea that my aunt had become the occasion for their unity.

I hope that those books will introduce some new ideas, some different ways of seeing things, to young people who haven't yet ventured far from that small town in Maine: kids like my sisters and brother and me, twenty years back; like my aunt and her sisters and brothers were, fifty years before us. Closing one of these books, I hope that such a kid notices the dedication and nods in appreciation, connecting, for the briefest moment, with my aunt's life, and my family's memory of her.

All through our lives and even after death, the gifts we give have the power to connect us. Whether kept on shelves, consumed, or passed on to others, they strengthen our relationships and enrich us, young and old. Even now, at ages two and five, my children are enchanted by gift exchange. Mostly, they experience the gifts given at birthdays and Christmas-time, when so many carefully chosen books or trinkets move back and forth through the mail, constructing and maintaining relationships with relatives clear across the continent. In the bathtub they wrap toys in soapy washcloths, which, passed from one to the other, are opened with surprise and delight.

# Home

In his essay, "The Trail Home," John Daniel addresses that mystical shift in surroundings as fragrances become familiar, feet feel their way along known trails, sounds are anticipated, and the place becomes "something more than a passageway." Home is not, for Daniel, "the place we were born, or that perfect somewhere else we used to dream of, but the place where we are . . ."

In the same essay, he describes a phase through which many of us born in the later twentieth century have passed:

> We skim freely from place to place, home to home, reasonably happy and very possessive of our independence, but also just a bit baffled, a bit stifled by our easy movement, sure of what belongs to us but not at all sure of what we belong to.

Home, for me, is more complicated than the place where I am, and is much more than a shelter from the elements. I have taken shelter in places which did become familiar—a smelly trailer, a cramped cabin which shook when the wind blew, even, once, in a damp basement room of a Frat house closed down for summer—but which never did become home. Maybe I condemned myself to temporary dislocations; maybe they were homes, but I would not believe it.

Home most definitely is, for me, the place where I spend time with my family. It's where we read, sleep, listen to music, laugh, shout at one another, eat soup, colour pictures, play. It feels as familiar as stepping into a well worn running shoe.

Home is the place where I'm inclined to stay put. It's where an accumulation of the most mundane things reminds me that I belong. If I poke my head out our back door, instantly our dogs and usually a cat or two, will greet me. If I step over the sticks the dogs have dragged there, ready for play, I can see the garden and, if it's spring, the topsoil my husband and I fairly wrung from sod and flinty ground. There might be asparagus poking its tender way through the last cover of snow. It was started from seed in 1980 because I didn't know enough to buy crowns.

And home is where our stories dwell. Along the east side of the garden, for example, rests the outhouse we brought on the back of a truck from a friend's place where it was no longer needed. You can see the hole punched in the side by a rock in the field where the outhouse fell out over the tailgate as we took a corner in the laneway. The dilapidated structure now houses garden tools and hoses, and sometimes kittens. The seat we cut from Styrofoam is still in there. Several litters of kittens have been born in a box which rests on that toilet seat in that outhouse/garden shed. Last week a squirrel scared the wits out of my daughter when it jumped from the hole in the south wall.

᳗

As a kid I envisioned home as a two storey dwelling of dark wood, with a high peaked roof. In the small towns in Maine in the 50's, families lived in two-storey homes, with children's bedrooms upstairs. By the sixties, split-level homes had begun to spring up. On our Sunday drives, we'd study them.

Eventually one appeared on our street. The woman who moved in there used to entice small neighbourhood kids with sweets and promises. I only went in once, but a sense of oddness scared me off. I remember feeling betrayed that such an ordinary-looking house could actually feel like a threat.

My own childhood home was a source of security and pride. The fact that we had wall-to-wall carpeting over the oak floors of the sitting room, a front *and* back stairway—and that our basement was "finished"—gave me the cock-eyed notion that we were rich. During the hurricane of '59 many of our relatives took shelter from the battering winds in our basement. It was—for the kids, anyway—a glorious pyjama party.

Our attic, all rough wood and sloping ceilings, was lit by bare light-bulbs hung on chains. The stairway up was steep. I felt it was the most romantic place in our house, as much for its spookiness as for the mysteries contained in the several heavy crates and steamer trunks lurking in its shadowy spaces.

When I was about nine, someone discovered that my younger sister had been taking things and hiding them around the house. This distressed our mother, who no doubt worried as much about the intimation of insecurity as about the impropriety of such behaviour. I remember thinking I understood why she hid small stashes of coins, cheerios, or candies behind trunks or the cushions of the couch: She was making the house her accomplice, yanking tighter a bond which felt threatened by marital discord, financial worries, talk of moving.

༺

Perhaps because my notion of home issues from childhood memory, giving over our home to our children has seemed natural, nearly irresistible. Our living room—unlike the proper and ornate sitting rooms I remember from when I was little—positively erupts with life. Tiny dump trucks and tractor trailers line up along the backs of chairs. Plastic widgets and metal gadgets cascade from containers of every sort.

On the highest shelves of an indescribably beautiful pine bookcase built along one wall, a dusty sock puppet sits up on a volume of Yeats. Lower down, a full four shelves hold nothing but kids' stuff: rows and piles of books; stacks of toys and puzzles; dogs and elephants, snakes and dinosaurs; a heap of tools complete with chunk of wood. We straighten up this room almost daily, and once a month we throw our combined creative energy and ingenuity into sorting, stacking, and tidying. But despite fine furniture, inherited lace doilies, and reading lamps of brass, the room defies all effort to civilize it.

❖

We share a certain sentimentality, my husband and I. That, and we have learned that a good way to keep ourselves on track is to align a goal with an immoveable date. So every step of the construction of this home we've built is intimately tied to the development and growth of our relationship and our family. Usually we can determine the year of a particular stage in the building of our home by remembering what pregnancy was pending, or where our oldest child was sleeping just then.

We moved onto our property on our first anniversary, in 1980. On that night, I'd came back from my job as surveyor's helper to discover our first real home together: our just-finished twelve-by-twelve plywood shack. We had no running water, no electricity, and no furniture other than a bed fashioned of log ends, and a plywood table. We built a bonfire and dug through our boxes of wedding gifts for plates, pots and pans, and candle sticks. It was late and dark when we settled in to enjoy steaks barbecued on the coals from the fire, a bottle of champagne, and salad.

Later in the month, we were talking by candle-light one night when a gust of wind blew down through the soffits and extinguished our candles, leaving us in smoky darkness. The next morning my husband was up on a ladder, wedged between counter and bed, pounding boards in to close off those soffits. He dropped a two-by-four, taking down a wine-glass rack he'd built and upon which I had just placed three rows of fine, gleaming new stemware—more wedding gifts. We could tell it was good crystal from how beautifully it shattered. That shack was a long way from luxurious, but it served us well. It was home until early December of our second year of marriage.

We hooked up a hose to the end of our water line, and brought it down over an unenclosed soffit so we wouldn't have to haul water. The drain ran out a hole in the wall to the ground. We even had power, via extension cords running across the yard and plugging into a temporary power pole. Our black and white TV sat balanced on the corner railing of the porch. When the power surged, or the refrigerator (also on the porch) kicked in, our picture would recede to the top of the set, the characters becoming short and fat. Mont did the fine tuning on that TV by twisting a piece of kindling he'd wedged into the console. It made a sickening grinding noise, but did the trick.

Preparing dinners was an adventure in the little cabin. Often there'd be a crew on hand to help erect the big timbers, or to raise the heavier windows. Maybe it's an aspect of rural living, or maybe we are blessed with good neighbours, but we never lacked for a helping hand. When work stopped, everyone would be famished. I'd make up a pot of chilli, or stew and bread— whatever we could afford *and* I could figure out how to make. We had little money, but thanks to the remainder of our wedding gifts we did have some beautiful dishes; evening might find us sitting on upturned buckets, eating lentil soup from crystal bowls.

I did more entertaining than ever before or since, cooking

in the narrow space between bed and wall. People stopped by to help, and perhaps out of curiosity, too. One night just the two of us sat eating our dinner when there was a knock at the door. Mont pushed it open to confront a startled pack rat in the midst of a recreational leap from the top of the fridge to the television to the porch.

It got cold that November. We kept warm by opening the door of our propane oven, set low for an hour or two, and lightly roasting ourselves. At night we'd shuffle around in bed under our down comforter, trying to generate enough heat to stop shivering and fall asleep. I also remember waking up, easing my face out from under the tent of blankets and taking a first breath of frosty air, only to have it condense and fall back on my face.

There were mornings when my husband's quilted flannel work jacket, hung on a nail by the door, would have the same skiff of snow on the shoulders as when he'd hung it up—not a sight to inspire one back to work. One morning my contact lenses froze in their case and once I had to use a nail-puller to pry a box of pasta from the hoar-frost which had settled in along the lower three feet of each wall. Still, I regretted moving out of the little cabin.

Late in November, when afternoons darken up so quickly, the carpenter friend who'd been helping my husband with the framing moved back to the coast. Mont was nailing cedar shakes, row upon row up to the steepest part of the roof, as the first snow of the season fell. We'd made it to the stage carpenters call "lock-up." But we weren't able to pour the concrete floor in time to move into the basement as planned. So we partitioned off the north half of the main floor, forming a room sixteen by twenty-four feet—a manor after the twelve-by-twelve cabin. Our manor was humble, to be sure. It was enclosed with plywood and poly, and heated with a terrifying wood stove: Its walls would glow red, groaning and shuddering with the effort of combustion.

We had a concrete double laundry tub bought from the area *Buy & Sell* (a publication to which we paid a good deal of attention through those early building years). That tub was hefted up onto four chunks of log and with some primitive plumbing, served as the kitchen and bathroom sink. Later, with a small hot water tank installed in the corner, a salvaged shower head rigged to a stud along the wall, and a plastic curtain hanging from a doweling rod, we had a fine shower. Making a graceful exit required some coordination, should company have dropped by. But this was a far more satisfying arrangement than dragging ourselves, armed with towels and shampoo, over to some friend's place for showers. No matter how accommodating our friends were, knocking at their door in the evening, tired and dirty, was plain awkward.

One of those friends dropped by for a beer one evening while we were sitting on upturned five-gallon buckets, eating supper from a table of plywood balanced on the stereo box. The next day Cameron arrived to present us with a proper table he'd built for us. It's served as my sewing area since retiring, after four years, as our dinner table.

In the eighteen months we lived in the top half of our home, we took what would become defining steps in the lifestyle which would be ours. So casually, it seems, we brought home our first animals, and set out farming. During these months, interspersed with building, Mont was up north working for four weeks at a time. I was doing whatever work I could scare up: substitute teaching, planting or harvesting plums or corn, tomatoes or pickling cukes—or pounding stakes as a surveyor's helper.

Then, in the summer of '81, the basement floor was poured. By that time, I was working away from home week-days, teaching in Merritt. Mont continued to work away for much of '83 and '84. But most often one of us would be home, along with a friend who'd reside in the little cabin. From our first anniversary onward, the home place has always been occupied.

It was during that first cycle of seasons on the property that we built our garden and began to fight the sod for the topsoil. After studying endlessly from books and magazine articles, I ordered over thirty packets of vegetable seeds, and made the decision to plant them in raised beds. The tidiness of the beds appealed to me, as did the long history (from ancient China, according to one article). Also important to me, they would in no way resemble those immaculate and lavish gardens I remembered from childhood. I knew, even then, that my nature and also the disparate focus of our lives didn't fit with that particular standard of gardening.

Yet I learned that I loved digging in the ground. Still resisting a disciplined approach, I dabble with a garden, experimenting, daydreaming, really. For months of that first gardening year, I was unemployed and gardened with a furious energy. The beds were an untamed profusion of zucchini vines and lettuce, raspberry canes and bushes of beans. In the central bed, enclosed by log walls remaining from a homestead cabin, we even grew marijuana one year. We grew more of everything than we could use, so we shared with friends, bringing them bulging bags of lettuce in a multitude of colours. I learned to cook soups and stews from the things we grew, learned to dig and trench asparagus roots and to wheelbarrow manure and mulch. That was a wonderful season—though it might be that memory has compressed several summers' happiness into a single summer's recollection.

I also learned to can while we lived in the top half of our house. I'd never eaten home-canned peaches—didn't even know that one *canned* in jars—but I knew that women who lived in the country put up food, and so I bought a book, three boxes of canning jars and lids, and a cheap canning pot (still in use). The lid to that canning pot flew out of the truck when I was bringing it back from the home of a friend who'd borrowed it. I bicycled back and forth along the side of the highway, searching until I found it, across a ditch and off in the bush. There's a dent along one edge, where it must've hit the pavement before rolling away.

The first fruit we canned was cherries. Cherries are still the favourite family fruit and we can several batches, if the crop is good. Now I simply wash, stem, and prick the individual cherries—fast and easy enough for the kids to help—before packing them tightly into jars, covered with hot light syrup. But back then, I would pit them until my fingers were raw from the rub of the spring-driven pitter. And our syrup would be spiked with brandy or rum. Poring through cook books, I'd try anything from green tomato relish to dilled carrots. Now, though, with three growing kids, I can fruit and more fruit; fancy now means a couple of cloves tucked in a jar of pears, or some raspberries in the crab-apple jelly.

That first summer, our root cellar was finished, so I could carry the boxes around the house and into the basement, lining the shelves with rows of fruit, jam, pickles, relishes. Though I've worked lots of jobs, I've found little to rival the sheer satisfaction of wiping clean warm jars with a cloth dipped in vinegar, to reveal the deep fruit-dyed syrup of a batch of canned cherries.

On that night when I'd finished our first-ever batch, we lay in our bed counting off the fourteen loud pops, as lid after lid sealed off the cooling fruit. We'd nearly leapt off the mattress at that first pop. Now, though, we're well acquainted with those small implosions—the sound of a good seal.

❧

Our original plan had been to live in the basement for the

years it took us to finish the main house. But like so many plans, it just didn't work out that way. One consequence of our having taken up temporary residence in the upper half, was that the big timbers for that portion of the structure would get exposed to temperature fluctuations which would affect the way they dried, cured, and settled.

Until we began to build a wooden home, I had no idea that wood dried, twisted, checked, and shrunk to such an extent. I didn't know that carefully stained and nailed pine panelling would change so dramatically over the years. In the basement, where we did our first interior finishing, the pine has mellowed from clear blond to shades of amber, then golden-brown. The boards have shrunk to expose paler, unstained strips of the tongues between the grooves. But kiln-dried lumber was beyond our means. We settled for fresh timbers, cut locally, which we would stack to dry for as long as we could wait.

But in that upper floor where we set up our second home, we had no panelling—only pink fibreglass, poly, and plywood stamped "D Grade." What dressed up the place were the exposed beams and posts which, at eight foot intervals, form the frame of the home. Occasionally, in the stillness of the night, one such beam or post would check, sending a resounding crack throughout our room which could vibrate the sternum itself.

In the fall of '82, we did finally move downstairs to the basement, aiming for a Christmas in our new home. We moved gradually, so that for a week or so my stove and dishes were down there, but we were still eating in the upper half. Because the opening above the stairway was left covered until the very last—to keep at least some of the sawdust and dirt of construction separate from the food and clothing—I hiked clear around the house to tend to meals, and back up around carrying the pot of soup or pan of brownies.

The last thing we did, in preparation for the final move down, was to paint the concrete floor—to seal it off and also to dress it up. The paint we chose was dark green. Or at least that's what the exterior of the can promised. We painted all day long, and then left the paint to dry while we went off to Vancouver for a weekend's indulgence in a fine hotel where we wouldn't have to remove dishes from the laundry tubs to take a hot shower. As we were driving along the Trans-Canada, the traces of paint around our fingernails and under our cuticles dried, and we watched with horror the evidence that back home, our floor was transforming into a hideous shade of green, somewhere between lime and pickle. With our next chunk of savings, we sprang for linoleum.

In that downstairs suite, we had a normal, enclosed bathroom, the root-cellar, and a separate bedroom. The kitchen had plywood shelving. Our washing machine (previously outside, with a light bulb to warm up the motor) was brought inside. Our television and stereo sat on proper shelves, and we had room for a couch (salvaged from a friend's pick-up, en route to the dump). Best of all, where our basement extends to ground level (as the hillside drops southward), my husband had built a greenhouse. So we had lots of light, and more sunlit warmth than we'd had in either of the two transitional homes.

Like most features of the place, though, that greenhouse offers us stories, most from the large and small disasters and miscalculations of its design and finishing. It is formed from four rectangular roof panels which slope to meet four shorter rectangular front panels. Along each side, two rectangular panels are topped by triangle panes. The innermost window units, on the opposite sides, open outward, a smaller square upon a long rectangle. The panes are all twin sealed, and represented a heavy investment for us.

Like much of home building, installing those window units was awkward and time-consuming. The greenhouse juts out over the top of the second roll of hill which falls steeply from the south face of the house. There's barely room to walk past with a laundry basket or load of kindling. This was where my husband was standing, hammer in hand, tapping the very last window unit into its fir frame. Giving one final tap at the top, he heard hammer head contact glass nipple (where the twin seal gets closed), and knew, even as he stood there, that the window would shatter. This kind of thing happens, we know now, more times than one would ever anticipate. It means, more often than not, a day's delay, phone calls, a ninety minute round trip to town, a dint to the budget and another to the morale.

The greenhouse, though, affords us a profusion of greenery and bright sunlight. Its floor, meant to store sunlight and release its heat to us in the evening hours, was originally made of stone. We laid that stone ourselves. But the crudeness of our masonry was an affront to my husband, who buried our amateur effort beneath concrete, painting it grey, which is how it has remained. The insulated curtain I sewed and hung still has the large hole chewed by our daughter's hamster. So as a passive solar unit it's a compromise, as most things in home-building have turned out to be.

❧

Our daughter was born during our years of living in the basement suite. We walked her up and down the thirty-two foot length of the place night after night through the colicky months of her early infancy. Her cradle was moved from our bedroom floor to the floor just outside, and then to the back of the couch. She grew from a tiny infant to a busy, alert baby surrounded by love and attention, and always in view.

Those months in the basement suite were a flurry of changes, into parenthood, a more extensive farming enterprise, the jobs we would end up staying with, and more socializing than we've done since. Our friends divided into two groups: the established ranch families of the valley whom we were so fortunate to be welcomed by; and those who, like us, had wandered there from somewhere else, and were seeking jobs, homes, adventure, direction, the ultimate ski run, or something less tangible even than those things.

Being married, employed, with land, home and child—but still adhering to a fairly crude, make-shift lifestyle—placed us comfortably between those two groups. We had friends of every description, any of whom might drop in to see how we were doing. Our hospitality had two bases, the kitchen table our friend had built, and the couch we'd scavenged. We finally brought that couch the rest of the way to the dump, but not before using it for years. It was sinfully ugly, but memorable.

You sat *in* that couch rather than on it. Its springs had fallen, so that you sank down until its arms were at your ears. And when you sat, if the light was just so, you could watch wondrous billows of dust rise up and slowly settle. It would make me sneeze for the first ten minutes or so, missing the first scene of whatever we might be watching on television. Those fine particles of dust probably spanned generations.

I remember wondering, as we held our baby girl, what impressions might be forming in her tiny new mind. When she hears a sneeze or smells old dust, does she conjure up, from distant memories, an image of that hideous yellow brocade?

By November of our basement year, our daughter was six months old and creeping around at a good pace. Her head would knock up against the top of her cradle when she stretched herself. Her change pad, sitting up on the drier, was too small and slippery for a busy, mobile baby. We needed more space. So we set ourselves a date for the big move into our full home: her first Christmas.

We worked long days to make that date. It's mostly a blur, but clusters of detail stand out. I remember two days before Christmas, painting the chimney stones with a clear, quick-drying solution, while Mont put the fourth coat of Varathene on the living room ceiling, which rises to form a peak some twenty feet from the floor. We worked through the night. That dawn I felt light-headed, exhaustion mixing with fumes as I swayed on the top of the stepladder.

We rushed to town on Christmas Eve to do our shopping. We had no gift for our daughter yet, and not enough sense to realize that, at six months, she wouldn't really care. I remember being dizzy with joy at seeing my good friends out for a snowy run on that mild afternoon. I pulled over and jumped out of my Honda Civic to greet them only to realize, as the door slammed behind me, that my baby was locked inside.

Early the next morning, after hours of carrying up mattresses and boxes, Mont went out for our tree. There is a photograph of our baby girl sitting on the floor of her brand new home, with wide eyes, watching her dad drag an enormous, snow-covered tree into the house. Later that day, we shared a wonderful meal with good friends, despite the fact that we had to barbecue the turkey and to broil the pies, since the newly installed oven wouldn't seem to bake. And I had to cart dishes to the bathroom and wash them in our lovely refinished tub, because the new sink my husband had spent the morning plumbing turned out to be missing one fitting. Over the years, our Christmas traditions have smoothed out, though we do seem to retain a telltale bit of the frantic and frenzied.

❦

Maybe because we did so much ourselves, the work we hired others to do for us took on a particular significance. This may be simply because of the expense, but I think it was more because—when you build your own home, progressing board by board—there's an exhilaration, an element of magic nearly, in witnessing a substantial leap of progress that derives from the talent and energy of another.

We hired others to do a variety of jobs, from laying the carpet to pounding out our copper ceiling hood for the kitchen fan. On the day I arrived home from work and looked up the hill, in the dusk, to see that the stone mason had finished, the sight of that beautiful stone chimney took my breath away.

That same stone mason, a tall and quiet man not given to talk, left me a panicked message at work one day. I returned his call to learn that a huge white pig had just walked by the front door. As we spoke, she was looking in the window at him, leaving muddy snout prints. I could tell he was scared of Petunia, so I resisted making light of it. All I could do was assure him that she was quite harmless. I suggested that he *could* try to lead her back to her pen—or he could simply leave her be, for the five hours until I got home. Which he did.

I arrived that night to find that Pet had eaten the dog and cat food (a binge for an otherwise strict vegetarian), up-ended the wheelbarrow, the kindling bucket, pretty much everything tip-able, and left a snout-sized trail of slobber which revealed a foray around the entire house—finishing with a lingering examination of the greenhouse. Looking longingly at her own food and shelter, she was waiting by her pen. She seemed put out that I'd taken so long getting back to let her in.

When we got to the finishing stages, we needed the expertise of other tradesmen. An old man and his son built and installed the wooden railing that runs from the basement up to the main floor. An iron-worker fashioned the wrought iron railing that rises from the main floor to the second. A fine carpenter who lives hours north of us built, transported and installed our kitchen cabinets. Another master carpenter built the floor to ceiling bookshelves which grace our living room and den. During this phase, as the details emerged in all their perfection, home transformed again. It began to feel permanent.

I never would have imagined, after adjusting ourselves to this new sense of stability, that the chimney our stone mason had built could fall. But it happened, twelve years later—the result of a particular combination of the climate of our area and our home's design. The roofline angles down steeply at the front half, above the living room. In the back, the angle widens, providing space for the upstairs bedroom. Since it's so much less steep, the back portion has metal roofing, to prevent the accumulation of snow.

Because the living area is open and it's ceiling so high, when the snow gets deep and climactic circumstances are just so, the snow slides—first from the back, then with less regularity but more drama, from the front. This seems to occur most often in the dead of night. When it does, it sounds just like Bob Marley's ghost dragging those infernal chains across the dark bedroom of Ebenezer.

The big slide happened years later, after we'd grown complacent. One night, conditions were such that a crust of ice atop mounding snow managed to crest up over the lip of the chimney. When it all slid, the ice tugged the chimney along, breaking off eight feet of it. The slabs of masonry cascaded down, clear through the lower roof of the east wing, which was under construction. We slept through the whole thing, awakening briefly when our son, whose bedroom adjoined ours, cried out before dropping back to sleep. From his window, in the morning light, we could see a ragged hole clear through the layers of roof and ceiling, and a dump of snow and masonry on the decking below. Hours of phone calls and paperwork for insurance purposes, and days of labour for reconstruction, and the whole incident is but a story to tell.

Those twin roofs lend our home a lovely silhouette from any distance. But they have caused me fright of other, less dramatic kinds. Sometimes I'll look up, while hanging laundry, to see my husband leaning out from a rickety series of footholds, cleaning the chimney. The sight, even now, makes my gut clench. It's a blessing, I suppose, that I wasn't at home the two times he did slide off; a greater blessing that he lived to tell me.

～

During the stages of building our home Mont learned everything about this work he now does for a living. He learned to wire and to translate building codes, to design stairs and to install tile. Because he was learning, he now seems to see nothing but the flaws when he looks around. The den and master bedroom (twin additions to the west and east, built ten years after the main part of the house, and so after years of learning) were more skilfully done, no doubt.

I learned things too, but managed to forget all the particulars of what I was so proud to have learned. I have vivid memories of framing the south wall of the root cellar and wiring what's now the boys' bedroom (while pregnant, so that I had to lie on the floor to *see* the outlet I was working on). I even wired a three-way switch, perfectly. During the earliest stages, I bedded in sections of our three-quarter mile water line—packing the pipes in soft sand to protect the PVC pipe from fracture—and applied the thick black tar to seal the basement walls.

Before we had children, I was determined at least to understand what lay behind the walls and beneath the floors of our home. But over the years, division of labour crept up on me, until I gave in to other responsibilities. Yet it satisfies me, still, that I grew to understand how a home came about. Though now I couldn't wire an outlet if my life depended on it, I do remember that it felt good, knowing.

~&~

When I think of home, I think of this dwelling. And because, for me, thoughts of home are so inextricably connected with reading and writing, I envision the places where I read and write.

My writing place is at the front of the basement, where my desk tucks in under the wood chute, by the greenhouse. It's well lit by day, though a bit draughty. And if someone's throwing firewood down the wood chute, which slants down over my head, the crashing of that first chunk will startle any thought out of my head. But it's my writing place, a place where I feel content and productive.

My thoughts of home extend from the interior, from the three floors of this structure, outwards to the clothes line strung between trees, up to the garden and down to the pens. Home expands from there, taking in the community of Heffley Lake and on down to the Creek where our children go to school, and outward to encompass Kamloops, where my job has been and where many dear friends live.

I harbour a geo-political and cultural sense of home, certainly, which is more expansive. But I've gleaned much of that from radio, which emanates from within our house, and so brings me back inside.

Barbara Kingsolver, in the title essay from *High Tide in Tucson*, examines dislocation and survival, want and need, drive and desire. She calls herself "the commonest kind of North American refugee," one who has flung herself far from her original home, and learned to love an unfamiliar landscape. Kingsolver explains that over the course of seventeen years she has become embedded there, within a family made up of friends, co-workers and neighbours, and a child who is native to the adopted land. She sees herself as there for good.

Having arrived in this unlikely place exactly seventeen years ago, I acknowledge both the tug of truth and the shudder of coincidence in Kingsolver's recognition. I can remember so vividly, whenever I approach Kamloops on the Trans-Canada and see the tawny hills surrounding that city, ringed with their sparse mane of grass and sage, how I once found them utterly strange, ugly and forbidding. Now they signify that, after a half hour's drive north on the Yellowhead, I will be back at Heffley. They have taken on the beauty of the familiar, and they beckon me home.

# *Echoes and Reflections*

That falling down cabin around which our garden has been built—the old homestead—has its own story to tell. It took us years to learn the fragments we know. It was built by the McDonalds, who came to homestead it during WWI. Though born in Nova Scotia, they'd been living in Kamloops since 1906. Archibald and his wife Effie Ann had three children. A sister of Effie Ann homesteaded close by.

The McDonald's didn't really homestead the one hundred and sixty acres around us, but seemed to have come here to wait out the Depression. The fact is, though, they stayed for years. Though Archie McDonald didn't farm, he did log a bit. The evidence of his logging could be seen when we first moved onto our property.

Mostly, it turns out that he dreamed of mineral wealth. He was convinced that the ridge rising behind us, the one we call Embleton, was volcanic, and rich in copper and gold. He bought four stakes, and waited and dreamed of his prospects. According to local newspaper records, in 1929 the McDonalds moved back to Kamloops. They left behind a stove, some dishes, and their small log home. We have been finding things they'd probably discarded over the years: bits of their dishes, parts of tools, the wheel of a baby carriage.

Archie, as he had come to be known, died in 1956 at the Royal

Inland Hospital in Kamloops. Effie lived to be eighty-four. When she died she had nine grandchildren and four great-grandchildren. For years after they had died, the ridge we call Embleton was known as Mount McDonald, for the man who had dreamed about its wealth.

# *Things Learned on a Family Farm*

Our twenty-eight acre parcel of land forms a long narrow band, rising southward up under the iron streaked ledges of Embleton Mountain. This is no big mountain. The highest point on our property is two thirds of the way to its crest. As a hike, even with young kids, it takes only a few hours to climb.

From the top of Embleton, you can look down and see our home and a scattering of outbuildings. This is one of those terms that conjured up visions of farm life for me, before I ever imagined life on a farm. Our outbuildings include a two-storey shop, the little cabin, the old homestead (gradually becoming little more than a heap of blackened logs), a wood shed, a farrowing shed, and a two-part hog shelter (accessible from two separate pens, condominium style), a weaner shelter, a dog house, and the outhouse/garden shed. The shop is the newest structure, and the one farthest from being finished.

Our home, in amidst the outbuildings, is finished, to whatever extent a house ever can be. What follows completion, we have learned, is the long slow process of disrepair. My husband's work is never even close to done around here, but that doesn't dissuade a certain meticulousness in the work he does. So while the grass grows too high and areas take on a hillbilly quality, there's a pervading order to things.

And everywhere—between buildings, around the perimeter, up behind—stand tall fir trees. So while the ground beneath us slopes ever upward, there are clean lines as trees rise straight up, and fences sweep across horizons. Our home is mostly wood and stone, with a roof line sloping like the land, and rising at steep angles. Because our valley runs east-west, we get long days of sunlight, and because it is rural, long nights of starlight.

I began a ledger in 1980 when we signed for this property which we purchased from Rob and Rose White, along with the water rights to the spring which provides our water. My ledger is powder blue, wire-bound, and while I stew about how paper accumulates, I wouldn't consider throwing out those pages of notes and calculations. If we'd kept a farm journal, the way Rob does, and used to advise us to do, I suppose it might have begun with descriptions of gathering firewood in my husband's first truck, a green '57 Chevy half-tonne. My ledger does show that he'd paid three hundred and fifty dollars for it, fifteen dollars less than the cost of his first chainsaw. Loud and robust, that truck ran well for years. Someone had written "Rust Never Sleeps" on the driver's door, a finger tracing through layers of dust and dirt while we were getting groceries at Safeway one Saturday morning. You can still read it where the truck sits, resting on its haunches in weeds which grow up past the gas tank. A truck like that doesn't get sold; it gets driven to the end.

There's an entry for our tractor, too. It cost four hundred dollars, back in '81. The price was low because it was old, and had once rolled into the North Thompson River. So a guy might expect there to be problems. But it ran, with constant coaxing. You'd be able to hear it long before it chugged into view, driver enveloped in a plume of diesel.

What I didn't know—about buying land, building a home, starting a farm—astounds me now, but didn't deter me then. I had no idea of what a two-by-four was. My vocabulary expanded further, in those first couple of years of rural living, than it did in four years of university. It grew to include culverts (one hundred dollars a piece, in 1981), three-point hitches, temporary power poles (what easterner could imagine inhabiting property not serviced with electricity, let alone a source of water?). Back then I could, and regularly did, stop at a hardware store to pick up nails, or tractor chains, or Varathane. I've since lost the confidence to field the inevitable string of questions (what gauge, what weight, aluminium or stainless, galvanized or not?).

Neither of our fathers drove a truck, owned a chainsaw, raised livestock. You wouldn't have to go back more than a generation to find farmers and builders in our families, but such know-how just doesn't jump across generations. We learned *everything* the hard way. Our learning all began with two pets.

During the summer that we lived in what is now our kitchen area, we acquired a kitten, Jasper le Mieux, a tortoise-coloured runt from the market gardeners I'd been working for; and a Golden Retriever named Lincoln who was a gift from my brother in Maine. The dog was brought across the country by a young fisherman headed for the Pacific. A month later we also had three fat young weaner pigs (Pork Chop, Bacon Bit, and Vinnie—for his deformed ear). We had never, either of us, owned a pet. I didn't even know that I could grow to love an animal.

Jasper le Mieux may have been small, but she was hardy. Usually just called Pusses, she lived for nine years and blessed us with litter after litter, each a predictable foursome almost always including one tortoise runt, a calico, and two black-and-white males. She was a merciless hunter, and taught her kits well. Once, after we'd moved into the basement, I'd climbed to the upstairs—closed off for construction and so unlit—and groped my way to the box left out for her, to check out Jasper's new babies. I felt for each kitten—one, two. three, four, five . . . *five?* Number five turned out to be a headless rabbit, deposited in amongst her brood. It seemed she began her hunting lessons even before their eyes had opened!

Lincoln, our puppy, was a big male, and pure-bred. He was beautiful, gentle, and splendidly goofy. I had expected such a creature to be well equipped for country life, but that proved not to be so. It broke my heart when he went missing, shortly before Christmas in his second year. I put in calls to the radio stations and SPCA, and left notes at the post office. But it wasn't till the next year's spring thaw that a neighbour, out for a trail run, called to tell me he'd found the remains of our retriever.

Lincoln had been shot, chasing cattle—a serious offence in open range. I had only just learned how deeply I could love a dog, before I had to learn to lose one. The experience left me bruised. While I've been fond of a good many pets since, none has managed to claim such a place in my heart as that dog did.

Pigs are quite another matter, though I did become immensely fond of one. Petunia was a sow worth knowing. It was 1982 when Mont brought her home, the bringing an adventure in itself. He met up with the friend who was selling her, in a parking lot just outside of Kamloops. Petunia no doubt had had far more experience with being loaded into trucks than either of those young men had with loading a big pig. She may have decided it was *not* going well; in any case, she balked. Slow, stately, and pregnant, she walked right on out of that parking lot. She made her way down the highway before they managed to get her in the truck.

Pet must have passed along a bit of wanderlust in her genes, because a few years later a skier pulled in our driveway on his way home from the mountain, to ask if we happened to be missing a pig. I asked what this pig looked like—half in jest, half wishing this might *not* be ours. But Petunia's daughter, Ten Spot, wasn't hard to recognize from the description.

I left on foot to find her (while an amused skier called from his car window "To market, to market . . ."). She'd shuffled all the way down to the fishing camp before I met up with her, turned her around and accompanied her back with my arm draped across her neck. Though we never repeated the experience, I like to think we shared a pleasant memory of that brisk winter walk.

The matriarchal sow, Petunia, besides providing lessons in loading a pig, taught us a lot about birthing, known in pig circles as farrowing. The birth of her first litter was complicated not only by our inexperience, but also because we never did know the date she'd been bred, nor her age, nor even, for sure, if she was pregnant.

Despite our ignorance, that first delivery went fine. Since my husband was working away from home, I attended to Petunia myself in her first day of labour. On that occasion, as with all her subsequent births, she defied every single so-called *fact* set out in our primer on pig farming.

Over twelve hours passed between the dropping of the first slippery piglet, and the final expulsion of the sac. And then she lay there, nice as you please, resting on her side for two full days. Though she didn't demonstrate the kind of nurturing which might have inspired some degree of confidence, her piglets did find her teats and drink. When she still hadn't risen to eat that evening, I opened Pet's lips and spilled in grain pellets from a yogurt container. I served her water after her grain, which she took, though with no evidence of gratitude.

Also vivid in memory is the occasion of traveling to Armstrong to buy our first boar: Another Vinnie, this one was part Red Wattle. We were driving the second in our line of dilapidated farm trucks, on this warm sunny day in July. Our daughter was just over one year old, and she loved a road trip. On our way back from Armstrong, we took a northern route, past Shuswap Lake.

We were hot and dusty, and pulled off the highway at a small cove for a quick, cooling swim. To us it didn't seem strange to be travelling, on a Sunday afternoon in the summer, with three hundred pounds of boar in the back. But to the other family on that beach, it must have seemed very odd indeed. They were quick to pack up and pull out, leaving us all to ourselves.

During that first year or so of our farming, when every experience was new to us and to our friends, the entertainment value was high. There was fanfare for every phase, from the farrowing to the castration to the slaughter. In between, there were more mundane pleasures like checking out which foods got the pigs most excited (prawn heads, melon rinds, egg shells, beet greens—in that order). We discovered that pigs love beer, and handle it well. Ours also seemed to enjoy water-play. One friend would drive out from town just for the joy of spraying them with a hose.

Our first slaughter was a gruesome event, which we did our damnedest to disguise as a festive one. We'd invited friends and neighbours, for muscle and moral support—and also because no one would want to miss this. We had a pot of stew simmering, and cases of beer chilling. Mont got up at dawn to start a fire under the tank of water which had been suspended from a tree limb. We had learned that you scald hogs, so the bristles will scrape off from the hide. We had clothes-line pulleys rigged on a board nailed to another tree, with ropes hanging down, to hoist the carcasses for draining. We had knives sharpened and ready, and the twenty-two loaded.

The day emerges vividly from memory as a jumble of

squeals, stench, sticky black blood, slippery guts, broken ropes, and cold rain. I remember racing back to the house to scare up some razors. Our tank of water had cooled and the bristles no longer yielded to the knife blade as illustrated in our soggy handbook. At some point in the process, my husband lay on the ground beneath a mutilated carcass, the rope suspending it having neatly snapped.

It's a wonder we still eat meat. But squeamishness, we have learned, has little place on a farm. Yet that first time, the stench and the grease got to me. It took a few good washings to get the smell out of my skin. I've since learned to rub salt and then lemon juice into my hands. But you learn those things late, often when you no longer need the knowledge. It's been years since I've had my hand in the killing of animals.

Even my husband's gotten out of that aspect of farming. As soon as we could afford to, he began contracting out the killing and butchering to professionals. Our farming was—still is— rather a shoestring operation. We're in it for some ambiguous lifestyle factor, for the good and healthy meat, and also for the simple reason that once you set up it's no small matter to turn back from farming. So we got out of the killing but remained in breeding, acquiring a boar and later—to diminish a level of incest you don't even want to think about—venturing into AI (artificial insemination), which yielded boar catalogues (think mail-order sires), and stories only my husband can rightly tell.

But when we set out, we decided that we needed to know the whole operation, start to finish. Over the next few years my husband performed several minor surgeries and even a major one (certainly from the pig's perspective). He would telephone or drop into the vet's, and follow whatever advice he could gather. He scraped out an infected ear with a soup spoon, until the swelling reduced from tennis ball size to a more ear-like dimension. He stuffed intestines and other internal organs back into whatever orifice they had burst from. He did what was necessary to facilitate troublesome births, or coax weak piglets or lambs to survive the first days, often in boxes in our furnace room or entranceway.

Pigs seem neatly designed for birth, yet poorly equipped for nursing: The sow can't see around her, and is neither overly agile nor much given to fussing over her dozen or so babies. Too often morning rounds revealed one piglet squashed flat, oddly two dimensional, underneath his suckling siblings. Inevitably, and perversely, the sow typically would manage to lie down upon her largest and heartiest piglet. Maybe it's some quirk of evolution, to ensure more milk for the rest of the litter; or maybe just bad luck, to ensure lower expectations for rookie farmers.

I've grown attached to pigs over the years. I like the sounds pigs make when you drive into the yard, or return from a run. It's a sound a quartet of badly strung cellos might make, strummed lightly as their players simultaneously murmur in disdain. Besides their endearing sound, I like watching pigs lined up at the trough—every couple of seconds one of them shoving out another, who struggles to insert himself at another place in the line—each one of them always and forever seeking the prime position for getting snout to slop (expecting, perhaps, the odd sampling of chocolate mousse or lobster bisque amid the daily repast).

Maybe it's because they are so engaging that I also enjoy saving scraps for the pigs. It's more than a matter of ecology. I *like* sorting the succulent vegetable peelings from the dry peel of onions: one for the pig bucket; the other for the compost. And I enjoy imagining their pleasure when I pour in pickle juice, or the remains of a kid's porridge with brown sugar. Composting is gratifying, but not nearly as much fun.

Twice we've had to sell off all our pigs, to prepare for a trip back east. Pigs are a good deal of trouble, but when we haven't had any, I have missed them, though I suffer no delusions about how little actual contact I have with farming any more. Sheep are easier to leave: Fenced in a field, they'll graze for weeks in the summer, needing only fresh water replenished occasionally. Sheep, unlike the pigs, have failed to earn my affection (and seem not in the least dismayed by this).

It's hard to love an animal as dumb as a sheep seems to be. I once watched from my kitchen window as a ewe, stuck between two lines of cable connecting the antennae to our television, pushed again and again into the cable. I got distracted, only to discover, a full hour later, the same ewe, held fast by the same cable. She had only to take one small step backward to find freedom. The next week a sister of hers was as ridiculously trapped in my pea vine, a flimsy nylon affair. She had ripped it to shreds pushing her nose through one square of mesh, only to encounter another one. I never did forgive her for mutilating our first tender green peas of the season.

When we set out to build our first pens, in a flat area just west of our home, we got help and plenty of advice from our rancher neighbours. "Hog tight" is an expression for fencing standards which we quickly learned to understand. We gained new respect for the ingenuity and restlessness of pigs. Finding the flaw in that fence-line is a lot like searching for the pinhole in your flat air mattress in the chilly darkness of night: It's damned near impossible sometimes, and never what you feel like doing, but a lot depends on it.

Pigs do most interesting work with a pen. Once they are in fact contained, within hours they upend and eat any vegetation (first tender grasses, then mullein and daisies, and finally, thistles and wild rose bushes). In a day, the area reverts to a plain of dirt and they begin on roots and stones, surfacing and rearranging them.

Eventually, what was firm ground resembles a moonscape and will barely support the fence posts defining it. But at this point, rather than pushing the fence over the pigs will more often begin to work from beneath, tunnelling out. It's probably only because they fail to organize themselves and coordinate their strategies that pigs are ever to be found in pens at all. Once a pig *does* escape his enclosure, you will find him waiting to be let back in. Their ambitions don't run far: A pig never likes to be more than a moment from the trough.

The sheep are another story. Mont had always planned on fencing our entire twenty-eight acres, so our sheep could graze freely for the summer months. Finally came the summer when the fencing was done and the cattle-guard in our driveway was installed. It took most of a weekend to dig out, cover with posts, and secure. The sheep were released.

Within the hour they were gone, leaping directly across that cattle-guard as though compelled by some innate drive. Instead of taking our kids to the lake as planned, we all chased sheep up the road, down the road, across the road. Once they were brought back in, barbed wire was strung across the cattle-guard. So they shambled up the acreage, following the fence up steep scree slopes and over rugged brush, as if drawn to just the spot where they could jump over to the neighbour's scree slopes and brush, wandering back down and out onto the road in front of *his* place.

Our kids have evolved their own relationships with our animals over the years. Children who grow up on a farm have to come to terms with all aspects of life: birth and sickness, worms and manure, copulation and death.

Each of our kids has had a turn falling or being swept by a gate into a pile of manure (understandably horrifying for each, though worst for Nicole, who got knocked into the pile by a gate swinging open, and then dragged *back* through the manure by the returning gate). They've gotten worms, a far greater trauma for parent than child. They've discovered that pig heaven is actually the deep freeze, and that while we enjoy raising animals and aspire to care for them well, farm animals are not pets.

And there were tougher things to be learned, the protocol of peaceful co-existence: awareness, familiarity, and respect. Our oldest was once showing off for her younger brother. All of six, Nicole was demonstrating her climbing skills, working her way up to the top rail of the fence, when she toppled forward. She landed in the ram pen, surprising Leo, who made the quick decision to charge her. Needless to say, she was frightened. Her brother, however, was terrified. He kept a wide berth from that ram for years.

Not long after getting attacked, Nicole ran to alert me that Andrew needed to be rescued. He had jumped up on top of the dog-house roof in a panic, sure he was about to get charged. Leo was tethered at the time. But Andrew would not be talked down from his haven. I had to lift him off and piggy-back him away to safety.

Still, this was progress for Andrew, who himself got chased by a hen. He was trying to catch a chick, and though he didn't stand half a chance of succeeding, our hen couldn't tolerate some mere kid scattering her flock. For the rest of that summer a cluck would send him running. These incidents have taught the kids to respect the animals—in a way that no explanations or rules could do.

Andrew may be the most timid around the animals (still, at ten), but he's also the one who most enjoys doing chores. He will spend hours with his brother, inventing games around the pens. Since he was four, there's been a "fire station tree": a tri-trunked tree with hoses wrapped around it. So not surprisingly, it was Andrew who insisted that I come down to the pens one morning this past summer, when his dad was away, to free a ewe who'd forced her head through a square of the wire mesh fence. It is a universal principle of farm families that once the farmer leaves for a weekend, some catastrophe will occur.

The catastrophes spill into memory: Take, for example, that time the pipe burst, flooding the weaner pen so that it resembled a garish sketch in a child's adventure story—swirling muddy water, around which swam rolling, screeching piglets, one trailing yards of bandage. Or the time that a lamb fell through a window-opening of an addition, under construction, falling ten feet into the basement. I was nine months pregnant and not about to crawl down into the hole to hoist it up. Instead, for several hours I listened to the mauuing of a distressed ewe, synchronized with the bleating of her lamb.

Perhaps, then, with five years of experience, Andrew's urgent news of a pregnant ewe stuck in a fence should have been no problem. And you might well think so, if you've never tried to push a sheep backward. Though frantic to get free, no doubt thirsty and hungry (being too firmly wedged to reach around for any nourishment), she would *not* budge. Her eyes were wild, and probably mine were too.

I resented failing, and the thirty minutes of time lost, besides which my arms ached. My daughter and I tried quiet reason, and we tried gentle prodding. Then, desperate, I sent the boys for the wire cutters.

After another thirty minutes which failed to turn up wire cutters, Andrew triumphantly brought me pruning shears. They worked, only by so crudely prying apart the wire that it's a wonder the stupid beast didn't slash her neck getting through it. But we had succeeded: The fence was mangled, and the ewe was freed. She drank with gusto, cast an evil look in my direction, and walked away.

Before we ever had sheep, back when we still lived in our

basement, we brought home our first chickens. Banties are beautiful birds with spectacular colouring and elegantly ruffled leggings. Though small, they're surprisingly hearty. We raise them not for the eggs or meat, but for colour and interest. Aside from receiving the occasional handful of pig food in the winter, they are self-reliant, digging for insects in the ground. They're quiet, peaceful creatures, except for early dawn, particularly in those times when the rooster population grows. And except for the oddest of phenomena which I call their chicken conventions.

Every so often chickens will set to clucking, carrying on until they've all come together. Once gathered, they will make an enormous racket, not quite jubilant but not distressed or mournful either. These conventions seem to take place during the summer months, out back by our gas tank, where the old trucks rest. I can offer no explanation for this behaviour.

Our chickens usually roost high in trees, which I never would have believed if I hadn't seen it myself. There are two particular trees down by the pig pens which the kids call the chicken trees. (Once, when I was reading to him, James scoffed at the barnyard picture which included a henhouse: "That's silly. Everyone knows chickens live in trees!")

Sometimes, probably in response to insect cycles, the chickens relocate close around the house, or up to the garden. But they seem always to lay their eggs in the shavings by the pig pens. And they coexist remarkably well with the pigs, sheep, and even dogs and cats on the property. It always amazes me to see a flock of fuzzy chicks pecking at the ground around the hooves of an enormous sow. Kittens will do the same, crowding in for a drink of water. My husband tells of discovering, on a frigidly cold January morning, a rooster, a dog, and a cat all huddled to sleep in a single frosty ball under one of the retired trucks. At first glance, he was sure the dog had killed the rooster.

Those chickens adapted well and survived, as a flock, cold winters, coyotes, neighbours' dogs, plus whatever unnoticed frailties and tragedies befall a chicken's life. At least, until the summer when a silver fox showed up in our area. He cleaned out all the free range chickens in the area, ours included. For a year we had no banty hens; we had a neighbour fox instead. Story has it there used to be a fox farm down on Little Heffley. Because of that, red, white, and silver foxes still roam wild. All I know is that we see fewer coyotes now than when we first arrived, but lots more foxes. At least now, though, they leave our chickens alone. We think that's because our geese scare them off.

Unlike banties, geese are definitely *not* quiet and peace loving. They are loud, and can be outright hostile. But we like having them. We acquired them in the same haphazard fashion that characterizes so many of the directions our farming has taken. There was a call one night from the friend of an acquaintance, wanting to find a "good home" for a small flock of pet geese. We made a call to our neighbour, and it was arranged for him to take two and for us, three.

These were four large white geese, and one black African. Call me biased, but they are beautiful birds, graceful and robust. They have a surprisingly broad range of vocalizations, from a low throaty sputter to a full throttled honk to an open-mouthed hiss. Our ram displayed an instant and total aversion to the geese, and the pigs, after a few tries at socializing, also kept them at bay. But the chickens seemed to recognize a common birdness and would often hang around the geese pen.

Like the chickens and cats and dogs, our geese will be pets. Though there was one egg, we have stopped expecting more, and wouldn't touch it if we found one. For poultry consumption, I prefer buying our eggs from a rancher down the road, and our chicken and turkey, from another.

Our goose story is a twin tale of homecoming and reunion.

When the geese arrived from their former abode at Knouff Lake, they came in sacks in the back of our truck. At our neighbour's place, two were dropped off. At our place, the other three were released. We put out food and water. The next day, when the kids ran down to check out the new geese, there were none.

After work we got a call from our neighbour, who'd come home to find all five geese outside his door. His place is a good twenty minute hike across the road and along a path through the bush. It's steep in places, and rugged going. We didn't see or hear any of it, but I like to imagine those five geese honking back and forth, the two guiding the three through a maze of pavement and foliage.

Unfortunately, separating them was more complicated than merely recapturing and transporting two. Their previous owners had separated them into two couples, plus one bachelor uncle. We now had, for all we could discern, one black and four white geese. My husband picked three, and brought them home where they were fenced in. But our neighbour was convinced we'd mixed our couples, or worse yet, separated the sexes all together. His were, he claimed, looking melancholy. Ours still looked like geese, for all we knew.

But I got books from the library, and we studied. Our research reaffirmed what we knew: Geese mate for life. The books had little to offer, however, on the subject of recognizing a married couple from, say, a pair of brothers. As for gender, the sources agreed: Sexing geese is a tricky business. There's something about the relative arch of the neck, the noises they make, and some discrete difference of design, for those undaunted by the considerable bulk and strength of the bird.

Our neighbour and our son rounded up the flock and spent some hours studying arcs of necks and comparing sounds, which were mostly unfriendly. They did, in fact, arrive at a pairing that satisfied the two of them, and apparently the geese as well. Although our neighbour's geese behave with a good

104

deal more hostility than our three do, they did recently produce an egg between them.

The addition of a cow has been, so far, less eventful than other additions have been. Millie may not agree, but she appears to be settling in. She seems lonely, but will no doubt make friends with the sheep in time. When I drive down past her corral she gallops along beside the vehicle. She always greets my husband, as all the animals do. Typically, though, just as we're getting attached, the month arrives when she's to become the year's beef supply for us and a couple of other families. We haven't yet figured out how we'll move her to Brenda and Uli's for slaughtering and butchering.

This will be our last time taking our animals up the valley to them. They will be retiring, my husband tells me. I'll admit that we'll really only miss Millie for a week or so. Doing business with our neighbours, though, we'll miss for years.

I can't end an account of farming without talking about farm disasters, maybe because we've just suffered a few. They tend to go in spells, I've learned. So the news that my husband had discovered our favourite cat, progeny of Jasper, dead at the side of the road two weeks ago, came to me with a heavy sense of foreboding.

I was battling just this feeling when one of our hardiest pigs died, days before the arranged slaughter and sale. It had gorged itself on pumpkin, maybe, or swallowed the stem—the discarded jack-o-lantern our son threw in the pen being the only thing out of the ordinary.

My husband saw the whole thing. He'd just pushed the animal to the ground, forcing mineral oil down its throat to give it some relief from whatever ailed it. But, despite his efforts, she struggled to her feet, shuddered and died right there in front of him. He spent the rest of the afternoon hauling the carcass away. He missed half a day's work, not to mention our lost profit on an animal bought, then fed for six months, and on a customer's unfilled pork order.

I should know by now, should be inured. We have years of experience. There was the summer of the cougar. And the fall before that, a dog got into our pens and ran down our sheep twice before my husband finally had to shoot it, but not before one ewe was dead, and another had a leg chewed off. That ewe survived—three-legged—to deliver two lambs. But we lost most of the lambs of the remaining ewes that year, probably to the stress of being chased by a run-away dog.

Then there was the year that some imported animal brought in disease. At least that's what we figured had caused our pigs to lie down and die, small to market sized, one after the next, over the course of a week. We even paid a vet in town to dissect one carcass, only to learn that it had gotten some swine disease.

I know that my husband regularly copes with such disasters, though more often on a smaller scale, in his building and farming work. I don't know what kind of a toll they take on him. Me, I just become wary, then I forget about them, at least until the next time disaster strikes. But for every hard-luck story, there's some instance of survival to marvel at. For every creature that mysteriously drops dead, there's one hobbling on three legs, carrying on. Survival comes in so many forms.

# High Notes

Waiting at the end of the laneway one crisp October morning, I shared my daughter's eager anticipation of the yellow schoolbus pulling around the corner. Something about the schoolbus doors sealing shut, the bus grinding away from the gravelled road edge, its pairs of red lights still flashing, gratifies me. Watching those restless kids bumping against one another in their impatience to share all the moments since the evening before makes me nostalgic: For what, I can't imagine. I never got to ride a schoolbus as a child.

In another life I might like to be a schoolbus driver, though ideally, I envision them as men—greying, broad-shouldered, congenial. And the buses, they should always and only be yellow. For safety, of course, but also for cheer against the backdrop of grey winter mornings. Their brash yellow picks up from the autumn leaves, carrying that splash of pigment into the greys of winter and the browns of spring.

❦

On Christmas day this year, between the overeating and the frenzy of giftwrap and ribbon undone, we went walking on Heffley Lake. Our lake forms a bow tie, pulled off and dropped, slightly dishevelled, spanning about four miles. By some lucky accident of topography, its entire far-side remains uninhabited, except for loons and the occasional beaver. On its road-side, homes and cottages elbow at one another, all nosing out to the steep edge which drops down to its watery depths. From the lake, you see one ramshackle dock after another, braced by some arrangement of rope and wire, spanned by rickety walkways or log steps, and now and then interrupted by an orderly plot of flowers, or maybe a tree house or rope swing.

It's a mild winter, with not much snow. Neighbours tell us the ice is solid, and their tracks—slender parallel traces of skis, the single wake of a sled dragged, and the tenuous slice of blades—tell us they've made good use of it. We're dressed in felt-packs and parkas, the kids swishing in nylon snow pants. We park at the home of friends who've gone away for the holiday, crossing their yard, slipping and creaking down their steep stairway and over their ice-encrusted dock. The lake lies frozen in several layers, now and again heaving to an uneven swell, ripples arrested from the motion their form suggests. There are cracks, and small circles left by ice-fishermen. Spellbound, our son lies on his belly, peering into the blackness of one such circle, looking for fish.

A couple of inches of snow cover the ice unevenly. It's crusty, and crunches as we walk and run. The toboggan my husband drags behind makes a different sound, a humming. We trudge, run for bursts, pull the kids now and then until we've made it across to the far side, where we leave the toboggan, step into deeper snow and climb up the bank. I carry our son, who's slow and gets too easily frustrated by his inability to keep up. Aware of her new-found agility, our daughter marches off ahead proudly. Setting the only tracks in this small area—the only human tracks anyway—we move through thick underbrush, the branches dumping their accumulation of snow on us. Nicole finds bird and rabbit tracks and for a moment so brief that I never do share it, she sees a rabbit scamper by, barely breaking through the crusted snow.

The kids climb and poke and slide in and about the hilly lake-side gulch until a subtle shift in light prompts us to move along. We retrace our unruly path back out and across the lake, to our friends' home. There, we get out snacks and prepare for a hot tub out on their deck. Always on the look-out for opportunities for a work-out, I steal away for a twenty minute run back out on the lake's surface.

Maintaining a lazy pace I make my way beyond the sight, and eventually the sounds, of my children shrieking and waving. Even the deck they play on becomes a distant black smudge. I weave in and out of neighbours' tracks, finally leaving these, too, behind me. Soon I'm at the narrows—the knot of that bow tie—which links the two fatter, and inhabited, sections of our lake.

I turn back at the moment when the digits of my watch flicker to ten; just then, pleasing me in the way points of time and place have seemed to converge, I reach a tree which has been slowly bending out over the lake, in the dozen years we've lived here, as if at any moment to fall into its own reflection. The summer my husband and I lived in a cabin on the opposite shore, loons nested in the lower branches of this tree. Mornings, I used to canoe over here, watching the pair of loons watching me. Despite my respectful distance, they never did ease their vigilance. Now, the only signs of life are my own rhythmic footfalls, the curls of chimney smoke rising from the homes in the far distance, and the eerie groans and plinks of shifting lake ice.

All around me on this particular winter afternoon of Christmas, shading lake and sky and hillside, my favourite colours materialize. The spectrum has diminished to four or five hues: the brown and dark green of the conifers, barely distinguishable one from the other; the blues and several shades of grey against which are defined the blackest of blacks, and a white gleaming like tempera on water colours.

If I painted, I would paint only in these colours, and if I knit, I would wear sweaters of greys splashed with blue and brown and black.

The air, just below freezing, tastes sweet as I suck it in over my teeth. The running and the colours and the taste of that air all merge to send me still higher. I've lost all sense of time, but as I push each step forward to meet each of the tracks I set on my way out, I am propelling myself back toward husband and children, hot-tub and chatter.

Somewhere between my turnabout and my return all the thoughts that compact themselves to await spells of meditative aloneness unfold, like so many origami figures my Japanese students form in brightly coloured squares of tissue. Outlines of essays take shape, each comprised of its own angle and hue. All the while my steps are composing their own story, adding to the stories of other runners, skiers, and kids on sleds.

᠊ᢙ

Five days before Christmas, we attended my daughter's school concert. Her primary school serves our rural community which extends for about ten miles. The concert was to be a casual affair, participation required, we were warned. Without actually admitting it, my husband and I looked forward to the evening. My daughter and her little brother were openly excited.

Bleary eyed and braced by coffee, I'd just driven eight hours, back from a week of study down in Washington, where I'd been doing graduate work. As usual, I'd rushed to get everyone groomed and polished and fed, only to realize that I was dismally underdressed. Barely tucked in, hair springing out in too many directions, I looked around us in the town hall to see familiar folks in quite unfamiliar attire: Neighbours were all made up in velvets and lace, fragrant with perfumes that set my nose twitching. Luckily, our daughter was still too young to be embarrassed by my short-comings—but I made a mental note to be better prepared next year.

She herself looked lovely, small and pretty in a black patterned corduroy jumper. Standing up on a bench with the shorter grade one students, our daughter peered shyly out at the audience, then retreated to the more comfortable view of her classmates. Once, catching sight of us, she broke into a grin (shy a few teeth) and waved.

We could hear every word she sang, and our son, fairly dancing on my lap, sang along with her. The blues version of a Christmas carol they performed made me grateful that the school still resisted the popular aversion to religion. "Mary had a baby, yeah Lord . . ." resounded.

Clusters of band members and class groups moved on and off the stage, while the principal led us in song. Slight and balding, he spoke with warmth, but singing was clearly not among his strengths. Yet we enjoyed ourselves and sang along with whatever words we knew. Andrew had numbed my legs standing on them to see everybody. Nicole joined us and together we watched and sang and waved at kids we knew, in one group after another.

Midway through the evening, a blond boy walked onto the stage to perform solo on his trumpet. His face flushed red, first with his effort and then with the sheer fluster of having lost a note. With his last note still lingering, he hurried away to the loudest applause of the night.

Composed of four girls we knew well, a flute quartet followed, off-key and halting. Remarkably different in height, they were about eleven. Nearly spilling into each other, they rushed off the stage like the trumpet player before them. Clustered together, giggling, their programmes up to their faces, they pushed down the aisle.

Those girls startled me with their height and their self-consciousness. They were babies when we first knew them.

Their having grown so surprised me more than my own children's maturing. Looking around me I discovered that their parents, the ski bums and hippies we'd gotten to know years before, had grown greyer. They were the ones in seldom-worn suits and dresses, with hair slicked down or piled in buns, and camcorders in hand.

I'd never quite noticed just when they turned into such solid middle-aged parents. Intoxicated by the carol singing, by the children who fairly tingled with excitement, by the sense of belonging here, I felt a surge of contentment at this whole aging process. I've never shared—not yet anyway—some people's reluctance to grow older, or their fear of their own children maturing. The cycles evident all around me on that one evening, both reassured and mystified me.

⚬

Once again I'm awash in the pleasure of discovering how the simplest pleasures are often the greatest. Impressions lift off from so many fragments of my days, leaving me bright schoolbus yellow mornings and gently shading blue-grey December twilights. Perhaps this way of seeing reduces my surroundings, the way the origami maker reduces the length and elegance of a crane to one thin sheet of paper in a multitude of folds and angles. But a small hint of pleasure results.

Like that solo trumpet player, we won't always reach those high notes we strive for. And those that we do reach startle us with their sudden, unexpected perfection.

# Home, Revisited

After they'd graduated from university, my two older sisters lived within two hours drive of each other, one in New Hampshire, the other in Vermont. They were, and remain, quite dissimilar in personality, taste, and inclination, but are friends in the complicated way in which siblings seem to be friends— particularly when separated by barely a year of age, but a chasm of temperament.

The older of my sisters was newly married, sharing a cramped but tidy duplex with her husband, who was studying business at Dartmouth. She was teaching chemistry and physics to high school students, students who were my own age at the time. One of the many things that impressed me about my newly married sister was her energy for order. On their fridge door she had taped a list detailing their meals and the coordinated grocery list. (I keep such a list today, clipped on a calendar suspended from a magnet on, of course, the fridge door. Sometimes it's all that seems to separate our daily lives from utter chaos.)

The other sister was in Vermont, living in a commune called Misty Meadows. She was not married, but lived with a long-haired man, drummer of a band, with whom she owned a store and had a baby girl. Misty Meadows, a stately, sprawling old farm-house situated on acres of lush fields, housed a remarkable and volatile blend of personalities. My sister's small family had their own section of the house, but everyone seemed to roam freely with few boundaries, or imperceptible ones. Some meals were communal, but my sister did have a cooking space of her own, with jars of foreign looking grains and herbs on shelves above a counter (not unlike, I suspect, the jars of couscous, barley, and wild rice lined up along one shelf of my pantry). The others who lived in the commune were mostly male, a couple of pairs of brothers, and also a woman in billowing skirts who lived upstairs.

I remember watching my niece propel herself through the rooms of that house on a scooter and thinking that she was careening from safety to danger, as she hurled herself down dark corridors and toward remote corners. But she seemed so at ease, casual and as wilful as any toddler in her exploration of that rambling structure which was her home.

As for me, my childhood home was gone, sold and renovated, and the small apartment my mother and younger sister shared never did become home for me. A teenager, I was living on the campus of a boarding school, where I'd contracted mono—that scourge of studious teens.

I don't remember the circumstances, only that I was to spend my spring break recovering, one week with each sister. What I do remember is the fog in which I left school, traveling by bus to New Hampshire, where I must have been quite a sleepy, but troublesome intrusion, bedded in the middle of a small living area. By the time I got to Misty Meadows I was healthier, and anxious for more space in which to find privacy (in a place where it seemed little valued, but available). I was also more aware of how, for me, home was somewhere between the orderly and secluded, and the rambling and chaotic. It was neither of those places, and yet I'd needed both of them, though the distance between them threatened to fragment my very sense of identity.

Our original pig-pen, a flat patch to the north and slightly east of the house, has, for a couple years, been in the process of becoming a rink. It was on its way to being transformed into a tennis court, when it temporarily became a rink one winter, evolving from a crude surface of ice to a full-blown, court-sized rink—complete with nets, boards, lights and bench. The rink, known as the pigpen, has been a communal scheme and endeavour. With it came a steady flow of traffic, guys coming by first to level the foundation, then to flood the surface, clear the snow, set up boards, roast sausage and gaze out at their efforts, waiting for the cold to set in. Who'd have thought that a slab of ice could so drastically change a place as settled as home?

For an American woman, even after years of studying this Canadian passion—watching the boys play, take shots in the basement or on the driveway, watch game after game on TV—having a rink in our back yard has been an awakening.

I can't tell you first-hand what goes on at the rink because I think my presence there triggers a series of shifts in pitch, or passion. My impressions have been cultivated from a distance and so are mostly auditory in nature. They are a profusion of sounds: slamming of bodies into boards; clatter of sticks heaved aside; scraping of blades across a faulty surface; whoops and yelps and shrieks; and profanity that approaches exuberance. Added to this potent mix are the five or six dogs brought along by their city masters. And occasionally a toddler, wrapped to cartoon-like roundness in layers of soft clothes—protection from both cold air and hard ice.

Our own kids will virtually disappear to the rink. On days as cold as thirty below, I might not see them for five hours at a time. The sandwiches I prepare will sit drying on their plates, glasses of milk warming. Then, with a blast of chilled air, one of them will burst through the door—sometimes tottering on skate guards—eyes glassy and cheeks chafed red, lips barely able to articulate the request for a mitful of cookies to chase down whatever fabulous lunch "the guys" have brought to share.

The guys who come to play out at the rink allot an ample berth to our domestic life: that is, to the house and those who remain inside—namely, me. I've long suspected that this is not entirely due to their considerate nature; but as much due to the pursuit of the unadulterated hockey experience, which is, well . . . primitive. Thus the clubhouse with its rough-hewn benches and blackened stove, its heaps of beer and pop cans, its smell of stale sweat, smoke, and grease. Around its perimeter, the snow banks are speckled with pee holes.

The clubhouse, though surely enough a shelter, represents, for me, the polar opposite of the house. If our home is the place which sets us apart as a family, separate from tribe or community, then the clubhouse is where those other groupings assert themselves. For as surely as we are aligned with family, those other alliances must define us, situate us, and propel us. This certainly seems to be the case with the rink.

I'm not sure, but it might be that the proximity of our rink to our home—of the communal to the private—is sometimes problematic for me. The rink, I've come to believe, exerts an irresistible tug away from the house. So I suppose that would mean that the house exerts the opposite pull—the draw toward lethargy or indolence. A kind of restlessness, then, must oppose, and so balance, the unexamined underside of settling down.

Maybe, therefore, one must have a rink, or a park, or any place of wild combat and play to maintain the viability of home. Without such a place, homes would be abandoned, becoming dusty brittle shells, like the mud-coloured, waffled wasp's nests the kids find under the rafters of the shop.

And so our increasingly collective sense of home has come to embrace this backyard rink, which has, at last, also become a tennis or basketball court in the off season. But unlike some features of the house, it is *not* a one-time effort which settles quietly into permanence, sliding gently toward disrepair. Maintaining the rink is a long-term commitment, though not mine. I don't yet understand it, haven't really attended too closely; but even from the periphery I've learned that it's complicated and controversial. I was so foolish as to once believe it would only involve letting water flow over the area. In fact, the water might get drizzled or poured freely; in several thin layers, or one deep one; in evening or early morning. The snow that falls on the layers of ice can be tramped down or scraped off. And like other fine arts, those who practice it care deeply, and dedicate themselves whole-heartedly to it.

Just the other day I was at home, sick. By afternoon I was feeling better and went out back with the dog, to walk a bit in the late afternoon sunshine. Miles and I went up to the rink and tramped around, playing in the snow. That turned out to be an inexcusably stupid thing to do. It seems that one can only flood properly over a smooth and level layer of snow. I learned that I'd inadvertently cursed the whole enterprise for the season. Maybe this will change the circumspect relationship that has been evolving between the rink and me. I doubt, though, that my impact will be great or enduring.

෴

It's when I am away from home that I think most clearly about it. I have those vivid images of a duplex in New Hampshire and a commune in Vermont forming bookends for what I've come to know as home. There is another set of twinned images, also bracing what home means. They are the most fleeting of images, one gleaned from a glimpse through the windshield,

117

the other from a sign along the roadside, leading me to a note in a travel guide.

Somewhere in Northern Ontario, close to Elliot Lake and not more than an hour past Sudbury, I saw from my window a teepee being constructed. Rising from the ground and turning into one another were three strong poles. That was all—just three shafts of wood, the slight twist of their former existence as tree trunk still so obvious. Nestling into one another some thirty feet above the ground, they seemed to me the essence of simplicity—the starkest notion of home.

A day's drive west of there, nearly to the border of Manitoba, is the town of Ignace. South of Ignace is White Otter Lake, one of hundeds of lakes that dot a rugged and harsh landscape. White Otter Lake is the site of a castle. It was built before 1914, the story goes, by a Scotsman named Jimmy McQuat. In a picture in *The Reader's Digest Canadian Book of the Road* (1991), he looks pale, with high forehead and bushy blond moustache. Though intense, he seems rather awkward and pasty-faced. He had come in 1903 to prospect for gold, but ended up trapping and fishing. With his own hands this man felled and hauled his logs, squaring their sides and dovetailing the ends, importing heavy glass windows at God knows what expense and hauling them in by canoe and portage.

He captured the imagination of at least one writer, and of the townspeople of Ignace and Atitkokan nearly a hundred years later. It's not known what motivated such an extraordinary travail—possibly love. It is known, however, that he was a squatter who never managed to gain title of the land upon which he built his magnificent three-storied castle. The story only gets sadder. In 1918, barely four years after his castle was finished, he got tangled in his fishing nets and drowned.

He is buried close to his castle. Not even the law can dispossess him of that home now. Why does the story haunt me? At the furthest possible reach from the stark simplicity of shelter, it touches some nerve. McQuat, known as "the hermit of White Otter Lake," surely was compelled by passion and the deepest of needs. Even today it would require a day's travel from the Trans-Canada, by land and water, to visit the remains of this man's home and resting place.

~❖~

One Sunday last winter I went out back to our rink. The kids were up skiing with their dad, so I had the place to myself. I laced on a pair of skates and carefully released myself on the ice, hockey stick in one hand, shovel in the other. I slid around until I could detach myself from the crutches and actually propel myself. It was exhilarating! I hadn't skated since I was ten and don't remember being particularly good at it then. Around and around I skated, passing by the outside of the nets. I even tried shooting a puck.

Then the dog barked and I hurled myself back to the edge, lurched across the snow and fell onto the bench. I managed to get my feet, which were aching by then, out of the skates, before a car drove up the driveway. It turned out to be one of the guys, come to check out the ice.

Leaving the rink, I pushed the stick and shovel I'd used back in their place amid the twenty-three sticks and twelve shovels which form the peculiar backdrop of our rink. I replaced the stick with particular care, back into the snow-crusted slot from which I'd pulled it. The sticks may appear carelessly planted in cold disarray—abandoned even. But I have some inkling now of the potent superstitions and rituals that attend this sport which is housed in my own backyard. I have a better grasp, too, of how the sport holds sway in our home.

# Community

While I passed hours during the years I was growing up, pondering ideals of home, imagining the home I would help to create, and the family which might fill it, I had little more than a fleeting interest in what might be my community. So perhaps it's hardly surprising that while our home retains features imitating features of our childhood homes, the community we live in, which we've grown to become part of, is nothing like the communities of our childhood.

I can only think that we now call this place home because it's where Mont and his friend ran out of money. It was 1976, and they were travelling west to learn to ski. The two of them had spent most of their cash replacing two flat tires. So when they finally made it to British Columbia they had to find work. At Jasper someone told the two of them about a little place called Tod Mountain, an easy day's drive south. Word had it that the skiing was great and there were jobs to be had. So they came. It didn't take long for them to find a temporary home on the lake and to line up a couple of jobs.

That winter was the year of record-breaking late snowfall in the west. I know because I was living in Montana, waiting for another ski hill to open so my own job might begin. Up here, my husband and his friend waited for Tod Mountain to open, so that the janitor jobs they had gotten themselves could begin. Neither mountain opened for business until after Christmas.

Tod Mountain, a fifteen minute drive from where we live, was a family hill with challenging terrain, a scattering of hillside A-frames and a funky lodge where you could sit at a heavy wooden table eating a bowl of chilli, and where you would know most everyone around you, including the women cooking and selling the chilli.

Now it's a flashy resort named Sun Peaks, advertised all over North America, prospering from its new image, a devalued Canadian currency and dumbed-down terrain. The place resembles a Bavarian village, and you can get sushi or filet mignon, fine wine or handcrafted gifts. You can overhear conversations in an array of languages. You can rent a movie, go dog-sledding or buy real-estate. You will still run into friends or neighbours, or certainly the neighbour's kids, and you'll see ski bums in ratty equipment and wool pants, but that's the exception now.

One of the consequences of that change from Tod Mountain to Sun Peaks has been the traffic on our road. It roars by at all hours, in all seasons. It makes my daily drive to work more tense. My husband talks of moving to a more remote valley. Occasionally he leaves a leaflet, describing some rambling home complete with well and pasture, sitting conspicuously on the countertop. But I'm not able to leave—I can't even imagine it. This is home and this is our community. It's where our children are growing up, where my husband learned to build, where our neighbours live, our geese roam and our asparagus grows. How could we up and leave?

It is, though, a community in flux. The growth up at the hill has meant jobs and prosperity, though often not for the locals. It has brought new people. The school-bus route has extended, the school population has grown, and there are small businesses springing up even along our road. Many of the couples who arrived twenty years ago, like us—purchasing acreage or leasing Crown land along the lake, then building their homes—have moved on. Some split up, one or both leaving the place they'd built together. Some left when their children hit their teens, tired of the hours of driving for basketball practice or band rehearsals, or pressured by kids who wanted the social density of town.

As people moved away, others came, buying their rustic little places and gradually transforming them into more conventional houses. A variety of individuals have moved their families here, seeking acreage, solitude, or recreation. Land prices have risen dramatically, so instead of ski bums or teachers, they tend, now, to be surgeons or judges. Swiss and German people seem to find this valley attractive. Others have come from Vancouver or Toronto, often after retirement.

Yet we count among our friends members of those ranching families—here when we first arrived, and staying put, now spun off into another generation; also the man my husband first came out with; the surveyor I worked with; and five others who live within a single short stretch of road along Heffley Lake. Each one of those people, without exception, is settled on land not previously occupied: land with no water, septic system, or electricity; no foundation or driveway; nothing but bush, rife with gophers and coyotes, rocks and daisies.

꙯

I grew up on the rocky coastline of an open harbour. We knew lobstermen, fishermen, quarry-workers—but no farmers. Now, our neighbours include ranchers and farmers, butchers and back-hoe operators. Most people who work ranches along the two narrow valleys of our neighbourhood also work at other jobs. They drive school buses, assist the local veterinarian, lease heavy equipment; or they work for a logging outfit, cut meat in a grocery store, run a lift or manage a shop up at the ski hill.

The couple who've done our butchering also cut hay, raise

cattle, hold jobs in town, rent an apartment, and keep exotic birds. These are busy, versatile, inventive people. Some have come from vastly different places and pasts, as my husband and I have done; others have lived in farming families in this valley for generations.

One family we've been fortunate to know worked their land full time, man and wife, son and daughter-in-law. The man passed away not three years ago; his wife moved to town. But years of memories placed this man at the head of his dinner table, head turned toward the picture window just behind the table to his left, which opened out to a view any man might envy: river waters meandering along through his own acres, carving a graceful curve of grasses along which cattle grazed; bald eagles in tree-tops watching along with him, like sentries. He was sick for years, literally shrinking away, but he seemed to harbour a greater degree of peace and contentment than most of us ever do.

For nearly twenty years now, this family has provided us with Christmas and Thanksgiving turkeys, as well as selling us chicken, and occasionally turnips, eggs, cream, hay—and once, a pure bred border collie we called Patsy, who, fifteen years later, is with us still. She's lost most of her vision and doesn't hear much, but she's hardy and seems content to bark at the wind, or to nap on our deck.

◦

Ours is a peculiar community, with no gathering place, no social hub. But there's a network. When someone gets hurt, the phone calls are made: Firewood is split and stacked, dinners prepared, babies cared for. When someone purchases a new horse or builds a shed or moves a range fence, word travels faster than the wind.

123

On Halloween, our kids dress up, their dad too, and they go home to home in a well-established pattern; and at each stop, someone expects them. My husband and I grew up in the small town neighbourhoods that may have characterized the fifties. In two different countries, miles and miles apart, we both went Trick-or-Treating with a gang of friends, racing door-to-door for hours, hitting as many as thirty doorways.

Our kids, on the other hand, go to no more than a dozen places and must go in a vehicle, the distances home-to-home are so great. But they are greeted with bags of loot especially prepared for them, or a treasure hunt or spook house all set up, or individually decorated ghost cookies. They are the only visitors at some of those places, so the whole occasion revolves around them. At other homes the whole family will be out trick-or-treating, leaving a lit Jack-o-lantern and a sign above the bowl of candies that reads "Take a handful!"

# *Looking Back*

I've been privileged to read the journal of Rob White, and some pages from the records of his sister, for the years 1945 to 1950, during which their parents relocated from Vancouver to Kamloops, then to Heffley Lake, settling on the land of their Grandfather Shaw.

Rob's older sister's records are more succinct, mostly single line entries, detailing dates, significant events, and expenditures. They read like a ledger, providing a remarkable compendium of information—accounting for every zipper, nail, and loaf of bread purchased, to the cent. They depict the intertwining of life and work which may be unique to farming: cash flowing out and cash flowing in—for dog food, bread and eggs, hay and grain, birthday gifts, truck repairs, soap and taxes—all of which got balanced at the end of the month.

Rob's journals are prose passages, narratives. They are written in an even script, in pencil, and provide a glimpse into the valley as it appeared to a boy in the 1940's.

~&~

The last thing Dad did before we left was kill two or three rabbits and clean them. He hung them on the outside of the trailer side. I can still see them swinging to and fro in the pouring rain as we left the house to head up country . . . on Sat. March 27, Dad, Grampa Shaw and me.

It was the start of a new life. We drove to Heffley Creek on what is now highway 5 a dirt and gravel road . . . a slow drive up the Heffley Creek Canyon. . . . We passed Knox's and down across Heffley Creek, up past the old Lawrence place, a long hill. We started to see a lot of snow and it got pretty tough going. Mostly low gear to Little Heffley Lake. Finally we met Ernie Henderson with a team of horses and sleigh. We left the truck at Little Heffley Lake and went the rest of the way with team and sleigh. . . .

We were welcomed by Mrs. Henderson and sat down to my first country meal . . . deer meat, fried potatoes and cabbage, or carrots . . . and the big round lump on the butter dish: uncoloured butter, a 2 lb. roll. . . .

~

Walking to and from school . . . carrying a five gallon jug of milk . . . the longest mile I ever had to walk.

Two city kids had a tough time that first 3 months till June. We hadn't developed the leg muscles and breathing stamina to make it up the hills. . . . I took a lot of teasing, they all called me a city slicker. Seems like I had to fight Bill McAuliffe every day at noon. We had some pretty tough battles but there wasn't much blood. . . .

Fishing in Louis Creek during noon hour . . . spent much time in wet pants and wet feet . . . would fall in creek and then to dry out would take socks and pants off, wring out as best we could . . . put back on and wear them dry.

~

Dad had to go to town for parts and groceries and was late getting home. He was having trouble getting up Heffley Canyon. . . . There was something wrong with the fuel pump

126

on the car and he had to back all the way up the hill. This put the gas tank above the motor so the gas ran into the motor without having to rely on the fuel pump.

~❧~

When Eatons' Catalogue came in August . . . it was time to start thinking about the coming winter. . . . You could order everything from guns to clothing, harness, wagon parts, saddles, traps, all the necessities for survival in the 40's. We picked out heavy winter shirts, breeches, and long German socks that came up to just below the knee and tied. Winter jackets and the latest, a helmet to keep the head and ears warm. It was like a flier's helmet and buckled under the chin.

It was just like Xmas in the middle of Sept. when the mail man finally brought the huge brown parcel. . . .

We didn't think much of the breeches and long sox but Mom was boss so we had to wear them when winter came. They were surprisingly warm but they looked funny. . . . New rubber boots with two pairs of insoles to change every night along with 2 pair of wool mitts and leather outer mitts and of course, the leather helmets completed the wardrobe. The helmets didn't last too long . . . gave way to the handknit wool toques. . . . We still had a lot to learn about winter clothes and how to wear them.

One day in late October . . . chasing heifers home . . . cold, with 3 prs of sox . . . Genevieve McAuliffe told me to take 2 pair off and just wear one pair of wool ones. It worked . . . a lesson I never forgot, to give your feet . . . enough room to breathe and keep wool . . . next to your skin.

~❧~

In the summer we used to bathe outside on the back porch

127

in the round tub. . . . Old Mac from the place behind the ranch would be sure to come for lunch when you were sitting in the tub.

❦

Spring . . . I was asleep on the porch one morning . . . Dad had got up early to check a cow that was calving. We had built a small corral down at the creek and he hollered and whistled from there for help. His whistle would wake the dead. I jumped out of bed and into my clothes and ran down to help. He was up to his armpits in a cow trying to pull a calf. I had never seen this operation before and that sight along with the run down made my stomach turn over. I walked over to the fence and leaned my head on the top rail and the next thing I knew I was on my back looking at the sky through the trees. Dad didn't know whether to help me or the cow. However he got the calf delivered and I recovered.

❦

Summer of 45 . . . saw an end to the WWII and to months of anxiety. [We] had the only telephone in the valley and all the messages from the War Dept. came in to us. It was my job to ride to the different families . . . that had boys overseas and pass on these messages. Sometimes it wasn't a nice chore but most of the boys came home, though some families had very anxious times.

❦

I remember Dad going out to cut trees [for firewood]: standing looking up these big fir trees and saying this one

128

is no good, the limbs are too close to the ground, and it looked like they were 50 feet from the stump. We just got the biggest and straightest of these trees. Now you can't find trees like that.

๏

Ploughing . . . was one hell of a job . . . slow and torturous. The team wasn't broke to the plough and there were lots and lots of rocks . . . It was impossible to plough straight . . . and the furrows would have given a snake a backache. However Jack got 15 acres or so ploughed and disked . . . on to picking rocks, seeding, stooking, etc.

๏

This year (1947) at haying time Dad decided to try some new technology. Ben Wilson had told Dad how to build a sweep for picking up the hay. This horse driven machine eliminated the need to fork the hay by hand onto the sloops. It was homemade. It was 12 foot wide and consisted of a frame on 2 wheels that were near the balance point. Ten teeth slid along the ground under the windrowed hay pushing it into bunches of nearly 1000 pounds. There was a horse hitched to each side to pull the sweep and a rail on the platform . . . to raise the teeth. The hay was gathered and slid onto a similar frame on the slide stacker which was used to push the hay up the slide onto the stack.

This worked alright but took a lot to get used to, to operate it. It took a while to train the horses to work 12 feet apart but eventually we all became quite proficient at it. We used the method just the one year. Next year another improvement was built. A boom stacker. This again was homemade with wood material. All we had to buy were the

129

bolts. . . . We used this boom stacker for 2 or 3 years until we learned about the 'overshot stacker'. Again this was a homemade machine.

❧

There's page after page of such meticulous detail about haying and the implements used to swath, bundle, stack and store the hay; about every dimension, condition and type of rope and cable, horse and mower. It's not so much the machinery described that captivates me, but rather what gets revealed about the character of the men who built it, and the aptitude and understated pride in the describing of it. The pride reflects upon both the co-reliance of these people settling our valley and each individual's resourcefulness and tenacity. Those things haven't really changed so much, then to now.

❧

This journal ends with the early death of Rob's father in 1950 while Rob was attending school in Kamloops. As he says elsewhere in his journal, "Death came quickly in those days. There were few options and medical care was quite basic." Which is not to say that grief came any more quickly or less keenly.

It was a tough calving season this year. The calves were thin and weak after the long winter. On the 8th of May Jack was ploughing . . . Dad asked Jack for help rounding up some yearlings to brand. . . . Somehow Dad's horse Star went down, probably tripped by a little calf, and Dad flew off over its head and hit his head on the ground and broke his neck. No one saw what actually happened but afterward we went down and you could see where the horse had tried to stop and slid along the ground. Anyway they got Dad into the car and brought him to town. . . . There was nothing they could do. . . .

The next few days are a blur. . . . Two weeks passed before the realization set in that Dad wasn't coming back. It seemed to hit us all at the same time. We got up one morning and everyone could feel the strain and tension. However . . . on we went. The farming still had to be completed and chores done. . . . I quit school . . . and came home to work the ranch.*

---

* Some of the punctuation in these excerpts has been added; Rob tends toward an economy of punctuation.

# Notes from a Journal

## September '92

We're waiting for the birth of our third child, and watching the rapid approach of fall. Being home with Andrew, seeing Nicole off on the morning bus and Mont off to work just after, has become a comfortable routine.

This past Saturday night Mont and I were invited to a surprise sixtieth birthday celebration for Rob White, the rancher from whom we bought our land and learned to live on it, more than twelve years ago.

A wonderful evening—over forty of us were gathered in Rob and Rose's home, waiting for their return from the Armstrong Fall Fair. Grandchildren decked out in party clothes and hair ribbons tore around the garage and basement, full of the excitement of the upcoming surprise. Cousins, great-grandmas, friends, neighbours milled around, laughing and catching up on days or weeks of news and gossip—four generations of Whites, with friends of the middle two generations, including us.

The celebration enfolded two overwhelming events: the birth of Rob and Rose's granddaughter, and the shooting of that grandchild's dad, their son. He was shot in the gut sometime between giving out the invitations and the party. Our neighbourhood has buzzed with news and tingled with shock for the intervening weeks. Only a week ago had doctors first offered the assurance that he'd live.

I remember Mont's uneasiness the evening we returned home from a quiet weekend of camping, to our ringing telephone and the appalling news. He kept saying that this sort of thing happened in cities—not in rural BC. When I went in to work on Monday, I was surprised to discover that what had seemed a personal, or at least a local trauma had extended outward to town. I met the questions of colleagues, some of whom already knew more than I did.

There are various renderings of what transpired: rumours of theft of gasoline from trucks, too much drink, threats and accusations. The undeniable facts are these: Two men, companions from work, were both hospitalized with gunshot wounds—one, a quiet man, our neighbour, Rob's son. He was hit in the guts, kidney destroyed, intestines and liver damaged. In the wake of the shooting was left a stunned and frightened family. And a badly shaken little community.

Though we carefully avoided the topic on that night, it weighed on everyone's minds. Nonetheless, the pervasive warmth and humour of that extended family wrapped itself around us. It was a challenge to recognize White family cousins I hadn't seen for years—some several inches taller, some trailing new spouses. Dinner hour was spent sitting in a large circle of lawn chairs on the cement floor of the garage (built two years ago by Mont), figuring out who was who, and getting to know the family who'd just moved in to Rob and Rose's old place.

Mont teased one son-in-law for the silk tie obviously sent by his upscale Ontario family. But for most of the hours, he conversed with—listened to, mostly—Rob's brother-in-law, a man renowned for his quick wit and ready stories.

I'd hardly seen Jack for years, maybe even avoided seeing him, afraid to see a man so full of life aging. But he's hardly greyed or wrinkled at all, and the wit remains razor sharp; the keen interest in a wealth of subjects, undiminished. We like best his stories of making do in the early days of ranching around this lake we live on, back when the road was gravel and the roadside barely populated—by the older folks who sit smiling around this circle and others who have moved elsewhere.

One thing I watch for, with part of my attention, is how the younger new-comers react to these old ranchers. The in-laws or friends of young cousins are good kids, but they haven't lived long or hard enough yet to have the respect these people warrant. They react to Jack's promise of humour with foolish jokes which sometimes verge on condescension. My irritation rises, but Jack seems impervious. That confuses me, since I know that he hasn't missed what I've perceived. He simply accepts each exchange, volleying comments about most anything from babies to booze, and moves on.

At some point in the evening Jack let Mont and I know that he and his wife, Velma, had spent lots of time with, nearly raised, the nephew who had gotten shot. He told us how the boy had first learned to stand up in their home, how he struggled through repeated falls to the kitchen floor, and finally pulled himself back up by the drawer handles. We knew that while Jack crinkled with laughter again at the memory, he was letting us know that that month had been particularly hard on him.

He told us how he and Velma met at fifteen, married at seventeen. They had decided, in all their young wisdom, to write down a dream plan: to have two children, a boy and a girl, with names they both fancied—Barry and Brenda. A world war and other traumas and triumphs of adulthood interrupted those young lives. But I had only to look around and see Barry across from me and Brenda to one side, married and farmers both, their own children close by, nearly adults themselves. While so many times we seem to blunder on through whatever surprises life delivers us, Jack and Velma appeared to have exerted some control over their circumstances, perhaps merely by the simple confidence of their shared dream.

# Part III

❖

*Taking Root*

❖

. . . It may be that our marriages, kinships, friendships, neighbourhoods, and all our forms and acts of homemaking are the rites by which we solemnize and enact our union with the universe. These ways are practical, proper, available to everybody, and they can provide for the safekeeping of the small acreages of the universe that have been entrusted to us.

—Wendell Berry, "Men and Women in Search of a Common Ground," from *Home Economics* (1987)

# Being Married

A while ago I picked up a journal I'd been keeping back in 1982 and '83, before children and during a spell of unemployment. I had found myself between excess and restraint: between working and studying furiously, and waiting—waiting for work, waiting for children, waiting for life as it was supposed to unfold. My words capture my discomfort with that time. My voice, though, captures the way I am, still.

Identity does this trick of bifocusing: recognition of self, simultaneous with a stir of remembered time and place which so surely distinguish the self remembered from the self enveloped by the present moment. The same thing happens when I look at our wedding photograph. In the silver-framed snapshot we are gazing up at the camera, not quite smiling. We both look timid, tentative, uncertain about the trappings of the day and about all that attention trained on us. Our faces look so young, scrubbed, smooth and shining.

At different times over the next fifteen years, each of our children would study that photo and then ask, where were *they*? The middle child was sure that he was in the house, looking at books with Nanee. The youngest claims to remember playing inside my belly with the others. (Which would go a good way toward explaining some of my discomfort during the day).

For a wedding gift, I made my husband a quilt. Both sides are patches—one cotton, the other corduroy—quilted together with embroidery floss, pulled through and knotted. Most of the fabric was gathered from friends and family, though some came from the thrift shop. One piece came from the fabric of my wedding dress, one from a plaid flannel shirt of my husband's; some are from the garish curtains we had in our dorm rooms. It took most of a fall and winter to gather and cut the pieces, another season to sew and quilt them. Between shifts of various night and day jobs I sewed, listening to Jimmy Buffet or Jonathon Edwards, Van Morrison or EmmyLou Harris, on the stereo which was our first purchase as a couple.

One month before I packed to move back east to get married, I joined individual blocks of the wedding quilt. At my mother's kitchen table in Maine I did the final assembly, side to side, and in her living room I tied the knots with the quilt draped over TV trays.

Though the quilt still does keep us warm in winter, the fabric is wearing thin in places. Some pieces have been patched-over or replaced by my mother when she visited two years ago. Those new pieces stand out against their more faded background. I should spend a week or two this fall, replacing more squares. Maybe, like the marriage, the quilt ought to get restored, enlarged to include patches from our kids clothing and the fabrics of our home. It's daunting, though, to envision the quilt as a gift that evolves over time. I'm not sure I have that kind of ambition anymore. And—also like marriage, I suppose—the quilt has a function now, aside from and probably more significant than the beauty of the original design. If it goes downstairs for mending, how will we keep warm?

Besides, I don't sew much now. And what sewing I do is mending. There's always a knee to patch, pockets to replace, a button to sew back on, and hems to go up or down. I sew cloth which is thick and soft from wear, and smells faintly of diesel or pine pitch. My machine is probably obsolete. I've grown unfamiliar with fabric stores: can't remember the lingo of bolts and spools; feel helpless the moment I cross the threshold of those busy places.

Old journals also remind me of all the years of our marriage when one of us worked away from home. I spent the first three months of our married life alone in Maine, doing my teaching practicum. Then, after reuniting and moving west, in the spring of '81 I got my first teaching job—in Merritt, two hours southwest of here. I would drive home on Friday night and set out again at five a.m. Monday morning, to board with a woman for the four week nights till Friday rolled around again. Mont often worked away for weeks at a time, on construction jobs in Blue River or Valemount or Revelstoke.

Through the early years of our relationship we lived and worked on separate sides of the border, but over time the separations grew more difficult to cope with. I remember so looking forward to being together, only to be confronted by the awkwardness of realigning ourselves to being a couple again. For the first hours, the joy was precarious, threatened by the irritations so quick to rise. By the time we'd settled into a routine of co-existence, it would be time to part. Ease and affection would give way to a bleakness, sitting like a stone in the pit of the stomach as separation loomed.

When our first child was born, right there in the recovery room my husband declared that he would not work away from home again. We knew that the decision would cost us; construction work away from home, back in the '80's, meant living-out allowance and overtime, amounting to pay cheques the likes of which we never saw again.

And though we both believe in a certain amount of separation in a relationship, I'm certain it was for the good of our marriage that we decided to stay at home. We've maintained our separateness through individual athletic involvement, separate career paths, and distinct circles of friends: What greater contrasts than hockey from running, building from teaching, tradesmen from academics? At home, we now maintain a clear division of labour, which turns out to be an utter contradiction of my intended ideal: to be partners in all joint endeavours. But, together, I suppose, we have become more pragmatic, even in our ideals.

In fact, maintaining those separate realms often seems so much easier than carving out some time to be together. Finding a few minutes to talk, drawing even the most tenuous boundary around the two of us, has become the challenge. Those elements which keep us inextricably attached and mutually engaged— children and home, shared concerns and inclinations—can seem so much more intangible, at times, than the jumble of hockey gear, semester schedules, late night calls about work, stacks of marking, team dinners. Sometimes we joke that we're just too exhausted even to drift apart. But I'm fonder of the notion that the distance we span is testimony to the vitality of our union.

Lately, though, every now and then we have an occasion to be alone together. To celebrate our twentieth anniversary, we left the three kids alone for the first time—their gift to us— and spent four days in Washington State, exploring the Yakima Valley. It took most of the drive down to stop thinking about the kids and to begin thinking of us and our time together. But even in that, the need to shed concerns of home, we were synchronized. And gradually, we discovered how much we loved traveling together. We remembered the astonishing ease with which we negotiated the millions of decisions of travel. We remembered a shared past of road travel, which seemed so much more significant in the remembering than it had in the doing. It became a joyful thing just to decide to stop for lunch, and to choose, together, a perfect place. For two days we visited wineries, drove back roads, discovered motels and sampled cafes. Then thoughts of home filtered in and took hold, and we drove home eager to see our kids and sleep in our own bed.

When we got home, our kids had made us an anniversary gift. It was a painting of a gull's head, with the beak carved of drift wood and jutting out beyond the frame. They named the gull Sheridan, after a ship wreck. Both the concept and the shipwreck came from a family trip to Monhegan, a small island located far off the coast of Maine. We had seen carved gulls in an art shop there, and loved them, but resisted the high prices. Later, the kids had found a perfect driftwood beak on one of the beaches we explored as we'd hiked around the island.

Two months after that Monhegan trip, our four-day absence to celebrate our anniversary had given them the opportunity to turn their beak into art. Nicole coordinated the creative effort: James painted the blue background, Nicole and Andrew carved, and Nicole made the frame.

Sheridan hangs in our living room, alongside prints by Robert Bateman and Steve Mennie. Early in our marriage, we had set out to collect art, intending to acquire an evolving collection as we learned about western art and as our savings grew. Little did we know that we'd lose track of the art scene, and our savings would not grow. Instead, those first prints by Bateman and Mennie, joined by Sheridan, have become our art collection. And our shared pursuits have become so much more commonplace and casual—a family movie, a chicken dinner, and occasionally, a trip together.

There's so much more—but my concept of our marriage merges with my sense of our family, home, and even work. For better or worse, it has spilled into all those other realms. It's possible that they define it now. I think Wendell Berry has it right when he claims that we need "a broader concept" for marriage. As

Berry sees it, marriage involves the man and woman, "plus their history together, plus their kin and descendants, plus their place in the world with its economy and history, plus their natural neighbourhood, plus their human community with its memories, satisfactions, expectations, and hopes."

So maybe it's no wonder that what drew us together twenty-five years ago is not what holds us together now. It's more of a miracle, perhaps, that the bond remains fast, reinforced by the greater design of things. Like a particular segment of a quilt pattern, it's a balance of contrasts, holding its own in a context never imagined when plans felt so deliberate and simple, and choices hinged on nothing more than the joining of two single squares of fabric.

# One Day in the Life of a Family

July 27th, 1988 was a momentous day for us.

The date stands out because it happened to be the day our second child was born. The weather had been ungodly hot. Mont had spent the whole of the previous day picking rocks. The opportunity to borrow a seeder had arisen, so it was his chance to seed the three acre field he'd cleared the year before.

There was more than the prescribed loan of a seeder to contend with. We had just acquired our first sheep. And in two days we were scheduled to put our signatures on a business loan for the purchase of a butcher shop in town (a new venture for which we had scant experience and less capital). The timing was everything.

For a couple of days I had been experiencing mild contractions. On the night of the twenty-sixth we poured ourselves into bed feeling beat—Mont from long hours in the hot field and me from hauling my own weight through yet another day. We'd put a new sheep-skin mattress cover on our bed that day, hoping for some relief from heat and aching backs.

At one a.m. I startled awake, perplexed to find myself standing on the floor beside our bed, even more astonished to feel the gush of warm water between my legs. It's the oddest sensation when the waters "break," yet, although I had never experienced it before, I had not a moment's doubt what was going on. An hour later, we drove to the hospital. By four, I was admitted and hustled off to a birthing room. Andrew was born before seven, arriving moments before we'd settled on his name.

My husband had just enough time to say hello to his robust little black-haired son, before rushing away. The seeder was due back at noon. It's a wonder we had time to stop and have that boy, and *no* wonder that he is such a busy kid.

# Inside the Lions

Those who study child language tell us that talking with children—aside from its being an engaging and satisfying activity—will enhance their development. The idea is that the more attention you focus upon your child's utterances, the more those utterances will occur—sustaining both your attention and the child's efforts to communicate.

Formal studies in child language development offer perspective and raise some useful questions about that corner of human interaction. Still, I'm skeptical of too objective a focus upon such a personal and, in so many ways, magical process. For the adult, delving into children's speech requires a discerning ear, a keen mind, and the occasional leap of faith.

Listening to my children talk—riding the waves of their wonderment, ingenuity, and boldness—has been my privilege as a parent. Seeking out and following the pathways of their sense of things challenges and engages me. It's made me laugh and made me cry. It's given me great respect for the powers of language and thought, and for the mystery binding the two.

I remember the summer day when my daughter, a spirited and social two year old, kept me company in the garden. She was busy fashioning worm villages; I was in the less hopeful pursuit of young weed roots. We'd spent hours pleasantly distracted by our labours and surroundings when I lost the thread of some conversation we'd been spinning.

We were in the potato bed, one of fifteen rectangular raised beds which made up my garden. From what felt like another world—the school where I work, in fact—I reacted to her musing about the term "bed" applied to those raised mounds of garden soil. So I launched right into a language instructor's explication: "A bed in the garden is different from a bed that you sleep in." I explained how they sound the same, but had, in this case, quite different meanings.

"Oh" she said, perhaps eager to get us from pedantry back to pleasantry, "so someone *else* sleeps in these beds . . . worms, I think."

"Probably," I admitted, feeling more chagrined than defeated.

But I improved. Over the years I came to know that ours was a more subtle and complex relationship. When she mixed "line" with "lion," and "bounce" with "balance," I kept quiet. For months we were careful not to drive over the water lion, and to colour inside the lions. I take delight in those phrases, in their convolution of image and meaning. And I model clear articulation. But the child finds her own way, in her own time.

Where does our language separate from our ideas? A passenger on the back of my bicycle, that little girl explained to me one day how every new daddy must find a driveway and build a house at the end of it. Indeed, on Tod Mountain Road, along which we live and on which we were that day pedalling, most of the steep winding driveways lead to owner-built dwellings. They do lend an impression of so many balloon strings, just waiting for the "new daddy" to take hold of one.

My daughter's revelations are woven into the words she speaks, and listening to her, I can hear ideas taking shape. Her ventures into language have always seemed cautious. She never shared words without first having a sense of their meaning. She wouldn't, for example, speak that ritualistic "trick or treat" on her second Halloween, despite being a social child. Our costumed little fairy chose, instead, to recite a storybook incantation: "Moon, balloon, tickle the trees. . . . Four balloons, more balloons, blossom for me." To her, it made more sense, somehow.

Her brother, on the other hand, leapt feet first into the adventure of words. Only later would he chance upon meaning.

Andrew spoke in idiom, in catch phrases. Dazzled by inflection and effect, he aimed for context. "No way, Jose" was a favourite expression. The experts tell us that such "formulaic phrases" bridge the gap between knowing and speaking. They allow a period of grace for the smooth flow of linguistic development. This child made full use of his period of grace. "Knock, knock . . . Who's there? Mickey Mouse's underwear!" was one of his first sustained utterances.

The linguist Michael Halliday accuses us of entertaining, nearly always, much too simple ideas about language. For the child, language is an instrument of activity and control, of relationship building and maintenance, of self-discovery and outer awarenesses, of play and creativity and information transfer. For the adult, it tends to function almost exclusively as an instrument for conveying information. In the language of my children, and especially in the language between them, I see the multitude of uses to which they put their words. I can see too, how easily we overlook this complexity.

Take, for example, my son's reaction to his sister's ascent into the school system. Given weekly library privileges, Nicole radiated joy. Then one morning, Andrew announced to no one in particular that he was wearing library socks. He wore library socks for several days, and once, a library jacket. Later, Nicole's class got their immunizations, which were followed by an extended preoccupation with sore arms and mild flu symptoms—shared, of course, with kindergarten cohorts. Then one day Andrew revealed that he had gotten shot in the leg by a gun: It was a big shot too, and his head hurt. For him, no risk was greater than that of missing out. And words quite adequately served the purpose of connecting him to events that otherwise might pass him by.

In conversation, children find ways of collaborating to seek common ground. The success of their conversation depends upon the success of the collaboration. Failure results in lop-sided exchanges or in a breakdown of communication. Yet the whole notion of success depends upon the child's purpose in conversing. Because my children seem to speak for quite different purposes, their exchanges may well seem lop-sided to an adult listening in.

"I am *not* your brother!"

"You *are* my brother, and I am your sister."

"I *am not*, because I'm Andrew." And another time: "I love you daddy, because I have these big ears."

Just what, I wonder, does "because" signify to this child? And how long and winding is the path connecting ears and love?

One of my exercises in parental decoding—in freeing meaning from the words encasing it—was the mystery of the big footprint. Nicole was four. We were homeward bound, at the end of a day's work—mine teaching, and hers daycare survival. She was relating a story about their morning walk out to the big footprint. I could remember a previous story of another trek to a big footprint. But I couldn't find any other clues.

A week later at breakfast she told me about going hiking the day before with her dad and her uncle. They had tramped for a mile through the bush separating our house from her uncle's, nailing up "No Hunting" signs. They'd seen deer prints on the soft ground. "Deer footprints," she explained, "are just like deer tracks." Aha! If tracks are footprints, then the college's new four hundred meter track is, indeed, a big footprint!

Child language is rich and adaptive. The child knows language through the many-sidedness of his linguistic experience, says Halliday. But it all gets complicated as the child makes transitions from the familiar contexts of home, to those of school and the wider world.

I remember observing my daughter at kindergarten, feeling awkward in my new role as parent-observer. This was spring—lambing time—and her teacher had asked her when we'd be having more baby lambs. The implications of that question—when the lambs would drop, whether the ewe's milk was in, whether twins, or triplets, or a single birth—all fit in the world of our small farm, where they'd become familiar and ordinary. But in school, they didn't fit. "I don't know," she stammered.

Child language experts claim that the more sophisticated, interpersonally sensitive and linguistically skilful a person becomes, the better he'll recognize signals of a common ground. But such learning is a life-long process. The wisdom to make speech appropriate and meaningful in a given social situation—that's a rare and finely hewn kind of knowing.

One November evening we were driving home. Andrew was looking out his car window: *his* window in that way only a two-year-old has of possessing even the view from a car window. Night was falling fast and hard. But this child was joyful at the sight of stars, surprised anew at the darkness which dampens the spirits of those of us more vulnerable to the seasonal flux in our daily rhythms.

"I wish I could be a star," he exclaimed from directly behind me where he was harnessed in his booster seat. No suitable reply came to mind. Minutes later he allowed that next year he would *be* a star. I was still at a loss for comment, but was quite sure this was a projection with meaning. If only I could catch it.

"When I get bigger, I'm going to be a star . . . *next* time."

Then I understood! At least I thought I did; you can never be sure. I was fond of my theory, in any case. On Halloween, a month before, Andrew had been a clown. We'd expected him to love Halloween, assuming that costumes would delight him. And he did love it: the heaps of candy, the thrill of fireworks, the scramble of routine disrupted. But he never quite accepted the clown costume, sewn by his Nanee and handed on from his Colorado cousin. He pulled at the sleeves and squirmed when we painted his face. In the picture, he smiles tentatively, a tear tracing its way down the painted cheek. We were puzzled: Tentative just didn't characterize that boy.

Nicole and I had known for some time that for Andrew there were clowns in the sky. It was our unspoken pact, not to correct this lovely twist which yielded such comical images from the morning skies. Chilly November mornings particularly seem to require that intoxicating element of clowniness.

Now I could retrace the paths of association. If clouds are clowns, then—just maybe—this child believes we have dressed him up as a cloud . . . How absurd to paint the face of a cloud; how silly to sheath it in a baggy, brightly patterned costume! I can only wonder how he'd expect us to dress a star.

The journey from child language to the adult mind can leave us dizzy and exhilarated. We guess what's on the minds of our children. We assume intentionality. Then sometimes, leaping from word to image to idea and then back to word, we'll perceive those tremulous shimmers of connection. For us it requires a reversal of inhibition—that sensible process to which we've become accustomed, which allows greater conformity and efficiency by closing down the paths which are redundant or distorted. Children, too, must engage in that process of inhibition in order to enter the realm of language prescribed by their social worlds.

But until they do, we can witness our language in all its multiplicity of functions, its creative potential, its possibilities for trapping and projecting meaning, its power to reach us and to elude us.

# Between Outlook and Appearance

For years I've been teaching English composition to second language students. I'm often surprised at how easily I talk about writing, how I love to speak about it from every angle and any corner of consideration. I'm always trying to engage my students, using words to catch their eyes. Holding fast, I pull them toward an understanding of the underside of this language I speak, this culture that engulfs me, and, I suspect, of my own personal ways. Sometimes, from the inside, it's difficult to tell one from the other.

These students struggle to know—and harder still, to remember and finally to assimilate—the eternally puzzling distinctions between "outlook" and "appearance," between "since" and "ago." The intricacies of the English language are continually revealing themselves to my students, and, through them, to me. What frustrates them, fascinates me.

There's little certainty and few absolutes in the teaching of language. So I end up trusting myself and the process I engage in. I ride the crests of my instincts and energies, buoyed by my affection for these students who come in waves, semester after semester. And semester after semester, I am swept from the awkward doubtful beginnings to the regrettable release of rapport, amazed at what does transpire between us, confined as we are by classroom, class-time, curriculum.

Like a Rubik's cube, teaching is puzzling in ever-varied ways. One particular twist of the cube emerges from memory: a mid-level ESL composition class, made up mostly of adolescent Cantonese males from Hong Kong, and Annie, who is female, French-Canadian and deaf. More troublesome than her femaleness, French-Canadianess or deafness, but probably intrinsic to each, is her sullenness. Before her sits Margaret, the sign-language interpreter. Margaret enraptures the rest of us, while being largely ignored by Annie. Tall, lean, and poised, Margaret attracts the row of teenaged males—and me as well.

The students' desks in my classroom form a horseshoe, with my table at the front and slightly to the right of centre. I am short and so usually sit up on the table to teach; to speak in English about writing in English. Although I try to vary the modulation and tempo of my teaching, from the point of view of boisterous Chinese teenagers—their comprehension of spoken English still none too keen—it's hard to imagine a more abstract and uninspiring performance than mine. Insert into this picture Margaret: Sitting there in the centre of the horseshoe, opposite the sullen and inattentive Annie, she signs with her graceful, long and expressive arms.

For an entire semester, for four hours a week, I drone and she signs. Each class I start off bravely, only to eventually give in to the charm of her performance and to watch my words become a slow dance. That watching seems like an arresting dream state where words leap into three dimensional motion. I watch the literal becoming something physical, and the tempo I have trained myself to monitor unconsciously, becoming tangible. Once, with a startling decrescendo, the signing slowed to a halt. With a jolt of realization—mortification on its heels— I saw that, in the fascination of watching the dance of my words, I had stopped speaking.

❧

Listening to myself teach, I discover that more and more I sound like an Evangelist of prose. Rid yourselves of all those conventions and formulas, I preach. Coherence is intuited, not sprinkled like pepper onto a passage, I assert. Draw in your readers, I urge. They train on me those bright and shining gazes, only to go away and write yet more obscure and stilted papers. Then just as I'm about to throw up my hands and retreat, I find myself caught by a hint of promise: the awkwardly crisp and startling words of a student caught between two cultures—the coarse sophistication of Hong Kong, and the unwieldy rawness of BC. A tender victory for us both, it's almost always enough to renew me.

❧

These paragraphs have grown out of an experiment: I'm keeping a journal while the students write theirs. Can I write in a room so charged with fidgeting energy? All around me I see faces registering the effort of focusing. I know, watching them, that they are searching me out. Their faces frame questions: What does she want? What does she really mean? As their writing finally engages them, the faces register the more ambiguous feelings that I hope will be captured on the pages of their notebooks.

Their eyes get to me. Those eyes, beaming their promise and their demands. Barriers of language and culture keep us far apart, but those eyes seem to reach across, slicing through so much. New students, or distrustful ones, keep their eyes hidden from mine—a cultural defence or a personal immunity. It's peculiar that silence, more often than words, will gather them back.

But words are what I teach. I watch my students inch toward

comprehensibility and confidence and finally, on to clarity and competence. But eyes are a powerful vehicle for teaching. I can move students, chastise, plead with, or reassure them—if I can hold their gaze with mine. Such power sometimes frightens me.

❧

Another time—in the isolating hours before dawn, and in the domestic comfort of home—my thoughts return to teaching. It's four a.m. and I've been sleepless since two. I had fallen into sleep hard and fast, as though directly off a clean edge of wakefulness. But I was jolted out of sleep by a baby, aching with teething.

I comfort him back into his sleep and lie still as my husband settles back into restfulness; then I creep downstairs, book in hand. I read for a while until, earmarking bits to share with others later, I sense that I really want to talk. So I do the next best thing: I write.

I *know* that I threaten my equilibrium by stealing these hours of sleep time. I regret the excess of coffee and recognize the excess of student demands, arising from the pressure of midterms. But knowing that I will pay clarifies the moment's value. In another twelve hours, shifting from work to home, I'll have to pull from somewhere the capacity for patience and perspective. I'll maintain that balance, which I don't dare relinquish because it feels like everything rests upon it.

❧

My classroom has been the setting for harangues on laziness and complacency and pleas for attentiveness and vigilance. Students respond in their individual ways. The tangle of their emotions and the discomfort of their uncertainty of expression

155

all manage to surface through layers of difference. I am both privileged to glimpse into the souls of these people, and burdened with attaching grades to such a sharing. They are, as in most other ways, unpredictable in their reactions to my responses to their thoughts in words. It's a tricky business and I carry on with great caring, if not always great care. More often than not, impulse—a wily, nerve-racking guide—guides me in teaching as in raising my children.

What keeps on inspiring me is the courage of these second language students. They may never realize how they've taken on the coming of age in an unfamiliar country, with the fragility of adolescence, and the precariousness of student existence. They probably never appreciate the amazing strides they make in outlook, even as they change in appearance.

In my late night hours, as in other times, these students I embrace by the act of teaching mix up in my life with my children, my husband, my friends. I am still learning how to make a place for them, so that releasing them is not so wrenching. Gradually, I open up to them and let them go more easily too. They move in—claiming such a firm hold on my heart—then move on. A semester later they'll appear at my office door, like long-lost and once-dear relations. Sometimes, a year or two later, one will resurface by Christmas card or wedding announcement.

# Journal Notes

## April '92

Lately, Andrew is obsessed with bad guys, dedicating whole days to schemes to protect us from them. He comes home from daycare with pine needles, placing them by the basement entrance to prick the bad guys as they sneak in. Or sometimes, with balls of string or yarn jammed into his pockets, ready to tie up bad guys who may want to get us. A chicken-shaped plastic whistle is to frighten them off if he sees any from down at the sheep pens. I just can't figure the fascination, though I try. He says he's seen bad guys, long ago—back when he had a different mother!

Meanwhile, Nicole wanders around singing, dancing in circles with arms outspread, oblivious to most everything around her. She'll glance into mirrors or windows or pools of water even, fascinated with her reflection. Six.

## August '92

I found a journal entry from last spring that I have no memory of writing. Had thought, in fact, that I hadn't written through this whole pregnancy. Those last paragraphs remind me of the passage from spring into the sultry heat and heavy rains of summer, into new challenges of these past weeks at work and the final trimester of my third pregnancy.

Since April and the days of bad guys and ballerinas, we've

survived the birthdays of both kids. Already they pry me for details of next Halloween, projecting directly to the next big occasion—the intervening birth of a new sibling apparently too trivial to be the focus of their anticipation. Nicole wants to know shouldn't I dress up this year, so people won't recognize the family? Why don't I be Batgirl . . . or a mother pumpkin?

# Old Paths, New Tracks

This year Nicole turned seven, and burst into writing. She's in the grip of creativity. Having set aside the crayons that captivated her at the age of two, she barely leaves the house now without journal and pencil.

The regret I'd been feeling as the kids edged toward mastery of speech evaporates as we awaken to Nicole's ascent into writing. Again, we get to witness the process of grasping patterns and rules which govern discourse—this time, with a written record to map the path of progress.

Nicole's been lucky to have a grade one teacher who has encouraged her, without fuss. Her dad and I were educated in the fifties and sixties, when tired spinsters—themselves bound by rigid, even dogmatic, adherence to more rules and codes than seemed healthy for any living thing—forbade free-form ventures into learning. So we watch, amazed, as her teacher lets her fly into the production of words and sentences.

Soon, captions for pictures have extended into fragments of narrative. "Jan 20 thrid" seems a turning point: a page with no picture, only the words "Erin is coming to sleep ovr. at my house. We are going to hev fun. We are going to sleep on the hideabed." Some "g's" and "p's" are backwards, as is the "J" of Jan, but periods settle very nearly in their proper places.

Her teacher writes neatly in the margin, "I hope you have a good time with Erin."

Nicole adds "I will." The following Monday, she completes the story: "My hamstr spun all nuit [French?] wen Erin slepd over nuit. it wus noisy! So we hed thrubl going to sleep."

Mrs. C. comments: "Oh dear! Were you very tired the next day?"

"No" replies Nicole. What communication!

Reading Nicole's pages, I search out the thought processes underlying her grasp of the principles of composition. Jean Mandler, in a short essay called "The Code in the Node," explains how children absorb the narrative codes and temporal sequences from stories read to them. In Nicole's journal I recognize some of those narrative codes: repetitions and refrains; patterns of conflict and resolution. While Mandler downplays the significance of grammatical structure, from years of teaching composition to second language learners I can't help but admire how, already, Nicole has mastered our elaborate verb tense system and sophisticated patterns of sentencing. "He knoo he'd nevre see'n them fiting befor," she explains in one story.

But the creativity of the spelling enthrals me even more. It's a wonder coherence can sustain her manoeuvres through so many phonetic mysteries. She slides over such lovely compilations as "anamols" and "yewst to," even as she remembers an expanding stock of spellings. Thus, "noo" becomes "knoo," then "knwoo," before unscrambling to become, and remain, "know."

At the same time, her three-year-old brother is struggling with the effort of steadying his pencil on the page. His writing asserts itself boldly, if not often, in huge black A's and W's and what might be D's. But at the slightest spark of distraction, his W becomes a slash of lightning; his D's, dog footprints which trail, with his attention, off the paper's edge.

Looking through her latest journal, I see that Nicole is ten pages into a story that she can't seem to end. Pencilled words spilling line after line crowd each page: "Aprel 24" marks the first page, with a lamb born—a "vere" curious lamb who wants to "kno mour" and goes "evreewer" to see what he can discover. His mother exclaims, "Wot a crasy baby I heve!" and then teaches him to play hide and seek. Looking ahead at a page from the last morning of June, I see that the lamb is about to find the sandbox: "We'v hird of it, But we hevin't seen it . . ."

I count six blank pages that she's left free for the further adventures of her lamb. I wonder if she knows how it will all unfold. Next comes a new story titled "The Rose" and beginning "There was wuns a Rose calld Hart . . ." It's only one page yet and ends mid-word, where clearly she was pulled away. I can so easily imagine the regret of abandoning a thought, perched at the edge of realization.

But I also sometimes envy this child her clear-headedness: that ability to focus, to pick up her journal, left mid-word, and to remember just "wot" a rose called Heart was up to. Against the distractions of home and teaching and graduate study, I can barely follow the thread of an idea, let alone a story. Knowing that she can, gives me assurance—though I know assurance should run the other way. Maybe, though, it runs both ways.

In the last entry of her grade one journal I read:

Jun 16. I whent to Washingtin in the uoonitd stas. It was my mom's gradyushun selebrashun. We hed a motle whith a swiming pool, we whent swimming evree day exset the day that we lefd. On the whae home we soa elest eighte deer.

# Loss and Retrieval

There was a yellow Post-It note folded over the edge of four pages in my journal, closing them off. But the folded yellow divider all too neatly resembles my memory's trick of tucking away the messy bits, sealing them away. So I've retrieved from those pages this story, which began on the first of March, 1993.

It started with the jangle of the telephone, at nine thirty-one Wednesday night. The voice was a woman's; the message concise, professional, delivered with sensitivity. My husband had been struck in the face by the blade of a skate. He was in Emergency, waiting for a better assessment of the cut. She told me that surgery was scheduled for later in the night and they wouldn't know the extent of his injury until the surgery was under way. She told me that my husband was worried about me.

Not long after I'd hung up, our close friend who plays on the same team as my husband came through the kitchen door. He'd been sent by Mont. Though no doubt as shaken as I was, he went through the motions of brewing us a pot of tea, which we must have drunk. Funny, we've never before or since, in the twenty-five years of our acquaintance, shared a pot of tea.

Then I think I began making phone calls, sharing what little information I had with our families back east and our co-workers. I told each person I talked to that the injury was an accident, a case of being at the wrong place at the wrong time. A player on the opposing team had tripped, his skate caught on an edge. The back of his skate cut Mont's right eye. It was possible that he'd sustained only surface damage.

When the calls were over, I sat and cried. After I had stopped crying and was catching my breath, I looked through sore eyes to see Andrew sitting on the stairs, peering down at me. As I sat on a step holding him, the baby began to cry and the phone rang. The following weeks swirled past in an onslaught of competing demands typified by that moment.

After I got the kids settled down, I sat at the kitchen table sorting through a pile of mail and feeling disoriented. I opened an envelope from the Mountain Equipment Co-op and read an appeal asking us to take time to vote for their board of directors. Strange as it may seem, I did. As carefully as though our lives depended on it, I pondered each candidate's credentials and testimonial, examined the photographic images, and finally selected four candidates. I filled in our form, put it in the envelope provided, and sealed it. Every March since, notice of MEC's board election has arrived in the mail, triggering the memory of this occasion.

Later that day or the next, there was another call—two friends from work. They drove all the way out, from town. It was dark out when they brought me a basket of cheeses and fruit from my co-workers. It staggered me to realize how suddenly people had seemed to drop away from my world, and how quickly they had mobilized around me, turning up as if from another galaxy. When they did turn up—as these two had—I didn't know how to respond, possessed of neither the wit nor the resources to be gracious. So I just stood at the door and received their offerings dumbly, startled by the unexpected attention.

Over the next weeks I talked and talked to what felt like

thousands of family members, co-workers, friends and neighbours. I must have gotten the knack of recounting the news, of taking comfort and giving it. But it was hard to get my mind around people's concern for me. My family's insistence on sending someone out to help baffled me. It made no sense that I needed help, certainly not at the great trouble and expense of flying a sister from Colorado, who would herself be leaving behind work and family. But the telephone lines buzzed from Maine to Virginia to Colorado as my family made decisions and arrangements.

I'll admit I dreaded the intrusion of a sibling I'd barely seen in twenty years. Yet it wasn't long after her plane touched the ground that I felt both relief and gratitude to have her here. I realized from that, and the dozens of other small and big gestures of support, how much we have to learn about the protocol of disaster. Older generations probably suffered such disasters in closer proximity, and had the experience of extended family to draw on.

❧

That first night after the accident I went to bed earlier than usual because I couldn't think of what else to do and needed to get to morning, when I'd know what had happened to my husband. My eyes stung. When I closed them I saw a flash of skates and blood-soaked towels. By five in the morning, I had talked to the hospital and knew that the surgery had lasted for hours. The surgeon discovered that the cut had penetrated the eyelid to slice the eye cleanly, like a knife through a tomato. She had stitched layer after layer, working to save the eyeball. It was too soon to know whether there would be any vision, I was told, or whether Mont would keep the eye-ball itself. He'd be conscious within hours, and I could visit anytime after that.

Those details pulsed through me, in waves of panic and

nausea. I called my brother (an optometrist) to relay the information, as I would do throughout the following weeks. He asked me questions which seemed foolish or irrelevant: What had Mont said? How'd his voice sound? It's a blessing that I didn't have the wit to share his concern about brain damage. The day it dawned on me what he'd been asking I felt a terror hit for what I hadn't known to fear.

By the time I got the kids up, our doctor had called for the second time, this time to let me know that Mont was awake. This man's been our doctor for all the years we've lived here. He's seen us through lots, and knows well my silly fears and how the sight of blood and the smell of antiseptic can make me faint. Not surprisingly, hospitals frighten me. Anticipating my anxiety, he explained that I'd find Mont pale, bandaged, and alert. We wouldn't know much more until the bandages came off, later in the day. The greatest danger was infection.

Our doctor was also candid enough to let me know, right then, that our hope should be directed toward saving the eye; sight was beyond the realm of reasonable expectation. At the time, though grateful for his support, I resented what felt like undue pessimism. Soon enough we'd know that he'd advised us well.

Throughout, the kids were both a challenge and a sweet distraction. I had to nurse the baby and was worried that exhaustion and too many tears had dried my milk supply. It hadn't, and didn't. Despite the concern and advice of many to wean the baby and have freedom from that demand, I clung to breast-feeding, knowing how it soothed frayed nerves and grounded me. Having a baby to nurse requires that one adhere to routine and care for oneself.

The older two children were more complicated: They shared my fears and concerns. Nicole had been at home with a sore throat. I sent her to school that morning with a note to her teacher tucked in her backpack, though the flat sheen of her eyes let me know she wasn't recovered. But routine provides comfort.

My memory of the initial visit to the Royal Inland Hospital is murky. Parking was very nearly an insurmountable challenge. In the room, I held my husband's hand while tears streamed down my face, hard as I tried to be strong. He's usually a powerful man with calloused hands. But he looked frail and white and his skin felt silky soft against mine. That's a consequence of the fluids from the surgery, someone told me later. The tenor was gone from his voice, which distressed me more than anything. He seemed somewhere far inside himself.

By that time we knew how the end of a blade must have gone right into the eye, penetrating clear through to the back of the eyeball. And we'd learned the extent of regret of the other player, as he stood shifting his weight from one foot to the other at the foot of my husband's hospital bed.

Other people came and went, and I struggled through the awkwardness of hospital etiquette, meeting the other patients in Mont's room while averting my eyes from anything that might increase my light-headedness. After that first visit, I got a bit better at it. At least I learned to notice where I'd left the car.

The next afternoon I met my sister Jeanne's plane. We went directly from the airport to a mall, and picked out a present for Andrew to take to the first birthday party to which he'd been invited. It seemed ludicrous then, in the way normal details do, in an abnormal situation. We picked out a plaid flannel cowboy shirt and a yo yo. Later that night, we wrapped them and drank wine. After four days, when my sister left for home, the two of us were closer than we'd ever been. Good things come from bad, as they say.

Five days after the accident, Mont came home to await a second operation in Vancouver. The kids were bursting with excitement. They hadn't been to the hospital and had no concept of his weakness or fragility. I think they did overwhelm him, with their balloons and stories to share. The nice meal I'd prepared also turned out to be overwhelming. Mont looked weaker at home. Against the warm colours and wooden walls of home, the pallor of his skin and the sterile bulkiness of his bandages seemed so wrong.

And he *was* vulnerable: The baby I'd placed on his chest whacked the bandaged eye with a small fist in a random exploration of Dad. That night, Mont banged the eye himself, running into the bedroom door I'd left ajar. I was vulnerable too, doing both our work and trying to appear just fine while feeling as though I might disintegrate at any moment.

Within days we were off to Vancouver. Leaving behind the bigger kids was hard, but I knew they'd be fine. Thank God for good friends: those staying to take care of them; those making ready for us in Vancouver.

Driving down the hill toward Kamloops, we lost a hubcap. We heard the ping of the hubcap hitting the road and turned back to see if we could find it. Driving up the road and back down, Douglas and I searched the roadside. But it was Mont, still sharp-eyed, who spied the thing, off in the bush. And we shared the first of many one-eye jokes (Keep an eye out for. . . Good eye, etc.).

❦

Our room was on the top floor of the hotel opposite St. Paul's. James was delighted to have me all to himself. I felt guilty about enjoying him there, but did. We shared a king sized bed, and I nursed him whenever the urge struck him, knowing it would play havoc with the schedule we'd evolved for work. I was exhausted and slept all I could. I tried to read, which was pointless; I tried marking a pile of student compositions, which was like marking from another galaxy.

167

The hospital was stranger than Royal Inland. I longed for the familiarity of our own town, our own doctor. In that place, nurses and doctors seemed brisk. No one explained things. Didn't they know how thick I felt? How many questions I needed to answer for the friends and family who called at night? Surgery was scheduled for the next day. Mont seemed subdued, looked pale and frail. My throat was thick with tension I could neither swallow nor express. On the wall of the hospital room hung a crucifix. Heavy feelings flowed down the corridor from other rooms. Ten days had passed since the accident.

James brightened things up. On the way to the hospital, he'd smile at himself in the mirrored walls of the elevator, black toque setting off his fair skin. *He* didn't think his dad looked strange in pale yellow pyjamas. And if he wondered why the smells of work—the diesel and sheep wool and pine pitch—had given way to the smells of hospital, he didn't let on.

Back on the ward that night, I caught up with the surgeon, literally running down the hall with him. He told me he might not be able to restore perfect vision, but should come close. His brusqueness inspired confidence in me, but I was careful not to irritate him with too many questions. Later I would hate him for toying with our hopes, for his boundless arrogance.

◦

Weeks later, in May, we were back in Vancouver for the follow-up examination. It took so much out of Mont, those two long surgeries, but by that time he was strong again.

That trip merely confirmed what we knew: The second surgery had not been successful; there was no restorable vision in Mont's right eye. Since we'd already come to terms with this, we were treating the trip as a holiday. We had a suite at the Sylvia. We used a cheque from my dad to treat ourselves to dinner at the English Bay Cafe, while friends came and watched the kids.

Before dinner, I headed out for a run along Second Beach. Outside the room, our shared sense of levity failed me. I was out of place: a country mouse in the city. My grey sweats stood out amid all the spandex. The roller bladers frightened me, flashing past so suddenly. One woman power-walked by me, a can of mace in her right hand swinging in time to her stride. A grey-faced man muttered to himself. A couple on a park bench smelled of patchouli oil, or pot.

It all seemed ominous. After a mile or so I thought I'd unwound when I mistook two older ladies in heavy brown coats for a bear. I hadn't relaxed—just forgotten my where-abouts for an instant and transposed a rural anxiety upon the city scene. The harbour was beautiful in the late afternoon sun, but from somewhere a beeper sounded, and my heart raced. So much for my relaxing run! Dinner, however, proved to be great.

⌖

Right from the start I mourned the damage to my husband's eyes for the simple reason that they are beautiful eyes, big and round and liquid brown. Laugh lines radiate from them, so that he has this way of smiling with his whole face. I was smitten the moment I set eyes upon him—as the saying goes— in the crowded dining hall of Willard Straight, up on the hill in the heart of our campus. I see those eyes in two of our children now. And in him, still.

Mont does have his right eye, though he sees nothing from it. There's scar tissue in the corner, and a milkiness on the lens. But we tend to forget about it. It's my habit to track the stream of wine with my glass as he pours. And he managed to knock over a couple of pieces of stemware before resigning himself to drinking from a tumbler. Sometimes, I'll try to pass him a cup of coffee as he drives, remembering—just as my exasperation rises—that he can't see from that side.

As traumas go, this was not catastrophic. People every moment of every day survive far worse. But it rocked our lives and affects us still. So I had to probe, defying memory's neat trick of sealing off such times, glossing over the edges until one can barely see the fissure that was surely there.

# Raising Kids

How peculiar a notion: that we raise our children. They do, indeed, rise. But through what action of ours? Their growth, physical and otherwise, continues to startle me: James, youngest, yet the most stubborn and opinionated of us all; Andrew, stretched and pushed by impulse, at one moment drawn, the next propelled, by whim or fixation or whatever's happening around him; Nicole, poised and thoughtful, creative, going steadily along her own way. Where did any of their ways come from? And what have we, their parents, to do with it?

I never would have imagined that one day I'd be watching my two boys, eating dinner side by side on stools at the counter, break into waves of uncontrollable laughter at a single fart. Who'd have thought such hopeless hilarity would result from a bit of gas? Their sister and I exchange exasperated looks, then give in to their laughter. The whole episode goes against the grain of every aspect of my own proper New England upbringing. As for my daughter, she has a more discerning sense of humour, and more couth. Yet even that fact flies in the face of all my idealistic seventies notions of sexual equality.

After James was born, we were absorbed by him, keenly aware that he was our last baby. I thought of this as a parent's perspective, until I heard Nicole say, "I wish he could just stay little, like this." She's always had an ability to jolt me out of some sense of my own boundaries by reflecting my innermost thoughts with her carefully chosen words.

Was it coincidence that James would later claim that he didn't *want* to get bigger? And could that vehement wish possibly affect the fact that this kid grows so slowly? At five, he remained under forty pounds. Last year, I retired his size four jeans when the second layer of knee patches had worn through, though he could still slide into them without unzipping the fly.

To raise, according to Merriam-Webster, includes: *awaken, arouse, incite, flush from cover, recall from (as if from death), levitate, establish radio communication with a higher place, elevate, invigorate, increase the strength of, or intensify the pitch of; to bring up, to rear, to cause to grow, to educate.*

I like the notion of raising kids, considered in light of such a broad spectrum of definitions. To my knowledge, we have never had occasion to *levitate* our kids, and I don't think we have the strength to *intensify* their pitch. Indeed, I often feel diluted by the very experience of having had them.

One of the diluting repercussions of having children has been a marked loss of memory. I've lost it in discernible chunks: The ability to calculate mentally and to remember numbers disappeared with the birth of our second child; the ability to fasten words to things adeptly vanished with our third child. And it's become worse in the last five years.

There's a quirky randomness to how I conjure up a number (take the "five," in the previous sentence, for instance), or to how a name or date comes to mind. If our dentist's receptionist asks for the kids' ages and birth-dates, for example, I prickle with anxiety, sometimes stuttering at the point when the names, dates, and ages are lined up and ready to file out of my mouth. An off-the-cuff answer really *won't* do. And how will it look for a mother to forget her own child's age?

The notion of *flushing* a kid *from cover* fits our experience. There was the time that all five of us had been engrossed in an afternoon movie on a rainy day, until we noticed that we'd lost James. Always independent, he'd simply crawled off to find his own entertainment. We searched, calling out for him, for maybe two or three minutes. I found him not two feet from where we'd been watching television, digging himself into the potting soil of a large philodendron. Still soundless, he peered at me, his eyes so white from the midst of a face masked with dirt. He was quite cheerful, in his mountain of mouldy soil. That was the first of many frantic searches for that mute and fearless baby. All of us became adept at flushing him out, though.

*Rearing, causing to grow, and educating*—those notions take me back to the fifties, when we were getting raised. We rose better, perhaps, leavened by the strong pressure of conformity. Guilt was the operative condition, the reflex of non-compliance. We have only to look at children's literature to remember how radically different a time it was.

Think of Robert Munsch, or Dennis Lee. The story *Sky Full of Babies* comes to mind. These are fun and silly stories, but inspired by a drastically different morality, or mentality, than what I'd grown up with. In these stories, harmless but silly parents are suffered and sometimes saved by wise and resourceful kids. Gone is all wickedness, and also magic. What's left? Whim and cleverness, mushiness or humour. I can't say I haven't enjoyed some of this literature, but it troubles me that we have abandoned an age old store of fable and myth, the influence of which we can barely comprehend.

When I was pregnant with our first child, our friend presented me with a heavy white volume of Grimm's Fairy Tales, translated from the German. Too harsh for little kids, I remember thinking as I read through it.

Then one day Nicole found the book on a high shelf in the boys' room. She spent a Saturday morning reading it, then spent the afternoon reading stories to her brothers. They have no scars from the experience. Come to think of it, neither do my contemporaries. So wherever did we get this idea that *our* kids were so tender and innocent?

In the nineties, we parents who were raised in the fifties turned ourselves inside out to model virtues of respect, tolerance, and gentleness. These were demanded of us when we were young, so we modelled them well, with proficiency. But somehow our kids have fallen short in their mastery. So either we weren't such great examples as we thought, or the whole concept of modelling is flawed. Or maybe the stories we've read them, about parents too simple-minded to come in from the cold, undermine us as models.

It was a challenge to convince our youngest son that children do not say to adults, "Get over here, *now*." I believe that he thinks we were being ridiculous ("wudiculous," as he would have said, then) and hypercritical. It wasn't that he wanted to offend, though he does seem to enjoy having an effect on people. Sometimes it's a shock reaction he's seeking; more often, just a good laugh. He'll repeat anything he's heard, watching for a reaction. And once in a while, he simply wants to stir the pot.

One work-day evening when he was two, we were running late. As the three kids sat, lined up at the counter for the interminably long dinner hour, I tried to speed things up.

"James," I prompted, "have you eaten your cauliflower?" (a rhetorical question, as said cauliflower sat, wilting on his plate).

"Yes." came the firm reply.

"You little liar," laughed Nicole, "What's *that*, then?"

"That's a duck," James answered her, not missing a beat.

Not surprisingly, cursing has had great appeal for James; he'd mutter "damn thing wheel," as he roared around on his tricycle. But then, our kids hear much more cursing than either Mont or I would have heard, growing up. That's probably as much due to the times as to the fact that their dad often works at home.

Both our boys have amazed and, I'll admit, impressed me by the inventiveness with which they have tried out profanity. When Andrew was three, the choice slam among his daycare crowd was "pee face." His brother recently called him "peanut-butter butt." So much for respect and tolerance.

Their sister, one evening, was driven to frustration by a craft she was working on and spit out "dag nabbit." We pointed out that the phrase wasn't much in fashion. She'd been reading *Huck Finn* at the time.

Maybe, though, our children are raised in the sense that they grow away, as if *incited by* that which engenders them. Perhaps it's much too subtle a process to recognize until the child has grown. In my background, for example, there is an ambivalent attitude toward travel. My mother's parents travelled from Italy: one eager, one reluctant. My mother is vehemently opposed to travel. Yet, her five children live sprawled across the continent. Oddly enough, I share her sentiment, yet am one of the furthest flung.

At twenty-two, when I was preparing for my first trip out west, I heard my mother telling a friend that she didn't understand why I had to go "traipsing all that way across the country." I felt offended by her words, but also strangely touched by the strength of caring I detected beneath them. And I knew that I couldn't begin to answer her question, even to my own satisfaction.

Influences on our children may run from depths we aren't even conscious of—by currents of myth and morality, trend and tradition. My youngest son once asked me, out of nowhere: "How will I ever grow up and find a mother like you to have my babies?" I can imagine my brother asking my mother such a question, and I suspect she might have responded with the same combination of laughter, fondness and alarm, as I did.

Maybe we raise our children in the sense that we *invigorate* them. And even as we do so, it seems that we are being awakened by the din of their growing. We might well be the agents of their rising, but it's all so much more mystical than the simple set of intentions for which we sometimes mistake it. Children grow to meet the challenges that face them. Sometimes we assist, other times allow or provoke them; but if we are vigilant, we can at least witness their rise to the demands of their maturing.

My journal records a particular image of our daughter, in her seventh year and getting ready for her school day. I was urging her to hurry, caught up in the general morning panic of getting her to the bus, the boys to daycare, and me to work.

She responded to my panic by slowing her pace to about the speed of chilled molasses running along a table-top. Then, at the last possible moment, she swung down from her stool, donned jacket and backpack, and—smiling sweetly to Dad—calmly sauntered out the door.

Still in nightshirt, dumbstruck, I watched this child, all long legs and gleaming hair, with a bounce in her step, and wondered how I had missed so many changes, and how I would ever rise to the challenge of keeping up.

# Part IV

❖

*Taking Stock*

❖

A settler clears a few acres, builds a hut of shakes and then moves away. If he returns a decade later he finds no clearing. Alders have taken possession of the damp earth, firs and pines of the dry. The hut has collapsed but the shake roof, made of durable cedar, is not yet rotten and lies flat on the ground.

—Bruce Hutchinson, *A Life in the Country* (1988)

British Columbia [with] its sleeping past, its awakened future, the gradual progress of discovery and habitation, the extravagant forests, prairies, lakes and mountains, the great beauty, the isolated and sometimes collapsed shack that speaks of human effort and departure . . . . The land is full of question.

—Ethel Wilson, *Love and Salt Water* (1957)

# Potluck

A yellow note adheres to the inside cover of my journal. On it are some phrases captured in haste, which prod some cache of memory, out of which springs the following story. I tell it with a belief that it may well be the story of any working mother, preparing for any social event, at the end of a work day in June.

Home early, about four-thirty, I'm hungry and tired, preparing for a pot luck dinner at a good friend's place in town. Pot luck, the worst of all worlds: a dish to cook for the scrutiny of others; the usual array of foods and gear to prepare for the kids; the less-than-eager anticipation of watching three kids in an unfamiliar surrounding where they either act worse and shout louder than usual, or just seem to do so. I've embarked on two new recipes, both marinated vegetable and grain concoctions. Our group of friends has conscientiously embraced a healthier cuisine, to support one of us whose heart condition has terrified us all.

As I cook, Nicole plays with Jamie on the living room floor, keeping him out of my way. While changing his shirt, she discovers a woodtick on his soft little back. Horrified, I pry it out, indignant that the tiny beast would victimize my baby, and guilt-stricken not to have discovered it myself.

"*Mommm!*" cries Andrew from the bathroom, interrupting my guilt. "I dropped the wash cloth *in the toilet.*"

179

"It's OK," I assure him.

With one hand I stir together salad ingredients, with another, fix a bottle of tepid milk to calm the baby. Reaching around to pull a steaming pot of couscous off the burner, I drop the bottle, the rubber nipple of which, mysteriously, pops off. Milk explodes everywhere. James cries. Andrew, now positively wailing, informs me that he has peed on the cloth he had forgotten was dropped in the toilet. James has crawled into the milk, the dishwasher has stopped whirring, Nicole is packing the diaper bag, Andrew is in the depths of despair, and I wonder for a moment what life is like in the households of our friends.

Scooping James up, I plunk him safely out of harm's way, snug in his seat, and give him Cheerios with which to entertain himself. Nicole reads to Andrew while I salvage the wash cloth, which I'm tempted to flush down but for the threat of a plugged toilet. Glancing into the mirror, I wipe off my face and brush back my hair. As I dry my face, I check the diaper pail and discover that our new babysitter has only changed the baby once in nine hours. Considering how I might instruct against such carelessness, I run out quickly to gather clothes from the line. Moments of fresh air and a task with little catastrophic potential restores me. I pull in sheets and sweatpants, underwear and t-shirts.

At the end of that very long hour, my husband returns from his day's work. As he washes up and gathers kids into the car for the trip to town, I discover that I've prepared my two salads ass-backwards. The dressing for one is on the other, leaving me pondering where to put the carefully roasted pine nuts, the small pile of crumbled Feta.

To my surprise, it's a lovely evening. James toddles from one friendly big person to another, curious, content, and charming. The big sibs play hard and long, enjoying newly mowed grass, which is a novelty for rural kids. My husband, holding a beer, engages in animated conversation, even catches part of a ball game on TV. The salads taste fine. And I drink wine, eat well, and attend, in a glassy-eyed sort of way, to a couple of hours of rambling conversation among close friends in the warmth of a June night.

❧

This other "memoir" comes from notes jotted on both sides of a flimsy, patterned napkin from a coffee shop. I was waiting for my friend to meet me and remember my relief at finding a pen with which to write.

The previous night I'd been up five times in seven hours, to tend a teething baby. The notes on my napkin record the ministrations—rock, turn on belly, sips of milk, Tylenol drops, cuddle. Waking up early, I'd managed a quick work-out on my stepping machine—the up-and-down, up-and-down of which became an eerie chorus recalling the night's interrupted sleep. As I showered, I reviewed what I knew about the new sitter who'd be arriving in thirty minutes. Over breakfast, I prepared the kids for her arrival.

"I can't get used to a name like Simone," said Andrew, lending strength to my own misgivings.

When I'd met her, Simone had seemed fine to me. A grade ten drop-out, she appeared slow and sweet; not bright, but not pretentious either. To prepare her for the job, I'd revised my three pages of notes and instructions, detailing routines, meals and snacks, covering every possible calamity.

As we waited for Simone, I thought about the work day ahead. One challenge that loomed was a lunch meeting with a visiting dignitary from Korea. My new job as department chair—which included such duties as The Wooing Of Important People—required a certain style and polish very much at odds with teething babies and new babysitters. Striving to rise to

181

the occasion, I stole a glance at myself in the kitchen window on the way out the door, and rehearsed the exotic syllables of the name "Chol Kim."

Midway along the thirty minute drive to town, I made a stop to drop off the week's diapers at the Diaper Service. I was running late for a student interview, and the gas gauge read *empty*.

When I arrived at work, my office was filled with the boxes of papers and books to be hidden from view for the Important People's campus tour. The boxes seemed to encapsulate the tenuousness of my transition to the office of Chair. I hadn't quite manged the time to unpack them; to disguise the heap and jumble that actually reflected my sense of that new role. But that level of disclosure wouldn't do for a campus tour. So the boxes got dragged across the hall and hidden in a colleague's office.

After the two student interviews, I left for lunch. My notes mention a freak hailstorm. But I'd need no notes to remember the absurdity of being pelted by hailstones while racing to my car, and how hail filled the pockets of my blazer, melting as I drove to the restaurant and leaving me a sodden mass of dishevelled hair and damp cotton. I arrived late. Just behind the guests and shortly before the college president, I was apparently the only one to get caught in the momentary storm.

I shivered as I dried. But our lunch passed in relative calm. Mr. Kim himself seemed pleasant and content, talking mostly to our president. I was only required to smile and occasionally to nod, and never even had to say the name I'd practised. Lunch went late, so there was no campus tour.

After dragging the boxes back into my office, I did manage to unpack one. Then I received a phone call urging me to attend a meeting which I'd hoped to escape. Finally, there was late afternoon coffee with my friend. I don't know what prompted our rendezvous, which I awaited as I scribbled those notes on a napkin. But she's a good friend, and a busy one, and the moments we find to share are moments I cherish.

Leaving for home a bit late, but fortified by coffee and companionship, I did remember to pick up the week's supply of clean diapers. Dinner, was simple: a casserole pulled straight from the freezer.

The challenges of that day and the interrupted sleep of the night before had left me as frayed as the napkin from which I read these notes. It's hard to make out all the words, but the last lines, scrawled along the folded line on the side of the napkin, prompted me to try.

*Do I exist in the sum of the parts of my days, or in the gaps between the parts?* Unfolding the napkin to see how I might have answered, I find only a list for the weekend. The list reads:

      laundry
      kids' baths
      next size clothes for J.
      Sun. dinner?
      garden—weed, replant
      update baby book
      bills, letters? new essay idea?
      bn. rice casserole, spinach salad, lamb stew
      use up broccoli.

As to whether I exist in the sum of the parts of my days—life as a kind of potluck concoction of work and home—or in the gaps between the parts? Either I didn't know how to answer, or I had just lost interest in the question. Or maybe the question will require a greater expanse of coherent reflection than I have time for in my life now.

# The Road Less Travelled By

Two roads diverged in a yellow wood
And sorry I could not travel both
And be one traveller . . .

Oh, I kept the first for another day!
Yet knowing how way leads on to way,
I doubted if I should ever come back.
I shall be telling this with a sigh
Somewhere ages and ages hence:
Two roads diverged in a wood, and I—
I took the one less travelled by,
And that has made all the difference.

—Robert Frost

Today my kids and I went wild berry picking. I threw sun hats and yogurt containers and the baby's bottle into Nicole's pack, got James in his stroller and the big sibs on their bikes, and off we went. Andrew, nearly five, refused to ride past our ram, Leo, who's free ranging these days, taking advantage of high green grass. Andrew edged along, bike wobbling beside him, never taking his eyes from Leo. My words of encouragement didn't speed him up a bit—indication of the limits of my credibility beyond the walls of the house. So James and I waited, watching Andrew barely managing his red two-wheeler, pant legs trailing on the ground, the waist twisted sideways, shirt half tucked, half not. At the edge of the road his sister waited, her long legs astride her bike, her face the very picture of tolerance.

After carrying bikes and stroller over the cattle-guard that marks the end of our driveway, we set off the half mile down toward the big lake, to a berry patch by the side of the road. When I was out for a run yesterday, the fragrance of strawberry nearly stopped me in my tracks. I used to go picking there in the leisurely summers before we had kids, and again when each child was a baby. But for the past three years my work and the kids' attention spans wouldn't permit it. This summer, though, I'm impressed by how the kids have grown: how they'll head off together, returning as much as an hour later with containers partially filled with wild strawberries, as well as with bits of dried weeds, and those tiny green bugs that emerge, so surprisingly, from the mushy sweet pulp.

Funny how those fragrant and powerfully flavoured berries recall the Junes of my own childhood, and hot sunny hours spent in the field that stretched from my backyard down to the Atlantic shoreline. Here, some thirty years later and three thousand miles west, my kids were gathering the fabric of their own memories. Maybe that's why I'd orchestrated that awkward journey—to ensure some degree of continuity between my memories and theirs.

At our destination, I broke off a piece of a Saltine for James to chew on and angled his stroller away from the sun, on as level a spot as I could find. He hunched forward in his seat, not exactly happy to be immobile. Andrew took a while to settle in. Wiping berry juice from his sneaker he philosophized, "Too bad I stepped on one, but you gotta step *some*where!" He picked a few berries, then put the cover on his container and ran the distance to his sister, to check out the picking further down. I wondered how many containers he'd dumped before adopting the caution of lidding that make-shift bucket. Back he raced, nearly tripping on a mossy crop of rocks between us. Nicole, he told me, had "a real mother-lode." I stretched my back and watched her for a while. Lately she likes to be off by herself.

Andrew looked serious: Bent over his own patch, he was surprisingly deft at searching out those tiny prizes that hung over on their stems, their blush of ripe red just beyond view. While he picked, he sang, thrusting away the silence with his refrain. "Speed the power, *pow-pow-pow-power* . . ." became a part of the atmosphere.

As I watched them, what surprised me even more than the berry-picking ability and endurance of the kids, was *my* growing impatience. While even the little one sucked contentedly on his bottle and watched, I felt myself getting restless and mentally rehearsing a quick trip home. My knees and back ached and a mosquito bite on my neck was itching. My mind traveled from the breakfast dishes waiting at home, to the unfinished programme proposal waiting at work. I planned the next class I'd be teaching, and began a mental checklist of what needed to be done in preparation for our trip back east next month.

Then James, too, showed signs of growing irritability. The sun was shining in his face now; his bottle lay on the ground beside him. His big brother and sister, however, remained fully engaged, and neither the blotchy red bug bites which dotted their foreheads and arms, nor the wind which was blowing dark clouds over the warm sun, detracted them from the task at hand. I announced that we'd move along soon, proposing for the third time "ten more berries each."

The rain felt just minutes away. James was howling as if to support my nagging. A few heavy rain drops fell, and my big kids were still just finishing "this one more perfect spot."

Finally, I gathered the red stained containers, along with rain-drenched sunhats. And we were off.

The return trip was uphill. Twenty minutes felt like ten days, and managed to dissipate all the restfulness and all the restlessness our venture had stirred up in me. Andrew's training wheels kept pulling him into the soft gravel at the road-side, and he fell again and again. He was brave about it all, but clearly struggling, while his sister rode on ahead, stopping now and then to wait. I was pushing the stroller, then running back to push Andrew's bike. Back and forth I went, shoving stubborn tires through gravel that felt like quicksand.

At the end of the day, this is a memory as sweet as a wild strawberry. But I wonder: Had I known what lay ahead, would I have ventured out along that road? Or would I have been tempted to put it off for another, better time?

❖

Six months have passed since that berry-picking day in the summertime. Today, snow pulls down the boughs of the spruce trees outside the window by which I sit writing. I am waiting for James to wake from his nap. The big kids are skiing. I've spent the past hour leafing through my notes and journals. The moment stretches open and the snow in the trees brings to mind Robert Frost's poem which I had memorized back in the years when memory's ink was indelible. Both a guide and a reproach, the sense of lingering at the edge of "the road less travelled by," which Frost's words capture so vividly, rises from page after page of my journal. Yet the complexity and subtlety of daily life far outstrips the simplicity of Frost's poem. Never, for example, do just two roads extend. And rarely does "all the difference" rest along any one roadway.

Parents *know* that "coming back" is not possible. In my journal, so many entries embrace that knowledge. An entry from the tenth week of James's infancy consists of fragments, "Holding him, my attention snagged by the rough edges of essays in progress, always pulled by so many conflicting demands . . ." Sitting here at my desk, I can't help noticing how those essays *remain* "in progress," while James has progressed quite nicely indeed.

Several entries speak about holding this baby, yet also about holding the memory of his babyhood. The writing itself serves to capture the memory, while also creating yet another demand on my time.

Last week, near the end of the Christmas holiday, I was having trouble settling James down for his nap. He threw his head back with the ache of cutting teeth. I lifted him from his crib, heaped two additional pillows on his brother's bed, and laid him down on my chest. He rested his head on my neck and fell soundly asleep. As I soaked in his warm sleepiness, I could feel the tiredness flowing out of my own body. Weighing just over twenty pounds, his little body has the satisfying sturdiness particular to toddlerhood. In his legs, draped over my stomach, I could feel firm muscles taking shape against soft baby fat.

Yet even the sweetness of that moment couldn't dispel a tug of guilt. After just a few more seconds I roused myself, laid the sleeping child down in his crib, and returned to the pot of simmering applesauce, the stack of unfolded laundry—the heaps of demands on a working parent's weekend afternoon.

But for just a couple of minutes I had ventured down that road so seldom taken and now, preserving the memory in words, I do so once again. Like the surprising sweetness of wild strawberries on a roadside in early summer, such moments entice us. And the enticement is a blessing. And yes, I am telling of it "with a sigh."

# Camping Tales

We are a camping family. It's taken me years to understand this aspect of Canadian leisure. Consulting a dictionary didn't help. In addition to the standard definitions about temporary shelters and ideological positions, there are less common definitions of the word as verb: *to put into a camp; also: to accommodate*. Then, there's the more obscure adjectival definition: *something so outrageous . . . inappropriate, old-fashioned, or in such bad taste as to be considered amusing*. Maybe that does get closer.

Here's what I have arrived at. Camping: the relaxing family activity for which Mom and Dad prepare for days, first digging out and then repacking old dishes, toys, towels, clothes, tent, bitter-smelling rubber air mattresses. Then jamming everything into the car. Then driving for two hours (having insufficient courage for any greater distance from home)—to pour out of vehicle, unpack same old dishes, toys, towels, tent, clothes. The rest: wondering what essential item has been forgotten and whose air mattress has the slow leak; and the relief when we do discover just what it is we are up against.

Camping: a creative exercise in accommodation.

Picture camping with a family of five. Now picture the same scene, with no dish soap. Or no sleeping bag for the oldest child (substitute, instead, a rather interesting assortment of car rags). Or no peanut-butter (peanut-butter being one of the few foods that child will eat). Or no clothes pins. Or no hatchet. We've experienced all of these. We'll be taking on new challenges this summer.

Someone might reasonably ask, "So why *do* it?" Certainly my mother has asked that question. Well, that's even harder to answer. Perhaps family camping is like other traditions—things we mindlessly do because others have mindlessly done them before us. Maybe it belongs in the category of Things Character Building. But then, my husband and I have quite enough character, and even if we didn't, our character-building potential's all used up. And the kids, well, I can't see how an experience that tests and retests *us* does much for them. Do they learn from their dad and mom the finer arts of graceless tenacity, the creative repression of irritability? No, it must belong in that other category—Things From Which Memories Are Made. Maybe there's some perverse relationship between things memorable, and the forgetting of stuff.

I recall one day last July. It was the end of our stay at a campground. While their dad dismantled the camp, I took the three kids to the beach for a last swim. The day was a brilliant blue and green, brightly sun-lit.

We took the high path, across a stretch of woods to the change huts above the beach. Andrew, close to six and alert to both signs and gender, insisted on using the men's change room. Nicole, Jamie (not yet two), and I crowded into the women's room. After we'd changed, the three of us—ready for swimming, our clothes rolled and stuffed in sandy packsacks—stood waiting outside the men's changing rooms. First patiently, then awkwardly, then frantically, we waited for our small man to emerge. Whole families came and went, traveling off toward the beach to swim and play. We waited. James drank from every fountain in sight, sucking, of course, on each spigot. At last Andrew came out—wearing nothing more than one water shoe, and carrying the other. After some help jamming his foot into the second shoe, he disappeared back into the change room. James, meanwhile, managed to scoot beneath the outside wall, into the change cubicle of a surprised young girl.

Finally, and proudly, Andrew reappeared in his swimsuit. "Where are your clothes?" I asked, carefully modulating my voice.

Sighing, he turned back. "Don't forget your underwear," I added. Heaving a second sigh, he looked down at his swim-trunks, beneath which poked the waistband of underpants. Back he went.

Not more than five minutes later, Andrew came running out from the change room, quite naked. He was shrieking, "Spiders! A whole *family* of spiders: I think they're *Tarantulas*!!"

I was treated to my first visit into a men's change room, to gather my son's scattered clothing. After which I helped him into his suit, and we trooped past all those other families, swimming and playing along the beach.

Which trip was that? The one where it rained for two full days and Nicole, hot with fever, was the only warm camper before she threw up, and then—like the rest of us—became chilled? Or the trip on which Jamie was sick—flushed, irritable, hot, then racked with diarrhoea? Or one when Andrew, refusing food, fished alone for hours, so determined in his white t-shirt and canvas hat, casting again and again . . . until I made him eat a sandwich and some watermelon?  "Eat," I said. "You'll feel better."

He threw up all the way home.

Much of child-raising revolves around the toilet, at least after toilet training. Before that, it's even more elementary. Camping only seems to strip away any vestige of civility a family might have preserved. So, not surprisingly, many of our camping stories involve toilets. Or throwing-up. This stuff is *not* for the delicate. But then, neither are our children.

I remember the second camping trip we took after the kids

were born. Our campground of choice was full. We had to drive another forty-five minutes to another, nearly full, park. The irony is that we live on twenty-eight quiet acres. So one could argue that we camp to expose our kids to people and noise, to crowds and public toilets. And our kids are as fascinated by those things as a city kid would be with chickens.

This other campground was crowded. From where we slept we could hear the man in the next campsite belch. He, in turn, had the pleasure of watching our kids trooping past his lawn chair on the way back and forth to the outhouse. Not being used to neighbours, they had little notion of privacy. And they're friendly kids. Driving out the next morning, they smiled and waved good bye to everyone we passed.

We returned to our original campground that morning, and managed to find a vacant spot. Just after piling into our new site, the kids raced off to explore. Andrew, then three, shouted (across two fairly spacious and peopled sites), "These toilets *flush*. Come see, Nicole!!"

Our kids had never, except for that one previous night, known any but flush toilets.

That's the trip on which we learned that a family should never camp for fewer than two nights. *No* one slept the first night. The kids, unused to sharing a room, let alone a tent, laughed uproariously for hours.

I suspect that it is in the tent, in the muggy heat of late summer evenings, where the kids form the memories they'll carry into adulthood. They'll remember *liking* one another, shrieking with laughter, and, for two or three minutes after the hissed warnings to be quiet and go to sleep *now*, whispering their silly stories and scary tales, and muffling their laughter with pillows. They won't, probably, remember hating one another in the cramped back seats of the family vehicle until finally, in despair, a parent heaped mounds of pillows and sleeping bags between them, making a downy barrier over which they were forbidden to look or speak.

With my belly eight-months-round, crawling into the tent, then worming my way into my sleeping bag, was no laughing matter either. But then that was good training for later sharing our cramped quarters with all three kids, each with his or her own pillow (own pillows being more important, we'd learned, than milk or matches). We, who look with disdain upon those who camp in motor homes complete with air conditioning and television, will keep on camping in a tent, despite the challenge of waking up every couple of hours to pull one kid away from the damp tent wall, or drag another back onto an air mattress, or to extract the third, wringing with sweat, from the bottom of a sleeping bag.

I have to admit, though, the tent—filled with family, warm with sleepy breaths and the first light of day—is a cosy place. The kids, exhausted from their own antics of the night before, will often sleep beyond the squawking whisky jacks and blue jays. My husband, honouring a tradition I cherish, most always struggles up first, to drag out boxes and reconstruct kitchen quarters on the picnic table.

During our final camping trip of the summer of my third pregnancy, Mont and I shared a glass of wine (in rather scummy plastic cups) and talked about taking an occasional trip the following year, when we'd have an infant in tow. As I looked at our vehicle—bulging with boxes and bags, Coleman coolers and rubber raft—and recalled the heft of baby equipment, I felt discouraged. After a few early morning hours during which we lay stiffly, listening to some poor young mother trying to soothe a screeching infant, we decided to skip camping for a year.

But, other than a child falling backwards from a picnic table or spitting toothpaste on the foot of another child, last summer's camping went relatively smoothly.

Except for one incident.

Nicole was perched on a rock, reading. I was hanging towels from the morning swim. And my husband was making coffee, I think, when disaster struck. Jamie had pooped through the side of his diaper. He was a mess. The water heating on the stove for coffee had to be cooled, and the basin of dishes emptied for a bath. The picnic table, in service as kitchen, was converted to a change area. While I searched the car for rags and a clean outfit, his dad undressed James. Jamie did his part by arching his back, which moved him backward so that his head landed in the just-removed diaper.

At about that moment, Andrew tore out of the toilet stall with his shorts around his knees and crashed headlong into the gravel outside, scraping himself from forehead to ankle.

At moments like these, there's relief just in knowing that things can only get better. And mercifully, in the peaceful months when the camp gear lies stowed beneath the bed in our guest cabin, if we even remember those moments, it's with a laugh. But as summer descends, I know it takes more than a few good laughs to keep us camping. Maybe it's the odd moment of sweet serenity that trails in the wake of the unpredictable and hectic, that keeps us camping year after year.

I remember, for example, one enchanted nightfall. Our camp-site nestled against a stand of ponderosa pines, with Nicola Lake lapping against rocks just below. After not more than three *zzzip*'s followed by a head extruding with some important announcement or random complaint, the tent stood quiet behind us. All things considered, the kids had fallen asleep remarkably fast. A light wind cooled the sand and rippled the water. The moon shone, nearly full, making a path clear to the lovely old Quilchena Hotel on the far shore. Our fire burned low and hot. Wine and wieners never tasted better than they did that night.

# Things That Fall from the Sky

In 1975 I took a course in modern American literature, taught by a man named Walter Slatoff. I dragged along four friends who had little interest in literature, but who indulged me for some forgotten reason by attending this class with me. Among them was Mont, who remembers how Slatoff, in the last moments of his final lecture, was about to read an excerpt from *my* paper, when he ran out of time. My memory—of a sweet, brilliant, and humble man who wouldn't have thought of holding his students back for a few moments—jives with Mont's.

One afternoon, about ten years later, I was browsing in the library when I discovered a lovely and utterly unpretentious volume called *The Look of Distance*, in which Slatoff muses on matters relating to reading and teaching. What seems to compel him is "a disturbing gap" between how we talk about literature and literature itself.

Probing the dilemma of teaching literature in those troubled times (the late 70's), Slatoff speaks about "the possibilities of human connection and the curious ways people have found to remain simultaneously together and apart." He carries on to describe the ethical aerodynamics "of highfliers like Icarus, Jesus, Vittorio Mussolini, and Joyce, and the impacts of all sorts of things—from boys to bombs to violets—that can fall from the sky."

Slatoff claims that, while we have "an astronomical number of assertions that literature is not life and should not be confused with it," we have almost nothing to say about the danger of separating the two. And likewise, while we have "recognized the values of detachment and the dangers of undue involvement," we have ignored the relationship "between detachment and coldness and between involvement and love." He asks us to remember that we turn to the study of books because we like the experience of reading them. His plea: to read with the full receptiveness of which we are capable; to read fully attentive to the possibilities for human connection.

～

During my first semester at university I had the good fortune to stumble into a Russian literature class taught by Patricia Carden. I was so very taken with her that I mistook her North Carolinian drawl for a Russian accent.

Five years later, as a young sub teaching in Montana, I was criticized by a principal for sitting on top of my desk to teach— exactly as Professor Carden always sat to deliver her lectures. The principal of that Montana high school was worried, he explained, that—looking so young and casual—I would not be able to control the husky Montana farm boys and dazed hippie kids who sat in rows of desks in front of me. He might have been surprised by the power of that slender brown-haired woman, Patricia Carden, to transfix hundreds of college students, while she sat up on her desk.

In Carden's Russian Literature class we read several short stories and a few magnificently long novels which included *War and Peace*. At the end of the semester, Professor Carden delivered a lecture on re-reading and gave us a lifetime assignment to reread *War and Peace*. She accused us of being consumers of literature. I suppose she meant as opposed to connoisseurs. Consuming books, as I still do—compelled by the scarcity of reading time and the press of unread pages—diminishes the potential of literature, at least of the literature written to be savoured, those stories composed for reexamination, remembering, and full engagement.

Of course, being also a consumer of courses, I have forgotten a good deal of what she explained to us. Yet, I remember trying, back in 1974, to be the kind of reader she had described. And over the years, I have made my way, page by page, through Tolstoy's *War and Peace*, as translated by Maude and Maude, not once, but three more times.

๛

Charles Lamb, in his essay "Detached Thoughts on Books and Reading," admits that "In some senses, the better a book is, the less it demands from binding." I think about this when I look at my Norton Critical Edition of *War and Peace*: dog-eared and battered, its cover is patched with tape which has become a part of the paper it once mended. Yet the very sight of the book evokes fondness. I found Lamb's essay on reading in a ragged and frayed cloth-bound 1911 edition of *Essays of Elia*, wedged tightly in a book shelf in the office of a friend.

"Much depends on *when* and *where* you read a book," says Lamb. He proceeds to set out examples: reading while anticipating a meal, listening to music, at a fine inn, in the company of a friend, out-of-doors, aloud. He goes on to describe "a class of street readers" furtively reading fragments at street stalls, much as we do today in check-out lines at Safeway.

Indeed, when and where I have read *War and Peace* has made all the difference. My first reading, in that Russian Lit class, remains both the most immediate and the most remote. Immediate because of my notes, scrawled in the margins, my hand-writing then, eerily similar to my handwriting now. Yet the sensibility prompting the notes seems so unfamiliar now, as does my studiousness, and the leisure I had, at eighteen, to explore and to analyze behaviour and speech.

I was enthralled by the romance, the spiritual ideals, the stable and mundane qualities of domestic life. Natasha, Petya, and Sonja had seemed so playful, the Countess larger-than-life. The social life in the 1820's fascinated me. The occupation of Moscow broke my heart. All those impressions of the first reading combine with impressions of freshman year of university, and of that extraordinary class.

Rereading the paper I wrote on *War and Peace* back in March of '74, was an exercise in humility. "The Comprehension of Reality as a Sense of Timing" it's called. And such hard thinking, such sensitivity to Tolstoy, such tangled, ambiguous language! I remember typing till dawn—that familiar sag of sleeplessness and despair; the sting of blood-shot eyes, forced to proof-read what I knew would only expose me as a fraud, unworthy of Tolstoy, of Patricia Carden, of the ivy covered granite walls enclosing me.

Now, comfortably grounded in my forties, safe from that haunting fear of exposure, I can appreciate the penetrating comments Pat Carden had penned in the margins of my paper. That wonderful professor managed both to probe at my tendencies for high-blown and obtuse diction, and to follow my thoughts with patient determination—no matter how challenging the path.

Yet, I can't deny that what I wrote then still interests me now. At the core maybe my sensibilities haven't changed all that much. I focused on two small sections of the text, on barely ten of the thirteen hundred and fifty-one pages. My topic: how people will refuse to face a reality (as does Pierre, with Karataev's death, and the old Prince with his son's letter of warning), because they simply can't face it at that moment.

Rereading those sections, I find that they still move me. In one, the Old Prince is distressed. He can't settle on the exact place to have his bed placed in the rooms they have moved into—until he has remembered, and then understood, Andrew's letter. "That couch was dreadful to him, probably because of the oppressive thoughts he had when lying there. It was unsatisfactory everywhere, but the corner behind the piano . . . was better than other places: he had never slept there yet." The sense of an impending reality gradually filtering through his peevish restlessness is heartbreaking.

~

All I know of war I know from reading. Reading *has* been, for me—as for many of us fortunate enough to live our lives removed from the direct impact of war—in the words of Proust, "the instigator whose magic keys open deep within us the door to those dwelling places into which we would have been unable to penetrate." I remember closing my slim volume of *All Quiet on the Western Front*, pressing it between my hands as though trying to absorb through my pores every particle of meaning, yet feeling oddly excluded by my gender and youth, distanced from sensations even as I understood them. I was in the tenth grade. Vietnam was a distant rumble.

~

I don't know what sort of change I expected to measure in myself, across the years, as gauged against the backdrop of Tolstoy's novel. At twenty-five, married, setting out along that long twisting road from romance to cohabitation, from passion to parenthood., I remember wondering whether, and how, all my reading of so many relationships affected my own.

Throughout my first reading of *War and Peace*, while still in

Carden's class, my heart had been with Natasha. Reading it the second time, I was surprised at how little the book actually focuses on Natasha. I remember how idyllic the hunt at the country uncle's estate seemed to me in that first reading as I shared Natasha's romantic flush; ten years later, the same scene felt shallow, even silly. Like the Countess at home, I awaited its finish.

Between being a child and having a child I lost my patience with Natasha and Sonja. Later in the story, they too become so *un*childlike, when they have their own children to care for. On the other hand, Petya and Andrew, who died childless, remained petulant, whimsical, tender—even as they approached death.

But at twenty-one, fresh out of university, Nicholas, Pierre, and Andrew engaged my attention. Absorbed by the grander scale, the historical and philosophical perspectives, I saw family and place as inescapable influences which essentially tangled up our lives and obscured deeper meanings. Freedom and consciousness: These were the questions to grapple with, in war and in peace. It fascinated me how Nicholas searched for glory; Andrew, for order and control; Boris, for social esteem; Pierre, for meaning and truth. What was I searching for?

⌖

In the sweet story "Flowers for Algernon"—my copy of which I can no longer find—the simple-minded Charlie loses the intelligence that was surgically bestowed upon him. He feels despondent and ashamed. Having learned to associate lack of intelligence with shame, he pulls out a small blue book and— with no memory of its content and no facility to decode its language—caresses it, remembering only the pleasure and delight it once brought to him.

Somewhere between my first and fourth reading of *War and*

*Peace*, I've lost track of many of the details I used to remember so easily. Unlike Charlie, I think I've retained the ability to interpret Tolstoy (though I have, without a doubt, lost the hard-won ability to interpret the language in which he wrote). Losing the facility to remember has been as perplexing to me as was Charlie's loss of intellect to him. He, at least, anticipated the loss. It's taken me ten years to stop feeling astonished by it.

Already I harbour lofty ideals for my golden years—images of leisurely reading and serene reflection. Yet how to reconcile this notion with the still peculiar loss of memory for what I read baffles me.

These days I record details and impressions in my reading journal—for no very clear purpose. But I can't help thinking how my doing so might not resemble the Old Prince Bolkonski thrashing through his papers, struggling to write his will—vaguely troubled, as he does so, by the nagging futility of trying to leave his past in order, while all around him, life as he's known it is crashing down.

᪣

On Memorial Day, 1991, I finished reading *War and Peace* for the fourth time. I remember how, in the same week, Nicole, then six, was searching for the meaning of war—wanting, like any inquisitive six-year-old, to know the why and when of it. "How often is war? . . . Why do people *do* war?"

I told her that war was like when she and her brother got angry and fought. I told her that while people might not want to fight, it happened, and always had. She said she'd wish, next time she saw a falling star, for no more fighting. She said that they'd been learning songs and poems in school to remember those who had died in wars.

My feeble answers creaked under the weight of her questions. And as I sensed the inadequacy of my answers, I wondered what she imagined about war and death and remembrance.

All that winter, throughout the months that the Gulf War raged on, I tried hard to keep the constant news coverage from my kids. One morning on the way to daycare, Andrew, three years old then, had chirped from his car seat, "I wonder how many died in the Gulf War today?"—as though he were asking what was for lunch, or how many days before his birthday. Those words, in that high little voice, shocked me.

❧

If I am to learn anything at all from what has happened between *War and Peace* and Tolstoy and me over the years, it would be this: Reading has *everything* to do with things external to the work. Proust once defined reading, "in its original essence" as "that fertile miracle of a communication effected in solitude." In our home, we read in a din, rather than a solitude, and, more often than not, through a haze of fatigue. The din and the fatigue both exert a claim, which more than competes—it commingles—with impressions of what I read. Whole stories and articles are wrapped up in my mind with the rocking and hissing of quart sealers in the canner, the hot fragrant steam of peaches, syrup and cinnamon, the August sunlight streaming through our kitchen window.

Impressions of my last reading of *War and Peace* formed a jumble, which got recorded in two pages of cryptic notes I recently found in a notebook. Some of those notes make no sense to me now, but what does emerge is a new-found awareness of the creative task of translation. My preoccupation with translators and their role probably reflects a growing fascination with language and with the act of writing.

The other thing that strikes me about those notes is how much broader my own demands upon the story were, at the later reading. While the details of the daily lives of the characters interested me less than before, I was captivated by how their narrative was interspersed with Tolstoy's philosophy of history and story-telling. I wanted summary statements, generalizations that would hold it all together for me. I made note, for example, of how Tolstoy's characters were constantly reinterpreting events and redefining themselves. And how history emerged as an egocentric rendering of the string of opportunities for choices which confront us.

Yet, I remember that at thirty-one I had felt a distinct impatience with Tolstoy's epilogues and preaching. The treatise that had seemed compelling when I was twenty-one, constrained and irritated me ten years later. I felt cornered by Tolstoy's rendering of history, by his meandering interpretations, by his subjective and selective remembering.

Then, another decade later, memory itself having become a trickier beast for me, I found myself more accepting of Tolstoy's perspective. I had become quite comfortable with his premise: that we lose more by deriding memory and history than we gain by accepting their limits and irrational subjectivity.

In the first epilogue, Tolstoy seems to reduce his main characters to mediocrity, but in doing so seems to elevate mediocrity to noble heights. The epilogues—one on the domestic life of the married couples and their children, the other a closing treatise—seem to characterize peace. Funny how at one time I loved those two parts, and in the next reading they rankled. But peace, after all, takes on a flaccid, mediocre tone. Particularly in contrast to war.

Peace provides the time and the perspective against which we can examine our lives and define ourselves. Domestic squabbles replace battle-ground skirmishes, as they do in Frank O'Connor's "My Oedipus Complex," when the father returns home to a wife and son who have shaped a home-life which no longer quite fits the man. Idiosyncrasies emerge and, in the suspension of grander action, become large as life. Reconciliation and redemption come only with the story-telling of war, during peace. This is the case with Tolstoy, as it was with Homer. Like Odysseus, one can imagine that for Pierre and Nicholas, as for the father in O'Connor's story, telling and retelling the tales of war—both real and imagined, both grand and minute—becomes critically important. To tease out the relationships between action and words—between the thing, the shadow, and the penumbra—that's homecoming, and homecoming is the challenge of peace.

❧

Thinking about Slatoff, and about the possibilities for human connection, I want to know what's happened between *War and Peace* and me over the twenty years from eighteen to thirty-seven. Surely the text hasn't changed—other than, perhaps, the paper cover having taken on a softer quality, the pages yellowed a bit, and feathered out to appear even thicker than they once did. But I have surely changed, mellowed and thickened, exchanged a keen edge for a certain blunt assurance.

Reading Tolstoy's novel, in my teens, I found romance and adventure; in my twenties, I loved the world of the men and boys, the world of action, larger than life, with its spiritual ideals and grand schemes. Then, somewhere between thirty-one and thirty-seven, what shone for me was the stability, the mundane daily routines, the ebb and flow of social life around and beneath which lurk the larger elements of war, political upheaval, and economic disaster.

❧

Walter Slatoff was small and fairly quiet-spoken, as I remember him, up on the podium of that lovely, semi-circular lecture theatre on the main floor of Goldwin Smith Hall. One peculiar scrap of memory I carry with me depicts Slatoff in a skirmish with Carl Sagan (already on his way to fame) at the first meeting of that American Lit Course. Apparently they both had classes scheduled for the same lecture hall. Slatoff may have been unassuming, but we stayed put.

Later that semester, standing behind the podium, Professor Slatoff told us a particularly funny story about his two young children, to illustrate for us something about the Oedipus complex. Now, twenty years later, I tell my students similar stories about my kids to illustrate similar human conditions. I like to think that sharing such stories reasserts the connections between the act of reading and the act of living, closing up, if just a bit, the "disturbing gap" between literature and life.

*Notes from a Journal*

Feb. '95

**Thoughts on War and Dreaming**

On our drive home from violin lessons yesterday, Nicole wanted to talk about the book she'd been reading, the diary of a young girl from Eastern Europe. Nicole likes these late afternoon drives to her lessons, when there are just the two of us. I think she saves up things to talk about.

She's been in the grip of this book, and war was on her mind. She told me that the journalist who published the diaries reported, in the introduction, that when the shelling started, the girl didn't even flinch. Nicole asked lots of questions about government, which I tried to answer.

Then we left war and government behind to talk about dreams. I made the move, by telling her how tired I felt from waking myself up, the night before, out of a deep sleep, screaming in a nightmare (or *out of* a nightmare, I suppose— I'd really been screaming). I tried to make it sound amusing, to deflect the eeriness that lingered from that dream.

She told me that she remembered realizing, sometime in grade two, that dreams were not really places you went to: Dreams happened in your mind. Since then, she told me, she felt more powerful, as though she had some control over the dreams. She enjoyed them more. Since that time, she said, if

206

her feet were bolted down with weights, she could simply decide to *fly* away.

This leads me to think about Alice Munro's story "Boys and Girls," in which the girl's dreams became less empowering and more passive as the girl became a young woman. I wonder how Nicole's dreaming will differ from that girl's, and from mine.

I wonder, too, if my own scream *was* a kind of taking control, willing myself away from what ever was stalking me through that nightmare. I don't know. All I know is how strange the scream sounded in my ears, how it alarmed Mont, how weird it felt in my throat. And how very tired I've been, for this whole day after it.

&

# The Chaos Theory

I am eternally behind in my current events reading. One fine thing about the reading of literature is that I don't fall behind in quite such a troubling way. People don't shoot you sidelong glances when you are reading a novel from 1962, nor do you feel compelled to hide the cover page of a Thomas Browne essay from 1658. It's quite a different story when you are seen, as I often am, reading a *MacLean's* from nine months back.

I contend that what is important enough will retain its importance, albeit as history. And so I carry on, a delinquent of current affairs. One night I was reading just such a magazine, dated a year ago November, when a science article caught my attention. Its title, "The Roots of Chaos," beckoned to me. How deep would the roots of chaos extend?

After pondering the latest in science's conception of chaos, I have found myself unable to differentiate between the degree of the paucity and audacity characterizing this theory, and the degree to which I've grown cynical about modern scientific thinking.

It seems that scientists have only recently attended to the complex and unpredictable state of the world. The article claims that "a growing number of scientists have become fascinated by unpredictable events." Their name for the phenomenon is *chaos* which they consider to be "probably intrinsic to most systems in the universe." Most scientists, apparently, are neither parents nor bartenders nor pig farmers. Those people would have known for generations that chaos prevails, and that most of life is complex and unpredictable.

Spend a full moon night in a back street Montana bar, and you will surely know chaos. In that orderly intersection of time and space, the lunar forces between earth and sky move people in the strangest ways. Add a few indiscriminate shots of whisky, and there will transpire bizarre and unpredictable quirks of behaviour. I've seen it time and time again. And yes, it's fascinating. Occasionally downright frightening.

Scientists are forging links with other disciplines as a result of this theory of theirs. The rest of us have known both weather forecasting and economic predictions to be largely unreliable, if absorbing. Our knowing that chaos is "the norm and not the exception" in these, as in other matters, should have long ago bound us all in a fraternity: If only that knowledge weren't so damned isolating. That's part of my problem with the notion that chaos is a revelation, and one which lends coherence to the scientific community, at that.

The physiology professor Outerbridge claims that scientists are now "forced to re-examine all of the things we thought were random or dismissed as unimportant." His admission exposes a serious failing of scientists: that they hadn't been doing so all along; that they had to be forced. How dare these people assume that "if they knew about all of the major factors involved in an event" they could then forecast that event, ultimately predicting "everything in the universe"! Not only do scientists distinguish between human beings and other kinds of beingness in the universe; they commit an appalling act of hubris by dismissing that other distinction—between beings and supreme beings, between mortals and gods.

I wonder, once I subdue my fury, whether scientists would consider as "random or unimportant" the vagaries of farming, for instance. Would they attempt to forecast, as a part of "everything in the universe," the annual livestock production from my family's small pig farm? Would they, then, predict the frosty morning in March when a weaner pig would cough like a smoker, then die? Or the week in September when healthy growers would, one after another, become lame of one limb, then paralysed, then dead? Or the mid-summer day when the kilometre-long water system would break at the pig-pens, lowest spot in our acres of vertical terrain, shooting forth glorious fountains of water amid which swine would churn and swim, one encircled by the Ace bandage applied to contain intestines which had, for unknown reasons, protruded from its belly the day before?

The remainder of the article expounds upon a few related curios. The "Butterfly Effect" explains for whomever may not have observed the phenomenon, that even "tiny" events cascade through time and space. Feigenbaum numbers calculate the points at which chaos interrupts equilibrium. And finally, fractals: the graphic representations of chaos which are, not surprisingly, magically irregular. Mandelbrot, a mathematician who gave us the term, tells us that fractals "bring chaos closer to the common person." I am of the opinion that, as a common person, I am quite close enough to chaos, thank you very much.

Perhaps the closest I've come to willingly facing chaos was at my daughter's ballet recital, in the spring of her fourth year. I can think of no better instance of the subtle unfolding of unpredictability. So much depended upon the synchronized compliance of overwrought mothers, many of whom had spent hours the night before, bent over miles and miles of stiff netted fabric, needle threaded with dental floss, intent upon poorly mimeographed pages of instruction. And on the attentiveness and careful cuing of a dance teacher so tense she might, at any moment, have shattered. And on the teenage boy responsible for the older and less reliable tape-player providing the dance music. And, of course, on the will and wit and wiles of those bedecked little girls. Even the variety of their shapes—from pudgy to gangly to sturdy—mirrored the variability of factors involved. To witness such an event is to look chaos full in the face.

But, of these phenomena of the chaos theory, fractals are my favourite. Although I hadn't known them by name, I have recognized these whimsical designs. Years back, when we were living in our basement, a pressure cooker full of deep purple Italian prune plums exploded. My attention must have been distracted by weariness from having worked all morning for the market gardener who gave me the crate of plums, or by my increasing state of pregnancy. And who knows what other tiny events may have butterflied into this wondrous explosion. In any case, for months after, we discovered plum coloured fractals engraved on cookbook covers, stencilled on bowls, interlaced around the workings of the small propane stove and cream coloured fridge.

Yes, I agree with the scientists that "turbulence has always been an acknowledged part of the natural order." It just doesn't seem astounding to me. Nor am I in the least surprised, or alarmed by, the idea that such "remote events" as "the death of a star in a remote galaxy" could lead to "enormous" changes elsewhere in the universe. It would surprise me more to learn that they didn't. And too easy an adjudication of relative degrees of enormity makes me suspicious.

This "basically new" theory of the universe claims to be "making a place for unpredictability" in the natural order of things. The intent is, no doubt, to liberate and advance our thinking. But the terms and the formulas it leaves us with seem so cold and impotent. What use can they be, for the bartender facing a tavern full of drunks, for the pig farmer mired in endless commonplace catastrophes, or for the mother wading into her first ballet recital?

The theory has none of the wiles and charms, nor the sheer

tangibility of, for example, Zeus, or that shrewd and capricious Coyote. And yet, for other peoples of other times, these beings have stood between mortal existence and chaos. That fellow humans, armed with calculators, can derive formulas to predict chaos—perhaps even to domesticate it—seems insubstantial and insipid by comparison. The power of their logic may be admirable, but that logic only addresses our ability to conceive of chaos. We are left on our own to cope with it.

# The Rhythms That Bind Us

They say that humans operate on a natural rhythm of twenty-five hours, and so are constantly functioning at a level of discomfort and disorientation within the twenty-four hour day of our prescription. Those of us who work the traditional Monday-to-Friday work week will, for example, sleep an hour later on Saturday morning and stay up an hour later Saturday night, often sleeping even later, then, on Sunday. On Monday morning, the alarm clock will jolt us awake a full three hours before we would awaken, if left alone. And so we struggle from the groggy stupor of Monday through to the eager anticipation of Friday, week after week, isolating ourselves from one another by repressing, even as we share, the same discomfort and guilty reaction to it.

Surrounded in time and space by evidence that existence is cyclical and repetitious—rhythmical—we westerners persist in our view that time is linear and progressive. I remember listening to a series of radio interviews with generation X-ers, during which they bemoaned the fact that they wouldn't attain the standard of living they had expected for themselves. I grew increasingly irritated with their whining, and more convinced of the truth of my own suspicion that they were living with the facile expectation that they could, and *should*, surpass their parents' standard of living: It was their God-given right to do so, and this deficiency was a grievous one. One young man explained that, despite being the best educated generation, many of his peers faced poor prospects for employment.

The *best educated* generation? How *could* such bunkum issue from any but astoundingly short sighted and foolish minds! What of the young Athenians who wandered in the shadow of Socrates? What of the African tribal youth, whose survival depended upon an intimate knowledge of the surrounding landscape, and the ability to read its signs and tracks? What of the many who have come before us, whose ways and wisdom have been lost to us?

But, when I take a step back from my flash of outrage, I suspect that these kids know all too well that their parents live better than their grandparents ever dreamed possible, and that their grandparents—often immigrants beginning a new life— surpassed the dreams of their own parents. These kids combine that knowledge with a hard-and-fast faith in the progress wrought by technology. Blind-sided by an educational system that reflects a culture all too enamoured of the dazzling present, they see only that one sharp, straight incline, grandfather to grandson. And they see themselves as the failing generation, sliding downward. It's as though, as a society, we resist a more humbling vision of the broader sweeps of time. In doing so, we deny ourselves the possibility of synchronization and the seductive comfort of being in harmony, of falling into place. Instead, we hold to metering out our lives in twenty-four hour days. We push onward, almost always slightly overtired, working to "keep up" and to "better ourselves," anticipating the rest that will "catch us up," the vacation that will ease our tensions.

We are governed by physiological and environmental rhythms: the physiological rhythms varying mostly over the day; the external rhythms of temperature and activity varying seasonally. Our biological rhythms themselves form intricate patterns played out over cyles of time ranging from milliseconds to seasons. Studies have confirmed what we already can guess from our own weekly work habits—that when left to "free run" we'll go to sleep one hour later each night, eventually adjusting ourselves to a twenty-five hour cycle. Freed from any awareness of clock time, most of us prefer to sleep an average of eight and a half hours daily. But, governed by the constraints of schedule as we usually are, we exist in tenuous synchronization of our watches and our biological clocks.

And who'd have expected both mathematical logic and biology to provide explanations for how time seems to pass faster in middle age than in childhood? Psychologists maintain that as the individual ages the mind correlates the perception of a year with a decreasing percentage of lapsed years. Children, thus, have fewer moments against which to measure a moment. Biochemists attribute the same phenomenon to the steady drop in circulation and oxygen in the brain which begins during childhood, and continues as we age: With less brain oxygen and slowed cellular metabolism, we seem to be passing through time more rapidly. A combination of those theories leaves us passing more rapidly through time, which we perceive as moving progressively faster—a dizzying prospect!

⟡

For years I've observed how our children, before they'd conformed to clock and calendar, determined their own peculiar means of grasping the cycles that govern the ebb and flow of our lives. I remember Nicole, one morning in her third year, opposite me at our counter, aproned, helping me stir and sift bran muffin batter. Out of nowhere, her question dropped: "The last time we made bran muffins Andrew was just big in your belly. How *did* he get out, anyway?" Her brother had been born four months before. Apparently, the making of bran muffins marked off some cycle of time and experience, prompting her inquiry.

215

Andrew, when three, struggled to come to terms with time. Waking from naps in mid-winter, he'd be irritated at the signs of nightfall, more so to be reminded that no, this was *not* the time for Cheerios. Past time was classified as "last night," distant past distinguished as "last night and last night." All sleeps were naps; the future, therefore, being "after nap." He showed little tolerance for larger increments of time, and had no patience for tedious attempts to clarify matters.

Yet, like his sister, every now and then he'd startle me by his sure grasp of cycles imperceptible to me. There was this morning in November—one of those surprising mornings in a particularly mild fall, when the taste of winter cools your first breath of outside air. Andrew demanded to know "Who are those guys again?" Twenty questions later, I had discovered that "those guys" were two friends of Andrew's dad's who'd come by the winter before, more than a full year back, for a couple of days of skiing. With just two winters in his memory, apparently that first taste of winter air had stirred a recollection I hadn't even suspected Andrew to have registered.

The children seemed to grasp seasonal rhythms first and most firmly, the rhythms of the work-weeks soon after. But then, those seasonal patterns so clearly and predictably govern the management of the family farm: gathering firewood in fall-time; mulching and watering berry patches and manuring and turning garden beds just before snowfall; and the spring's pruning of our motley collection of fruit trees and poking of spinach seeds through the last stubborn snow. Then there's the breeding of the ewes and sows, the shearing, and birthing and slaughtering—endless cycles in the raising of our livestock. Chickens and cats follow much the same rhythms, of their own accord. Those seasonal rhythms are punctuated for us all, but most significantly for the children, by holidays that have themselves evolved out of celebration of those ageless seasonal cycles.

Daily and hourly rhythms seem much less clearly perceptible to children, and even to adults—who, I'm convinced, all too easily violate those rhythms, suffering the consequences without awareness. I was surprised when my daughter, barely two, was offended by my going in to work one weekend. Caught by a deadline, I'd assumed that an extra four hours of work on a Saturday morning would pass by unnoticed.

When I was a few years younger and an inexperienced new mom, I remember learning how to nurse that daughter. Anxious to do things right, I tried to follow both the onslaught of advice, and the firm direction of my tiny, brown-haired girl, as well as the urging of my hormone-driven body. But the contradictions among those sources abounded. So I followed my intuition, dismissing the regimen prescribed by the nurses and by countless manuals. Imposing a neatly regular, time-driven schedule on the creature whose little head bobbed up and down my shirt seemed smug and callous, and utterly perverse. Far more sensible, I thought, to be guided by her thirst, and her keen nose for her mother's scent. Despite my disregard for "regularity," all three of our children thrived. The rhythms thrummed out by their individual needs proved to be neither capricious nor tyrannical.

Listening to a Saturday afternoon "Quirks and Quarks" show some time back, I learned about the latest understanding of Sudden Infant Death Syndrome, that cruel and silent killer of sleeping infants. It seems possible that SIDS may be caused by the infant falling into deep sleep before the body has adapted biologically to the phenomenon of deep sleep.

One researcher explained how, in the more natural sleeping arrangement where mother and infant remain in close proximity, the baby awakes to the mother's shifting breathing patterns, and vice versa. That intricate and intimate dance of rest and restlessness seems such a natural extension of the long nights that mothers experience in the latter months of pregnancy. Thus, the baby gradually "learns" sleep, while the biological systems become synchronized.

I didn't know about this when my babies were small, but I did know that separation from them caused me to panic. So I wouldn't have the infant sleep in a separate area, feeling somewhat foolish and emotional about that, until—at thirty-eight and with my third child's cradle so close to my bedside that I took care not to fall into it on getting up—I was simply too old and too tired to feel foolish any more. Many a morning over the infant years we'd awaken in a warm tangle of bodies, blankets, and pillows, having snatched a couple of hours of sleep since the dawn nursing—all three of us in our double bed. Thinking back on those mornings, on the loveliness of the contact with our infants, I'm left wondering how we ever could allow our reason to override such complex and compelling feelings that pull at us like some magnetic force, old as time.

At the other end of what feels like a hard-won sensibility, stands the rebellious rejection of predictability and convention which, when I think back, characterized my university years. At eighteen, the distortion of rhythms—biological and social—fascinated me. Studying for two days at a time with no sleep and little food, I teetered at the edge of lucidity, exhilarated by the strangeness of it all, by surges of caffeine, and by peers whose behaviour made mine seem normal.

I remember being terribly impressed by a dormitory acquaintance who organized her life by sleeping for ninety minutes every six hours, convinced of the super-efficiency of such a schedule. I can still see her, covered in a haze of cigarette smoke, pale and edgy, hunched over her desk, her alarm clock signalling the time to return to her cot. As for me, I see now that what began as the enticing urge to satisfy ever-increasing demands I placed upon myself, lead to a ludicrous disregard for the constraints of time and capability.

But then, no doubt larger rhythms propel our lives: Maybe that flagrant rebellion against pattern and predictability which characterizes the twenties falls into a natural place of its own, in one of the broader schemes of life. If so, I'm eager for the forties—for the years of coming to terms and settling in, which will fit so much more comfortably with my present inclinations. But then I suppose I will also have to watch as our children move through the wilder decades.

～❀～

In a book called *Body Time*, Gay Gaer Luce claims that in our century we have "set the time out of joint." As a result, the pace we live at is "dissonant with our inner needs." Since we no longer live in harmony with the natural cycles of life, we are, in a real sense, more primitive than our primitive ancestors. The "exponential surge of technology" has us travelling at the speed of sound, bombarded by media, and by constant change.

Our social life is dissonant with our metabolic processes, the internal organization of our cells and organs. While cycles and fluctuation and evolution pervade, our expectations remain static: Our self-images remain fixed, and so we expect consistency in our performance, health, feelings, and behaviour. Resisting evidence of a rhythmic nature and cyclic change, we confuse our own manifestations of that pervasive state of flux with abnormality!

Heartbeat and respiration keep us going. And yet, despite so much evidence to convince us, and so many patterns to observe, we remain perversely unaware that time organizes us. We've expanded our sensory range, and our range of consciousness, yet persist in holding a vastly underdeveloped sense of our timing—our immersion in the rhythmic flux.

～❀～

Over the past couple of months my own family has been moving. We haven't moved from our home, but rather have moved around and through our home, taking occupancy of two additions: shifting, in domino fashion, from one bedroom to another, one bureau to another, one bookshelf to another. It's been, like so many mundane experiences of home life, much deeper and more challenging than we'd anticipated.

The first task we undertook, in the month between the repainting of bedroom walls and the actual move, was to reorganize the bedroom bookcases for the kids. Nicole was to move to the room my husband and I had shared since she was six months old. Our books and bric-a-brac, framed photos and dusty boxes of jewellery, all got packed in boxes. My daughter's books and figurines slowly made their way up to their more dignified spaces, from the chair where they'd been piled for years.

For months, Nicole had been worrying about this move, apprehensive about leaving behind her secluded room in our basement. Upstairs she'd be only a wall apart from two boisterous younger brothers. In time, the new bedside table and the extra twin bed for overnight guests would win her over. But at that point, the move was only an abstract notion. So we were both surprised when filling the bookcase began to seem like an act of love. Nicole spent hours lining up and organizing her books, soon transferring piles into her brothers' room, then lining up and organizing those too. She worked the better part of a day, and when she was finished, the west wall of our bedroom belonged to her.

Later that night, standing in the bedroom which was still ours—but becoming hers—I admired her work. I'm not even sure I was conscious of the slight changes I made to her decor as I stood there. I do remember being pleased with the effect when I tipped the Japanese folded paper hat at a jaunty angle over the round wooden head of the doll a neighbour had given her.

Some time later, I noticed with irritation that my arrangement had been carefully disassembled: The origami hat had been pushed neatly against the wall, the doll carefully lined up beside it. Each thing had its place, forming one meticulous line across the top shelf. Not exactly proud of my reaction, I felt slighted. But that didn't stop me from quickly attempting a few small improvements.

In the end, if we ever do reach the end, I feel sure that my daughter's evolving taste will prevail. Her possessions remain lined up and neatly folded, in the manner she, at age nine, prefers. It's funny though: If ever asked to define my own style, I'd describe myself as conservative, with a marked preference for symmetry and crisp corners. So who, then, is the woman in me who pushes her daughter toward the relaxed and jaunty? Could it be *my* mother? I still can't forget the hems she re-hemmed as I learned to sew; the ornaments she rehung as we decorated the Christmas tree; the pillows she *still* redistributes as I decorate our home. Do we keep repeating the same dances even as we change partners? Can we be one way, while becoming another?

❧

Notes penned in my journal remind me how, two years ago and months after the birth of our third child, I was at battle with myself, struggling against acceptance of my aging body in its maddeningly slow recovery from childbirth. I had written in my journal, in the midst of a workout on my stepping machine, how slow and fat I felt, and how my mind seemed to hold my tired, flaccid body at some distance, resisting familiarity with its changed form. Then, lying on my back after a dozen sit-ups, I'd fallen into a study of our living-room ceiling. It's a lovely high, cathedral ceiling, of pine decking along fir beams and rafters. Following its aged golden boards, my eyes swept down the pattern of knots to the walls which, framed by eight-by-eight fir posts and beams, form elegant lines. Though the beams and posts had twisted and cracked over the years they still asserted themselves against the rigid lines of drywall, wrought iron, and glass.

I remembered how my husband and his friend had spent hours carving the joints that hold those posts and beams together. The joints were works of art, each different from the next, each connecting three, four, or even five of those members which provide the structural support of our home. We were all amazed then, at how that wood absorbed time—soaking in hours of the days, just as it later absorbed litre after litre of oil. The home stands aging but solid, changing year by year; colours deepen, lines shift imperceptibly, marks and gouges multiply, testifying to years of family life. Time moves so differently for such a structure.

Now, for me, time dictates and straight lines prevail. No patience in me for slow processes of change, for sagging body or weary, slowed mind. Yet, reading my journal, I can fall back to the memory of that infant time:

At my side plays a tiny baby, sitting so precariously on his quilted blanket. Some noise that escaped me startles him, and I watch his back arch, causing the toy he had gripped to fling forward, just out of reach. Adult time drops away as I rouse myself, and infant time engages me.

For minutes, or perhaps hours, Jamie explores a blue and red Duplo block with his toes, while I explore him—marvelling at how his entire body responds to the colour, or texture, or whatever he reads in that hard piece of moulded plastic. An extraordinary moment, outside of time, magical.

Babies—like passion, like wood—are great absorbers of time.

They have some power to shake us from our rigid, driven ways—if we will be shaken.

But we are stubborn as well as strange creatures, and we hold to our ways. Blinded to the ecological and cosmic view, which might ultimately be the more human view, we live out of touch with "the tempo of the natural world" and the rhythms of ourselves. We persist in forcing our lives to conform to patterns not consistent with the rhythms pulsing within or around us: "the rhythms that bind us" in Luce's words. Yet those rhythms will ultimately draw us in, binding us to a cosmos we don't even fathom.

# The Stuff of Life

It has happened again: My mother, an eternal pessimist, has managed to bring about what was very nearly a natural disaster. And disaster is just the right word for it—*dis*-aster: a failure of the stars, and so, related to ancient and compelling forces of faith. Despite my best efforts to consider rationally such phenomena as weather, superstition—all tangled up with stubborn traces of Catholicism—continues to haunt me.

For months my mother and I had been making plans by telephone. And each time my excitement would burst into evidence, she'd puncture it with dire predictions. I'd say, "We can hardly wait to see you," or, "You'll get to see Nicole's school concert with us!" trying to end our conversation on a high note.

"Well, I'm not going *anywhere* if it's storming," she'd quickly retort.

The down-side wins again, I'd think to myself, but she'll see, once she *does* get here, that things will work out fine.

On the morning she should have departed from the Portland Airport, we heard on one news account: "The worst storm in fifty years to hit the northeast." She was flying out to meet her newest grandson and to spend Christmas with us, and her birthday, which falls on Christmas Eve. My children were thrilled, and so was I, despite the heap of other feelings riding the crest of that thrill.

Since October, parcel upon parcel had arrived at our already cramped rural post office. Her frenzy of Christmas buying may just be her way of releasing anxiety wrought by the season. Or maybe it's natural for a child of the Depression, born eighth in an immigrant family, who grew up with so very few possessions.

⌘

My own uneasiness about *stuff* must, indeed, be wrapped up in layers of superstition, floated down to me from earlier generations. My nagging concern no doubt gained in intensity from the pervading environmental sensibilities of the 1990's. It's now a year since my mother's Christmas visit, which did come to pass despite airline delays caused by flukes of turbulent weather, or fate. This Christmas-time, again, I find myself wondering if we derive too much from our material possessions and clutter; too little from our spirits and our relationships with one another. I worry about my own fondness for every little plastic trinket that, for as many as thirty-five years, has served to reflect Christmas for me. Throughout December, conscious of my doing so, I carefully unwrap these various glittery wreathes and brass angels, aiming to create the sense of Christmas which our children will carry forth into their lives.

⌘

Given our attachment to stuff, I wonder, perhaps more than a normal person should, how we would survive a house fire. What would we do if suddenly we found ourselves with nothing but the clothes on our backs? What would we mourn? What would we struggle to replace? Would a certain freedom from constraint balance the sense of loss—the grief displaced by a lightness of being?

225

I think that what I would miss most is what we have created. I fear for my word-processor, and for the words it stores for me in our uneasy partnership. I would weep for the drawings my kids have done over the years, and for the cards they've made, and for the baby book we've all made for James. The baby pictures of our kids, of us and even of our parents—well, I don't know quite how I'd feel about losing them. What they really represent for me is carried forward in the individuals. I love having those photographed images cluttering the bookshelves, always in view. Yet I can love this family without them too, and I'd remember the phases of that love from the stories we tell.

The house we live in has been my husband's creation. It, too, is irreplaceable. He's probably a better designer now, certainly a more competent builder. So he could, indeed, build a new home, and it would be superior in many ways, stark and clean, freed of our possessions, and with a broom closet actually as tall as a broom, and cupboards and closets roomy enough for the clutter a family produces. Yet, for all that, such a house wouldn't be right for years. We *do* seem to take the shape of our homes and our stuff, or maybe our homes and our stuff evolve in trails and piles according to some scheme of personal or family identity.

❧

Last fall I made a quick stop at the Safeway on the way to picking up my kids for swimming lessons. I'd forgotten their snack. Looking for something tasty and even a bit entertaining to hold them for the forty minute drive home, I searched for fruit snacks. Should I look by the candy, or chips, or cereal, I wondered, aware that each passing minute of my search would proportionally reduce the time left to change from school clothes to swim-suits.

A store manager, apparently responding to my harried look, stopped to help. He sent me to a shelf above the frozen vegetable section, beside beer making equipment. To my parting comment on the illogic of the organization, he replied, with a harried look, that the profusion of new products and varieties pretty much defied systems of organization.

That left me thinking. The nineties often get characterized by the information explosion. That may well be, but perhaps every bit as extraordinary and even more insidious is our explosion of *stuff*. I don't remember fruit snacks from my youth, yet today we can choose from at least five brands. We can have bear snacks, shark snacks, dinosaur snacks, rolled snacks, or puzzle shaped snacks, cherry, orange, cola or tutti-fruity snacks, natural fruit- or simulated fruit-flavoured snacks, number or letter snacks, spaceship or Ninja snacks.

It's hard to imagine what might *not* be found in a grocery store. Looking for canning jars the other day I went past raincoats, socks, goldfish paraphernalia, hubcaps, and potholders. When will we begin to protest such an oppressive and incessant deluge? When will we notice that, in the name of convenience, our grocery stores span city blocks?

It's ironic that those of us who clamour for simple foods only add to the problem. Chemical-free vegetables now crowd the four kinds of mushrooms and six varieties of fresh won ton wrappers. Corn flakes, rather than dropping out of circulation, hold their place in three brand-name varieties, not to mention two generic brands. Beside them are Astro-flakes, Cocoa Pebbles, and Pro Stars. Up the aisle live the plain, unadulterated oats—quick, instant, rolled, slow-cooking, porridge, wild, and even apple-cinnamon flavoured.

When will we refuse to be attracted by the glamour, and actually see the clutter of our own surrounding culture? The pressure for eco-sensitivity has further complicated matters. The eco-sensitive products, boldly labelled in their recycled containers, compete for space with eco-callous goods, labelled "new and improved." Do we substitute more choice for better sense? Does this profusion of stuff result from a simple pride in our technological capacity to produce it? Or is it, rather, an inability to conceive of restriction of choice as a possible choice?

❧

This Christmas, our older children left Santa letters with the butter tarts and carrots and apple and rootbeer. Nicole, now eight, retains a staunch belief in all the magic of this season. She used her logic to wed fantasy to faith in the mysteries of life. Her letter read:

> Dear Santa Claus,
> I hope you have a fun Christmas. If when you come to our house you're too full to eat anything, take the stuff we leave out home. My hamster Dasher died [Santa's gift three long years ago]. I was very sad, But he was old. If you ever see Jesus, wish him a happy Birthday for me. I don't really care what I get, because I don't know what I want, give me anything. I'm having fun skiing. I made you a picture.
>
> Love Nicole.
>
> P.S. Please give all the poor people nice presents. MERRY CHRISTMAS.

Her brother is three years younger and more sure and easy in his belief. His letter, with a sticker in its upper right-hand corner to match the sticker his sister had used, went right to the point:

To SANTA—I want a new skiing snow ball.

From Andrew.

His manner was casual, and his request was straight-forward: The new skiing snow ball he required would be replacing one sent by his Nanee a couple of years earlier, another of so many decorative trinkets she had insisted that the children have.

"They're just little things, worthless really, that make them happy," she retorted to what I had intended as mildly discouraging comments, my futile effort to stem the tide of material excess that seemed to engulf us.

And there was my son, one of the children my mother felt was in need of happiness, asking Santa for another skiing snowball—a dimpled plastic ball decked out in red skis and a striped toque—to replace the one that had lost its ski when dropped to the floor by the self-same child, two years back.

The possibilities latent in that very circle of needs and wishes seem greater than my own ability to comprehend them. I'm struck, not for the first time, by the wisdom of my mother's irritating ways, and by the strength of what tugs between the Nanee and the grandchild. She knows him in ways I simply do not—knows how to delight him with the very stuff which threatens to overwhelm me. He responds with delight to those things which she sends him in the nooks and crannies of her parcels. And Santa, of course, will work the magic to repair the object that provides the glue in their relationship.

This season, once again, the family spent most of a surprisingly satisfying day pulling down the decorations, wrapping God-knows-how-old tarnished and pleasingly fragile tree bulbs in God-knows-how-old scraps of tissue and paper towels. We packed box after box, making a game out of ferreting out the one last ceramic choirboy resting amongst magazine and plant, packing and labelling and finally handing boxes up to Mont, who stacked them in the storage area above the back entranceway. The ladder was carried back through the house. All of the activity—the procession of people and boxes, followed by a ladder—fascinated our baby. One child pinched up tinsel from the wool of the carpet, while the other proudly discovered one last felt Rudolph hung on my rowing machine. We chased away the impending post-Christmas gloom with loud rock-and-roll and hot chocolate with marshmallows.

My feelings?

Tremendous relief, but also a sense of accomplishment. Once again, we had emerged intact and somehow enriched by this time of beauty and magic, with its undertow of excess and sham.

# Sweet Wine, White Barley, Sheep's Blood

Anyone can stop a man's life, but no one can stop his death; *a thousand doors open on to it.*

—Seneca

The first time I gave birth, I burst the blood vessels in both my eyes. That's how hard I pushed to expel that small creature out of me and into being. The energy and joy of the birth kept me aloft and oblivious to my own appearance and even to the little cone our daughter's head had formed. But I know now that I was quite a sight in the days of rest and recovery, shuffling up and down the waxed linoleum of hospital hall-ways, eyes red where they should have been white, with black half-moons etched beneath them. Gradually, my eyes turned from red to purplish-yellow, their itchiness matched by their ugliness.

When my close friend went to her family to be there for the death of her father, several years ago, and postponed her return time and time again, I remember feeling that she'd lost her will to come back home. It was a relief to drive down to meet her in Washington to bring her back to BC.

When I met her there, I knew she'd been altered by the experience. She seemed so distracted, remote. We went for a run and got lost. Her usually keen sense of orientation had simply left her. After we found our way back to her brother's house, she talked about her dad's death, sharing what seemed like a splendid, sacred experience. I hadn't expected the death of a parent to be like that. I was astonished when she told me how, when her dad was dying, she'd thought about how I had burst all those blood vessels in my eyes, giving birth. There was a similarity, she said, in the extraordinary intensity of those events: the birth of a daughter and the death of a father.

෴

From Greek and Roman myth we carry stories about how powerfully the loss of a daughter affects a mother. Considered by some to be about the genesis of winter, these stories remain, for me, legends of grief. Centuries after the story was first told, we understand Demeter's agony as she ranged the lands in search of her beloved Persephone.

Persephone, lovely and vivacious, disappeared while gathering lilies in her apron: She was the picture of innocence and youth. Unable to resist her charms, the lecherous Hades had chased her across the land and down into a ravine. She disappeared from the face of the earth.

So strong, so profoundly unsettling, was the grief of Demeter, that Zeus risked the ire of Hades by promising the return of the goddess's daughter. There was one simple condition: The girl must have eaten nothing at all, while in the underworld. But Persephone had swallowed seven blood-red pomegranate seeds, and so had violated that condition.

Streams of tears flowed down Demeter's cheeks. She withheld the sunshine—by her power and in her agony and anger—until Zeus relented, partially. Thenceforth, Persephone would live out her years between the love of her mother in the light of the land, and the love of Hades in the darkness of the underworld. Demeter's grief, and our winter, thus give way, annually, to spring and summer. And so the lilies bloom, the pomegranates ripen, and the tears fall to earth again.

෴

The summer our daughter was seven Mont and I took her and

her brothers back east to visit our families. We left behind her first 4-H lamb, Basil, to board at our neighbour's farm. Nicole had had misgivings, fretting that Basil wouldn't like being at our neighbour's, and might not eat well there. Basil died, within two days of our departure, of one of the many afflictions to which farmers lose lambs. That was the news to which we returned home. I held Nicole for what seemed like hours. I remember the way her body felt in my arms, all damp and hot, her shoulder blades jutting against me. It was her first such loss, and she sobbed with abandon. The experience drained her of any interest in 4-H, and two years passed before she allowed herself to befriend a lamb again.

During the fall of that same year, her brother Andrew shared with me a remarkable insight. He was four when he told me, with an assurance that surprised and impressed me, that yes, death happened to all people. Then he added the qualifier, "To all except *our* family, that is."

Now seven, his way of thinking about things hasn't changed so very much.

More recently, all three children were watching a nature show I'd recorded, about a family of elephants and the woman who had studied them for years. Included was the inevitable mating scene, and with bull elephants involved, it was conspicuous. I listened for the kids' reaction. When the youngest asked what were they *doing*, his sister explained that it was just like what the ewes did with the ram.

"Chickens do it too," contributed his brother, adding, a few seconds later, "Wouldn't it be funny if people did it too?"

The three of them dissolved into laughter, taking down all my notions of how wise in the ways of life farm kids would grow up to be.

❦

Last spring I attended the funeral of a colleague's son. It was a sudden death, a car accident that had killed both the boy and his girl friend.

It was only the second funeral I'd ever attended. The other had been a small gathering of friends, clustered respectfully at a doorway of a small dark church in upstate New York.

This time, there were no respectful and safe distances. And the church was bright and airy; light streamed in through stained glass. From where I sat, I could hear the father sob and see his shoulders shake. For a few minutes as the ceremony began, I couldn't catch my breath. Stupidly, I had not equated the service we were attending with the actual funeral, and the casket, not five feet away, shocked me.

The service was so moving that there were a few times when I wasn't certain I could stay. Emotions—agony, disbelief, anger, love, raw pain—defied containment. Odd and random impressions remain seared in memory. I felt surprised at how fresh and young the parents looked, as though grief had stripped away the slackness and the wear-and-tear of ordinary life. I remember what was said by classmates, uncles, friends, and neighbours who stood to speak. Their words and tears and music swirl in my memory of the event.

Toward the end of that long afternoon, after the refreshments were put away and as the last knots of friends and relatives were disbanding, one of the young men turned on some music. Spontaneously, magically, people began dancing. They held hands, enclosing the grieving family in a wide circle. My friend and I stood awkwardly in the background until we too were pulled into the dance. In the centre the family held one another and swayed beneath a circular sky-light. It was the strangest sensation, that weaving of ecstasy and grief. A spirituality, an otherness, radiated.

❧

Sibyl told Aeneas in *The Aeneid*, "the way to Avernus is easy; Night and day lie open the gates of death's dark kingdom: But to retrace your steps, to find the way back to daylight—that is the task, the hard thing." Aeneas made his way to the lands of the dead through a precisely prescribed series of offerings. Homer's Odysseus, similarly, ensured a safe and certain return to the lands of the living by appeasing Persephone the Dread. Among the libations: mingled honey and milk, sweet wine, water and white barley, and sheep's blood.

◦

The day after the funeral, I was driving past the place where flowers strewn along the road-side marked the site of the crash. A few kids I'd seen at the funeral had congregated there. I felt the strongest urge to stop. But I resisted, not wanting to invade their privacy, and continued on my way. That urge—to stop by the roadside and re-enter a community of grief—reminded me of when my friend seemed to lose her will to resume her own life after her father had died.

The other funeral I had attended, as a twenty-year old, was for a friend with whom I waited tables in a river-side restaurant in upstate New York.

"Douglas Scott Wallace," said a radio announcer, "died suddenly last night, when the car he was driving was struck."

I never made the connection between that bulletin and our Scottie until I got to work. Then, I was swamped by confusion and helplessness.

When my only surviving grandparent had died, I was eight, and sick with hepatitis. Shielding me from my grandmother's death must have seemed to my parents like the right thing to do. So, at twenty, I had never encountered death, except in books.

Desperate to *do* something to support my grief-stricken

friends at the restaurant, I offered to work Scott's shifts that week. I knew even as I offered that it was a foolish gesture. What could his shifts possibly matter? Worse, he had been a graceful and masterful waiter who could balance a full tray of meals above his shoulder, on his finger-tips; I was clumsy and slow, a rookie. But *doing* something seemed necessary. That's why, I figured out years later, people bake brownies and casseroles and deposit them in the kitchens of grieving families. The flowers strewn at the edge of a highway, the brownies delivered to kitchen doors: They might just be our own libations, not unlike the sweet wine, water and barley Odysseus poured into the ground for Persephone.

Scottie and I had talked about death just three days before he died. It was one of those lovely late night rambling philosophical conversations that restaurant workers share after long shifts, when the public is at rest and your own bone-weariness and adrenalin makes the notion of going home to sleep ridiculous. He had been so amazed when I admitted that I'd never been to a funeral. Then I was at his.

Two months after Scott's funeral, one sticky, hot August night, a rain storm broke. Suddenly umbrella-topped tables were overturned, dishes were blown everywhere. A drowned cow floated down the river. We ran around—waiters, bartenders, cashiers, even managers—frantically moving rain-drenched diners from the outside decks to the single crowded dining room inside the restaurant. In that turmoil, I saw Scottie's ghost, his back to me, standing right there along side the bar where we picked up our trays of drinks. It was as though he was waiting for his partner, our cook, to get off shift.

෯

Ceres, the grieving mother of Proserpine, was befriended by a young girl driving home two goats. The girl took the goddess to her old father, who beseeched her to come into their home and take comfort. There they found his wife, the girl's mother, in great distress. Their only son, who had been sick, lay feverish and dying. The grieving goddess Ceres, disguised as a mortal woman, kissed the lips of the feverish boy, restoring the colour to his face. Later that night, after sharing a hearty meal, Ceres took the sleeping boy and laid him in the ashes. The mother, ever-vigilant, sprang up and snatched the child from the fire. Ceres, resuming her immortal form, told the mother that in her fondness for her boy she had thwarted the goddess's attempt to render him immortal, thereby condemning him to mortality. Then Ceres, still mourning for her lost daughter, left them.

❧

My mother told me a story about a seventy year old man skating alone on a lake. "He was dazzling," she said, "as he carved pirouettes, his blades flashing in the sun." She said that people made a circle around him, watching his graceful performance, when he just dropped dead there on the ice of Chickawaukie Lake.

My mother told me that story when she was visiting us, three years ago. She said I was about my daughter's age when she'd taken me, my younger sister, and another child skating that day. The sky was a brilliant blue. My mother always liked to skate. I have her white figure skates now, but my feet have grown bigger than hers, and besides, I never mastered skating.

As she told the story her admiration for the man was evident. She must have been forty-two then: my age now. My youngest sister was her fifth and last-born child. In those first five years of her youngest child's life, my mother had nursed her own mother through the strokes that finally killed her, and had suffered the final ravages of a twenty-seven year marriage. There she was: left alone with five children on that sunny winter afternoon, watching a man skate himself to death.

She'd never told me the story until that particular visit. And though I was ten when it happened, I don't carry my own memory of that day. My mother was seventy-two as she told me about it—older than the man had been. I wonder if she thinks about his splendid, sunlit death, sometimes, on cold winter afternoons. I hope that she does. And then, I wish that she doesn't.

❧

During the Christmas holidays last year, Nicole came downstairs from her room one morning, her face contorted by misery. She was grieving for Walter of Ingleside, Anne's son, who died at war in the last of the series of L. M. Montgomery's *Anne of Green Gables*.

"It still hurts, but not quite as hard," she admitted, after a couple of hours of distraction.

This was a real and terrible hurt, and even as I resisted the easy assurances (It's only a story. It will be all right . . .) I was grateful that she was coming to terms with such grief.

On occasions like that, I've worried that she's too young. I've worried, too, when each one of our children has run headlong into the truth of the killing of animals that's part of farming. Surprisingly, they each met up with this truth before they'd even turned four. Coming face to face with undeniable evidence of death, each of them has revealed a sense of dismay, and of betrayal, expressed in their own individual ways. And then each of them has carried on.

❧

In a remote village in India, a woman was giving birth in a

238

hut, accompanied by two or three other women. No men were allowed to see her—not even her husband, who waited behind the hut. The women stood on the dirt floor, around a thick hemp rope which hung from a low ceiling. The one giving birth held on to an elaborate knot about the size of an infant's head, at the base of that rope. The knot looked like a monkey's fist (an elaborate knot I learned to tie as a teen, roaming among the sailing vessels on the Camden harbour). Squatting there, she could pull on the knot for balance and support, and squeeze it to release her fear, pain, and pent-up energy.

We hadn't had children yet when I saw the film of that woman having her baby. Now, after three experiences with modern childbirth, I know far better than I did when I watched that show just how right it seems—to give birth clutching a thick hemp knot.

It also impressed me how these particular people didn't name their offspring until the end of the first year of life. For that first year they seemed to avoid referring to the infant in any way—just packed the child around, fed and cleaned it. The reason, the narrator explained, was that infant mortality was so high during the first twelve months. Not naming an infant might diminish the pain of losing it; then again, anonymity might shield the vulnerable from death's grasp.

༰

In London, in the early 1700's, seventy-five percent of the children born died before they reached the age of five. Mothers had as many as fifteen children, hoping half would survive. Two common child rearing practices of those generations served the purpose of distancing mothers from the emotional and physical agonies associated with such harsh realities: wet nurses, and swaddling. Both practices, keeping the fragile creatures well nourished and safe from harm, would limit the parents' skin contact with the infant. And skin contact, we now believe, triggers hormones that release milk, while nourishing emotional bonds between infant and parent.

The last time I visited her, I sat in my aunt's living room, holding my newborn son while his older sister played with a box of spools kept under the sofa for kids just her age. My eldest aunt described how my grandmother had swaddled her babies. She explained that her mother would rub the babies with olive oil, and then wrap them in strips of soft fabric, finishing the wrap with a layer of coarser fabric. She remembers my mother and her twin, the youngest in a family of ten, bundled in this way, leaning against the kitchen cupboards like two small urns with faces. She said the babies would be unwrapped and washed a couple of times a day, and that though she hadn't swaddled her own babies, those bundled little ones had seemed so quiet and content. My son, meanwhile, squalled and squirmed in my arms, his black hair sweaty and his face red.

❧

These days, in spite of safer medical practices, doctors will still caution you not to tell friends you're pregnant until the twelfth week, so great is the threat of miscarriage in those first three months. So we push the pregnancy out of mind during exactly the months of greatest discomfort. We try to deny our nausea, our precarious mood swings.

For the first twelve weeks after my daughter's birth, we lived in an alarming state of vulnerability because we knew that was the time when infants were susceptible to all sorts of frightening weaknesses. It was also when they reached the twelfth week— and it can't be coincidence—that each of our three infants quit wailing every evening; a primal howl, which lasted for hours, and sounded like a mixture of anguish, fear, and misery.

But when they stopped that night-time crying, my husband and I experienced a peculiar sense of loss, a disorienting lightness. It was as though we had been ballasted by that cycle of tears and comfort.

# Journal Notes

January 1, '97

**New Year's Day**
The weather has stolen the show this Christmas season, sitting at thirty-some below zero without budging for days and days, (even while snowing)—today it's risen straight up to ten above, bringing howling winds and rain. We've gotten more snow than since the twenties, they say. Now the snow is compacted and crusted over by warmth and rain.

We took turns being sick last week, first Andrew, then Jamie, then Nicole and me. Fevers, throwing up, aching joints and wracking coughs. Seems like part of the holiday tradition.
Anyway, today all is well. Despite trails of crumpled Kleenex and rivers of snot running, general good health seems restored.

᠊ᴥ᠊

May 28th, '97

In what order to set out this tumble of reflections?

Next week, Donovan Baily runs against Michael Johnson, to determine who is the fastest man in the world. The next day the national elections will be held. I'm surprised at the level of interest and anxiety both events rouse in me.

Soon, too, we'll know if parts of Kamloops will flood. For months we've been watching Manitoba and the western-central states struggle against high muddy waters.

Yesterday Nicole turned twelve: our baby, our sweet round-eyed daughter—twelve!

Meanwhile, we carry on with soccer, and the birthday sleep-over, and district track meet, and Heritage Fair, and the piano recital, with all the attention and spirit they each merit and I can muster (the latter often falling just short of the former).

❧

## July '97

James's new expression, uttered repeatedly during the weeks of planning and reviewing our plans for our summer trip, back east: "I'm a western guy, from way back east."

It's a perfect rendering of that effort which I think begins in early childhood and takes us pretty well till our golden years to work out: figuring out where the hell we have come from, and where it is that we find ourselves.

# Two Small Stories

## One

James, on the way to the festival to recite a poem, anxiously asks question after question as he tries to picture what's to come.

They're peculiar questions, and remind me how much we overlook in our kids' processes of conceptualizing. He wants to know if he'll have a microphone (no). If he'll be walking up to the stage alone (yes). If all the cars on the highway are on the way to this event (no). If I know where we are going (no, so it turns out). If the judges will like his sweater (probably). If he should end with a line about the author having forgotten the title (no—that line *only* works with his brother's poem).

We walk in late, having gone first to the wrong hall. I search for strategies to help James out. I remind him he can decide *not* to recite the poem (Dennis Lee's "Goof on the Roof"): We could, I casually suggest, just watch the others, go for an ice cream, and go back to his daycare. But no: He *wants* to say his poem. Don't I want him to?

This church is a looming building—all spires and sweeping white heights. The stage looks as though it's five miles from the doorway. James wants to know how we will hear him. I tell him that I will sit at the back and he can speak directly to me.

"Just look at Mommy," I suggest, "and forget about everyone else."

He responds to my good advice by assuring me that "In Kindergarten we had our eyes checked. Mine are really good. I can look at *more* than one person out of each eye."

"That's great," I reply. "You'll do very well, then."

And he does. Of the three Canadian Poetry competitors, he ties for second place, and is enormously proud.

❧

## Two

It was the second day of the Arts Festival. That morning the van was already warming up as I headed out the back door with several things already on my mind.

I drove up towards the apple trees wondering about the wisdom of taking the back road, since the ice had been bad for the past month. But by then the van had begun to slide. Fortunately, it was a kindergarten day for James, and so he was safely on the bus. I was thankful for that, as I began the long, slow slide around the trees. By then, I'd shifted into low gear and was steering into the curve, thinking I could come to a stop and turn back.

But the Mazda wouldn't respond to my manoeuvres. It careened around the bend, picking up speed. With a sickening thud, the van hit a tree and I shot forward in my seat.

Before I could draw in a breath or begin to worry about how I'd get to work and how Nicole would get from school to festival, Mont was there. He'd heard it all from the house. He asked why on earth I'd gone out the back road. My answer was humble, and surprised enough to deflect irritation.

"Because," I heard myself saying, "that's the way the van was pointed."

I was careful *not* to say: because he hadn't turned it around, as he usually does. (What I lack in pride, I make up for in diplomacy.)

245

Has our division of labour evolved to such a degree? Sure, Mont gases up, tunes up, often even starts the vehicles. He looks after buying them, although he takes me along to share in final decisions. When he's forgotten to gas up on a Sunday, I have, on occasion, run out of gas on Monday; once I had to hitch-hike up our road with two kids in tow, a briefcase under one arm and a baby under the other. And so, when he hadn't turned the van around that day, I assumed he had considered the back road driveable.

But once upon a time I used to think for myself. I had bought and learned to care for my little red Honda Civic, for which I'd paid five hundred dollars that I'd earned picking field cukes and plums. I used to change my own oil, and could change a flat tire in no time. I travelled from Maine to Montana alone, in my antique car with its malfunctioning starter and vacuum wipers.

So what, I wonder, has reduced me to a woman who drives in the direction her vehicle is pointing, and doesn't check the fuel gauge because it's Monday? The blessing is that whatever has happened to me has also made me less interested in pursuing such questions too ardently. I'm more prone to be thinking about who I'm supposed to pick up at three-thirty, or whether the kid with the soccer game has his soccer gear, or if one more dinner of turkey soup would constitute negligence.

# Part V

❧

*Bearings and Benchmarks*

❧

"I'm a western guy, from way back east."

—James Templeman, 1997

. . . No matter how Canadians managed their estate, the land would remain, always the land and the impulses nourished by it from the beginning.

—Bruce Hutchinson, *A Life in the Country*, 1988

# Notes from a Journal

July '98

**From our trip to Barkerville:**

In the parking lot, Andrew read: "Gold first discovered here in 1862," and he and James angled their cameras to snap photos of the ground beneath the sign. Must be exciting, to have that kind of faith in details of historical account, especially when at a place like Barkerville.

Watching the three busloads of teenagers unloading at the front gates that first morning (ugh), A. asked, "What are cath-*ol*-ics?" The mispronunciation embarrassed him, but how could he know? That's how far he exists from the *very* Catholic world of my past. Interestingly, he isn't without faith—it's just so differently directed.

James, playing with big kids one moment (gold panning on the gravelly banks of a stream), running toward us with a bloody gash to his head the next. We rushed all the way back to Quesnel to Emergency for one *single* stitch . . . Last week he had the stitch removed and Doctor Meredith gave him the black thread to keep. He carried it around balled up in a Kleenex for a few days. Then I removed it to a safe place, to tape inside of the MacDonald's card he was given at the hospital. But when I took the card up to his room I couldn't retrieve from that damned memory of mine the safe place where I'd tucked the thread. He kept asking for it—wanted to take it for show-and-tell. I searched and searched (house and mind), sorting through balled-up Kleenex in various waste baskets, to no avail.

Yesterday, though, he brought me a gruesome bit of dried blood and skin, with short golden hairs shooting out of the edges: the scab. It was safely taped into his card, labelled and stashed in his treasure trunk. I do try.

# Notes from a Journal

## November '98

I've been contemplating the draft of a project Andrew did for school last month. He had to list all the requirements to create a town on an isolated island, attending not only to physical, but also spiritual and intellectual needs.

Andrew's brainstorming produced this rumpled sheet of paper sitting on my desk. He began in pencil, switching to blue ballpoint pen midway through the second of four columns. On the flip side are two more columns. Reading them provides a dizzying adventure in mental association.

The list begins: seeds, calf, NACl, animals (crossed out). Followed by: a shovel, a pick, an ax, then people (crossed out). Next: Black smith, metal, rope, compus, medicine, 1000 workers (crossed out), musicians, barells, wagons, plows, paint, paper, ink, butcher, pots, pans, buttons, leather, laws, bible, religion (the *idea* of religion, he explained), storekeeper, candles, oil, anvil, priest, rope, hooks, net, string, horses, dogs, turkeys, roosters, lambs, goats, oxen, donkeys, tents, storekeepers, string, education, spears, sundials, pumpkin seeds, apple seeds, pair (sp!) seeds, gloves, pants, socks, undergarments, hats, hope, drivers, wool, nitting needles, story tellers, books, violin, flute, sieve, flour, piano, sugar, soccer, chalk, hop scotch, sand, boat, doctors, builders, archeteks . . . arihitects, mirror, spikes, garlic seeds, silver, calander (colander, or calendar?), police, saw, sacks, rice, potatoes, jellies, a water witcher, bottled water, bakers, money (crossed out, then rewritten, then crossed out again). And finally: bees, and soap.

The list mesmerizes me. It reminds me of taking one of those *Magic Schoolbus* trips: Now we are inside the mind of your kid.

An interesting place, but I'm glad not to have to dwell there. It makes me tired. I've pondered how a child with no religious training decides upon including a Bible; imagines the "idea" of religion; gets from anvil to priest and back to metal.

Hats to hope, spears to sundials, leather to laws, saw to sacks—all sound like jaunts along alliterative lines. Clearly there was a run of animals, brought on, somehow, by string, and interrupted by the thought of tents. Mining was a theme at the start, as was farming, and later, building. Eating emerges again and again (no surprise, I suppose, for a ten year old with a monumental appetite). There are hints of our family life throughout: the soccer, the violin and piano, the gardening, the building, farming, and water witcher (one being hired, recently, to locate a second source of water). Equally evident is the fact that winter was still a distant idea: no skates or hockey sticks; no idea of hockey; not even a toque or boots. October was balmy this year.

On his final version, with all items categorized, soap appears off to the side of the second column, not classified. I think he forgot about it. Which does illustrate one thing about Andrew— how, in the haste of capturing the wild flights of a busy mind, he'll fall short, again and again, on tidiness and organization.

This is his quirk, and the reason why his ingenious projects fall out of his unzipped packsack and land on the floor of his room where they get lost in a heap of sports gear, gift wrap, or half-done science experiments. It's the challenge of being Andrew. But I do believe that he's meeting it with greater skill with each passing year.

# The Middle Age

From the moment I got pregnant with James I acknowledged that I was an old mom. On the January when he was twenty-seven months old my journal reveals the growing awareness:

It's time to stop counting J's age in months, thank God. Have had to count on fingers each time, no capacity to remember numbers left.

If he wakens me more than twice in a week, I look bedraggled for days after.

Survived sleeplessness for years with Andrew, but now, when I finally do get seven hours uninterrupted sleep, I feel as though I've just stepped out of platform shoes carved of stone—a wobbly, slightly elevated sensation, everything distorted.

Being rested doesn't even feel good yet—just odd, like I'm about to take off, or pitch forward, headlong. Vision even affected—colours snap into focus with clarity which dazzles. I'm giddy, sometimes drunk with rest.

I had an idea about writing a guidebook for old moms, when I was still in the hospital after James's birth. But one of the distinguishing characteristics of this change seems to be a who-cares-anyway reaction to nearly everything except the baby. I must have stopped caring about other ill-informed old mothers, because the idea fell by the wayside, relegated to an item—never checked off—on an old page of writing goals.

Another such benchmark is irritation. No more an occasional visitor, it's a live-in guest now. This became apparent while I was pregnant. One of many sources of my smouldering irritation back then was how maternity clothes are made for the glowing *young* mother-to-be: They're *cute*, with Peter Pan collars and little buttons; they say "I'm so delighted to be pregnant, and I want to share my delight."

However, I have learned that when you are pregnant for the third time, at thirty-eight—while your friends are having grandchildren—you feel so far from cute that you are in danger of falling off the edge of tolerable. What you feel is heavy, peaked, drab and old. That doesn't in the least mean you don't long for the baby. You also long for sleep, and privacy, and maybe a scrap of dignity too.

When I got to the hospital to have James I knew things would be different with this delivery. I didn't feel frightened, submissive, or subdued; I felt ready to give birth. I did not resolve to appear brave or stoic; labour pains hurt, though yes, there was a mystical rhythm to the pain. I did not withhold; I moaned and I complained. Yet it offended me to be offered painkillers.

I expected this pain, and wanted to be left with it. My husband seemed the closest to understanding me. Only slightly ill-at-ease, he stood by me. He didn't even wince when I sent a young lab technician packing with her clinking vials of blood. I wanted *nothing* between this baby and me, other than the birth process. In retrospect, I ought to have spared the well-meaning hospital staff and stayed at home. I had no interest in playing the roles; in being encouraged, or soothed, or told how well I was doing.

After the delivery, my hunger surprised the nurses. They

seemed disconcerted by my need for food, as if I were supposed to be experiencing sensations somewhat more elevated than appetite. But I *was* hungry, no question about it.

I can't forget the morning in the hospital that my eyes left the sweet face of my lovely infant, to meet my own reflection in the mirror. Mont was to arrive soon, bringing the kids with him. My aspirations were modest: Presentable was what I aimed for. But I was ill-prepared for the ghastly face peering critically back at me from the bedside mirror. How could such an unsightly apparition have given birth to the cherubic boy who lay, bundled into a pale blue egg-roll, on my bed?

I did my best to look presentable for my kids, who were the o. lance my way. It hadn't taken many visits to know that no one cared a whit for anyone but the baby. It wasn't long before I began to feel spent, like a cocoon left behind by the emerging offspring.

"No point," I thought to myself, watching one young mother swishing down the corridor in a fuchsia satin robe and matching slippers. I did wish, though, for the dignity of a long braid down my back and the billowing white cotton gown that I remember from birth scenes on *Little House on the Prairie*. It helped not at all to be subject to the constant probing attentions of a flock of nurses. They demonstrated an inordinate amount of concern for temperature, bowels, blood pressure. (Which made me, then, a cocoon with vital signs. And appetite.)

I did, however, find myself possessed of an impressive power to get rid of people who threatened to bother us. A well-aimed scowl would disperse pastor or photographer. Yes, I knew these were probably good and useful people. But I wanted none of them. Not at that time.

I knew full well how rapidly infancy would pass, and how hazy an impression it would leave. I aimed to focus on it, to savour it. And I did. For long stretches I lay, propped up on pillows, my baby in the crook of one arm. We studied each other, nursed, day-dreamed, napped, made small noises at one another. He was beautiful, with his round eyes and fluffy, reddish hair.

At night I'd return him to the nursery, reluctantly, so I could get a few hours of sleep. But the nurses, unable to console his night-time cries, would come and awaken me. For this, I had vast patience: I could sympathize with his hot fury and remember feeling pleased, through my exhaustion, to be rocking him.

His colic went 'round the clock, a phenomenon which I'd heard of and found fascinating. At home, four days after his birth, he was crying from about ten at night, to two in the morning. A few days later we shared pre-dawn hours from two to five. Yet even with this new spin on it, the experience of colic came easier the third time. It was no longer terrifying, only tiring.

When he wasn't ravaged by colic, James would tuck his head under my chin and suck the middle three fingers of one hand while his other hand would scratch the flabby underside of my arm. He'd breathe a shuddering breath, eyes wide but dozy, eyebrows arched as though to hold my attention, feet pushing against my lap. I could have held him this way forever—and for hours, I did.

With our first two babies, the intensity of my focus seemed to overpower even the object of that focus. Nicole was a sweet, precious baby who absorbed so much energetic affection, and grew well from it. But in all of our concerns about caring for her, I missed things—small things I knew to watch for with James.

Andrew was a difficult baby, tense, busy, and restless. I don't think we ever had enough sleep to see him clearly. The memories are fragments: the click-clack of the swing-o-matic as we gulped down dinner; his falling—from coffee table, stool, steps, change table . . . . With him, I was always startling into another level of wakefulness, constantly reawakening to his diffuse curiosity, lurching energy and quirkiness.

With James, though, everything felt different: I was old and tired; he was wilful, focused, determined. How much my temperament, at that time, determined who he has become, I'll never know. Do old mothers produce a particular kind of child?

At three months, his hair waved like wisps of grass in a breeze. It had changed, mellowed to the colour of seasoned birch—neither red, nor brown, nor blond. Everyone's sweetie, we all wished him to stay small. He had a slew of nicknames (Little Mudge, Jamie the Shark, Pud, Slobber-Dauber Slime Trail), partly, I think, because he was so self-possessed, even as a tiny thing, that there was no danger of a silly name robbing him of *his* dignity.

He grew into a solid baby, strong and determined, with one digit pointing in the air and a glistening strand of drool falling from his mouth. Sometimes I would wonder how all of the easy attention we bestowed upon him in his first months had shaped him. I still do. Now he's a small but strong five-year-old to whom people of all ages attach. At his school the biggest, coolest boys love him. In a confrontation, his siblings rush to his defence, gentling the way for him.

As for me, I kept my flabby arms long after James lost his fondness for stroking and scratching them with his fingers. Another full year would pass before I'd gather the will and focus to shed the thirty pounds I'd gained. Getting fit wasn't that hard—aside from the humiliations of exposing my body in a swimsuit; of sensing the flab reverberate with my footfall as I ran. I learned, beyond a doubt, that forty-year-old fat has a level of firmness, a capacity for endurance to which we might aspire.

During a low point in those months of reclaiming my body, we travelled, in a snowstorm, down to Kelowna to buy me a stair-climber. I was desperate for a way to exercise without going outside. That was our first outing as a family of five and, despite the storm, we enjoyed it.

Back home, we set up the machine in the living room. I wanted it right in the middle of things, not hidden away. After we assembled it, we watched our daughter and son climb up on my new machine and, one behind the other, pump the steps together, their muscled legs bending in synchronized grace, like the necks of blue herons nesting in tree tops. I also remember quiet afternoons while the baby, content in his loden green corduroy Snugly, uttered whispery breaths in time with my exertion as I stepped and stepped.

❧

In an open range, such as is the area around Heffley Lake and Louis Creek, there are cattle-guards along the roads. Common as railroad crossings in the western half of Canada and the U.S., these were a new experience for me, an easterner. Though I've lived out west and travelled the western states and provinces for twenty years now, I still laugh to see those phoney cattle-guards painted on the roads in parts of Washington State. Cattle down there must be pretty stupid. In our area, cattle-guards are mostly made from iron poles, though where ranchers put in their own, along driveways and side-roads, they're made from logs. (Catalogues, Nicole used to call them).

Cattle-guards mark range areas. As temperature drops and days shorten, cattle get moved to the top end of one range, and in a few weeks, will be found bunched along fences and cattle-guards at the lowest end.

❧

I swing like a pendulum these days, resting for a lovely, seductive moment before I push myself off again. Self restraint comes harder too. I hate myself even as I hear the rebuke I am hurling at my husband or kids for some trivial, real or imagined slight. Sometimes the moods remind me of that creature ripping out from the chest of the man in the seventies movie, *Alien*. The things which fly from my mouth, hissing forth, are no less repulsive, or surprising.

Though I pride myself on teaching with sensitivity, last week, when a student kept asking what caused the low mark on his composition, I heard myself answering, "It's not interesting. And it's written badly."

Who *is* this person I have become? Perhaps it's a godsend that I can so easily forget whatever I've said or done moments before.

Sometimes I can temper my surges of mood, sanding the roughest edges, moderating the rages and exultations too. But other times, trying to appear as I think I ought to be wears me out.

⌒

I read with hunger still. And as soon as the cover is closed, I forget what I've read. Sometimes I have to search the first chapters to remember some minor character, or some detail which will make sense of the conclusion. I read now in much the same way as I used to brush my forehead with holy water, on the way into the church: I want to anoint myself, ever hopeful for some lasting effect, an impression or essence to linger.

The synapses are wearing down and the gaps between them are widening. Those synapses don't fire as effectively. Or at least that's my mental image of it, cold comfort that it is. The ancient Greeks might have feared that a spiteful goddess or spunky nymph stole the substance of their thoughts—an act of vengeance or trickery, or playfulness. Me, I think of frayed sheathes, like the rubber coating on electrical wires, spraying that power every which way, transmitting weakly, intermittently. Sometimes an image or sensation comes hurtling forth, unbidden, surging from a time when the mind was nimble.

⁊

I know in middle age what I never suspected in my thirties: that the normal—the calm, eventless time I have been waiting for—is anything but normal. It's elusive, rare, and precious. Contrary to expectation, normal actually *is* the chaotic, disrupted, unpredictable time—more so, perhaps, for a family of five, with so many connections to so many communities. Normal is someone sick, someone having a birthday, someone crying, someone thrilled, something spilled, something not running properly, and the phone ringing.

⁊

In a way, all of these markers of middle age seem like those cattle-guards that mark the way along our road. They certainly rattle a person. And they mark off the territory where one will pass a spell of time. Crossing them on foot requires extra care and a bit of effort. And the effort heightens the awareness of transition. But it all recedes—the effort required, the awareness, the sense of change. Soon, the new ways feel normal, and not long after, you barely remember being any different.

This is what it was like for me, being a middle-aged, experienced mother. Each of the changes in myself felt strange, and then became ordinary. So it goes, I am learning, with body shape and eye-sight, sleep patterns and mood.

# Day of the Cougar

One steamy July mid-week night my husband and I had fallen into bed before eleven. I was suffering with a miserable summer cold. Mont had put in ten long hours up on a neighbour's roof, under the sun.

At around one a.m., the insistent ringing of our phone finally penetrated the deepest of sleeps and one of us woke the other. Our bedside phone turned out to be unplugged, so my husband stumbled through the blackness of our bedroom, on into the kitchen, reaching the phone just as the last ring jangled into stubborn silence.

For the remaining six hours we tossed and turned, pretending to sleep. Over and over I surveyed the relatives who might have died, or been in an accident so terrible as to warrant such a late night call. Not my mother, please, I prayed— something I hadn't much tried for thirty years. And not my father, who was, admittedly, old. And, oh God, *not* a sister or brother. We have many between us, and so are vulnerable to loss. Death played upon my wakefulness and then danced through my dreams.

I woke a bit late, straining my ears to hear the phone call my husband had just taken. It wasn't yet seven. The kids still slept. A friend who lived down the road from us was calling to tell us he'd seen a large cougar crossing the road just in front of our place as he'd driven past on his way home from a night shift. He was worried that, after more than twenty rings, we hadn't answered his late night call. The cat had swaggered, his wife later elaborated, as though it had no fear in the world.

Perspective can make the difference between surviving an experience and embracing a story. We live in cougar country. But the cougar, a secretive and solitary predator, seldom encroaches upon the domestic scene. In our sixteen years on this farm we have seen coyotes and bear, even an enormous owl. Hawks fly down from the iron-stained cliff which rises at the edge of our north boundary. Rabbits and groundhogs live close by, having relocated after failed experiments in cohabitation with barn cats. I once stumbled over a grouse that had shot out from the bush to detract attention from her babies. But none of us had laid eyes on a cougar.

And we'd been lucky, until that time, in our years of raising pigs and sheep. We'd suffered losses to disease and disaster I'd never have imagined before this lifestyle became mine. We'd lost unnamed kittens to unseen owls or coyotes over the years, and our banty chicken flock had expanded and contracted in its own barely perceptible seasons of birth and mishap. But thanks to the combination of watchful dog and good luck, we had suffered no major loss to cougar, bear, or other roaming carnivore.

So the morning of the phone call, my husband took the news lightly. He did ask me to send Nicole down to the pens to count the sheep, and he cautioned me to keep a close eye on James. Then, running late, he left for another long day.

After her cereal and juice, our daughter headed down to the pens. Andrew went along. In too short a time they came racing up the laneway, bursting in the back kitchen door, eyes wide, near tears, words tumbling from their mouths faster than my ears could untangle them. Dead lamb, sheep racing around, Rosie missing, Leo gone, lamb, blood, dirt. Trying for composure, I collected the little one and the four of us went down to assess the situation.

It was dismal: The sheep were in a frenzy, running in circles around their pen, kicking up dust. Ewes stamped out nervous warnings, their lambs bleating shrilly. In the midst of it all, unperturbed, our chickens wandered, eating bugs and bits of spilled grain. Oddly, they'd suffered no apparent damage.

The kids pulled me to the dead lamb, tripping over one another to stay close. Then we tried to take a count, to measure the losses. This resulted in useless but fervid arguments—sister against brother—about just how many lambs we'd had after having lost the triplets, but before the last lamb dropped. Then came a series of debates about how to distinguish the larger lambs from the smaller ewes. The two of them eventually concluded that we'd lost three or four lambs, including the one slain in the front of the pens, and at least one ewe.

James kept asking about his lamb, Wayne Gretsky (Gwetsky, as he said in his r-less accent). W.G.—a bottle-fed runt who regularly slipped through the fence with his sister Rosie for a private evening feed in the field—was vulnerable to be sure. James didn't know what to make of the situation, but had absorbed the bigger kids' fear and panic. He kept asking about the "coocker," which made us laugh—our laughter sounding only slightly hysterical.

We were barely back in the house when the phone rang. It was a neighbour who wanted to let me know that she knew about the cougar, and to find out what *we* knew. I had no choice but to tell her about our losses, and then to spend the next twelve hours running what felt like a chat-line, talking to more neighbours than I had imagined shared this rural lake-side community. I don't like talking on the phone. But an unfortunate consequence of rural living is the dependence on a telephone network to address work, safety, and social needs.

As soon as our first caller hung up, I called Conservation to report the incident. The man with whom I was connected,

Josh, turned out to be friendly and down-to-earth. He told me to keep the kids in view, and took down directions.

In British Columbia that summer, two gruesome incidents had been prominent in the news. Both involved cougars attacking children. A five-year-old in Nakusp was on her swing in the back yard when she was snatched up and dragged to the woods. She'd been rescued, as had a little boy from Lytton who had also been attacked by a cougar. Both remained in critical condition.

When I asked Josh whether these cases indicated some change in the cougar's behaviour which rural parents ought to be aware of, he said no. Cougars, he said, were large cats, unpredictable, predatorial, aggressive. He said we should *always* beware, particularly when we had little kids.

We love living here at least partly for the casual existence the country allows. We can lie naked in our hot-tub, out on our deck under the stars. We are under no pressure to mow our yard or to grow orderly rows of flowers. Our shrubs have never been trimmed. Things grow in wild profusion here, including, more or less, our kids. On our property they feel free to roam and explore, to dig holes and build kid things. The place is littered with balls and bone collections (cow bones, mostly), with stick and binder twine contraptions. Our kids don't have the luxury of a neighbourhood park, schoolyard, or town, but they do have the freedom of wide spaces and natural bounty. The notion of limiting that freedom or constraining it with fear unsettled me.

Cougars are also called mountain lions. I had imagined them as different beasts. The cougar (also known as puma, catamount, or panther), runs seven to eight feet in length. It's considered to be the most destructive of all the animals in North America, an efficient and precise hunter, able to leap a breathtaking expanse. According to *The North Thompson Journal*, there are approximately seven hundred and fifty of the powerful wild felines in this region.

There's also one in captivity in Kamloops, at the Wildlife Park. One night last summer he surprised and alarmed the caretakers by making his escape, leaping from a rock to a lone branch which had swung down in the wind, some ten metres above the back wall of the pen.

Within the hour Josh, accompanied by Mike, a volunteer, pulled up at the back of our house. Their trucks roused our dog, who alerted us with her frenzied barking. Patsy's eleven now. She's going blind, but what she notices, when she's awake, she announces with persistent enthusiasm.

The second truck emitted muffled barks and growls. Josh was in uniform, and carried a rifle. My boys were beside themselves with excitement: guns, hounds, uniforms—all at their back door!

The two men wanted to be shown the sheep pens, so we collected ourselves to go back to the crime site. Within minutes Mike and Josh had found two more bodies, ewes this time, over sixty pounds each, with their throats ripped out. They'd been dragged over to the field adjoining the pens to the east. By this time, spirits raised by the company of the men, Nicole and Andrew had managed to assess our losses. They agreed that we'd lost two ewes and three lambs. So two lamb corpses remained to be found.

The hounds, freed from the truck, led the two men off in pursuit of lamb corpses, and—we all hoped—cougar. Our two boys watched, riveted at the back door. By noon the hunting party returned, sweating and frustrated. They'd hiked up the northern side of the property, finding tracks, but nothing more. They'd been across the road to the south of us, where they discovered more tracks, but also where their hounds lost the scent due to a combination of too much heat and dog tracks intermingled with the cougar's. It seemed that maybe the neighbour's dog had chased the cougar across and into their property. No lamb corpses, and no more information to be gleaned from scent or track.

The two trackers packed up to return to town. Josh revised his earlier instructions, now telling me to keep all three of the kids inside. He asked me to stay in touch, and he advised me to keep the remaining sheep enclosed in our empty pig pens for the night, and to drag the three corpses further away. He suggested that we sweep the ground around the corpses, so a trail could be easily detected. He also recommended that we keep Patsy inside for the night, so she wouldn't chase the culprit away before it left a good trail. Josh and Mike would be back at the first light of morning.

I dreaded relaying Josh's instructions to my husband. After another hot day of roofing, he would not welcome the challenge of moving sheep to the pig pens and enclosing them for the first time. Nor would he look forward to arranging for Patsy—who had lived outdoors all her life—to spend her first night inside the house.

By late afternoon the kids and I were stir-crazy from the heat, the confinement, the excitement, and the constant jangling of our phone. I would no more than get us settled and distracted, when another phone call would renew the flow of adrenalin. We were instantly famous in the neighbourhood, and I hated it.

We set out for a swim, to escape, and to cool off. But we had only pulled out of our laneway when we discovered Mike's truck parked, and Mike emerging from the bush with the hounds behind him, all in a lather. He'd found the two dead lambs in an old bear den across the road from our place. Not only that, but the cougar had then found *him*, and had charged. Our cougar, he told us, was big and aggressive—and provoked, I thought to myself.

At our friends' dock we had a good swim, and also retold our story to the neighbours who had come to hear. The kids by then had competing versions of the day's events, which they shared with gusto. One dwelled on the dead sheep, one on the hounds, one on Mike (now a hero), and the guns. The boys insisted that they'd seen blood on the hounds from their encounter with the cougar. I hadn't noticed, or didn't remember. I was losing interest in the details even as they engulfed me. My worries went beyond, to the discouraging effects of lost income, the hours of extra work ahead that night, and the alien mix of fear and vigilance that loomed before us.

When we got back home, Josh had returned for another hunting effort. Trying to push my worries into the periphery of my mind, I carried on as though it was a normal dinner hour. By the time Mont drove in, the kids were sitting at the counter eating. With everyone talking at a furious rate and impressive volume, a wild account of the day's events unfolded.

Then Mont went back outside to check things out for himself. Moments later there was a blast of rifle fire, and the kids nearly leapt off their stools. By the time what passed for a meal was finished, we'd heard another volley, and then three distinct shots from a much louder gun. I heard strangulated moans from the hounds and I could swear I heard a low growl. James started to cry. The phone began to ring even as the last shot was heard—neighbours wanting to know what was going on.

Twenty minutes later, Mont returned. They had hit the cougar, but not before it charged again. They'd shot it by the bear den it had been occupying. It was big and muscular, though mangy and not, apparently, in good health. It had fought so fiercely that they'd resorted to using a handgun.

I left my husband with the phone and the wide-eyed kids with their millions of questions, and escaped for a quick shower. The ten minutes in the solitude of my bathroom were peaceful. But the house had grown eerily quiet. After hours spent in a state of wariness and anxiety, the focus of my vigilance was gone. Mont had taken the kids across the road to see the dead cougar.

We make an effort to protect our kids from undue violence, but in this case I was grateful to my husband for taking them to see the animal. Nothing they would ever see could equal what they might imagine after such a day.

They returned filled with awe.

"The teeth were three inches long," they told me.

"He was *enormous*," said James, "and ferocious too." Jamie had transformed from a quaking little boy who wouldn't let go of my hand to a ball of bravado. The other two were more subdued.

Bedtime was a many-staged affair. Mont and I took turns answering their questions and then returning the boys to bed. First one then the other needed a drink, a cracker, to pee, to ask just one more time about the second set of tracks one guy had mentioned, to ask if there were any rhinoceroses in our woods, to complain of headache, even of car-sickness. At last they slept.

❧

Two nights later, a cute grey fox we'd spied from the road a few times got into our chicken roost and killed every last banty—chick, hen, and rooster. When I bemoaned the loss (not of income, since they roam free, but of something harder to articulate), James comforted me.

"There's a place in the earth," he told me, "where, once a year, chickens come from: a chicken place. We'd get more, and then they'd lay eggs. No problem."

A month passed and life got back to normal for us, minus the chickens and five sheep. Andrew wouldn't go down to do chores alone. Otherwise, I ran along my normal route, and we went about our work and play, keeping a closer eye on James.

Andrew, when he did finally agree to run down to the pens, sang loud choruses of some song he'd learned from the radio. If Nicole felt afraid, she didn't show it.

Then, in August, a young mother of four was killed by a cougar, just outside of Princeton. She had been horse-back riding with three of her children. After rescuing her young son, who had been knocked off his horse, she had ordered her older two children to leave the area, taking the youngest to safety. A man who had come back to find her had been able to shout to her that her children were safe before the cougar fatally attacked her.

It's now February of what has been a remarkably long, hard winter. Yet I can still remember the look on the faces of that woman's husband and children when we saw them on the evening news: pale, stoic, their grief held back from the intruding cameras. I cried as I watched them, fought tears each time I read the story over the next few weeks, fight tears now as I remember her again. I can't reconcile this occurrence with my previous attitudes. I can't find my way back to complacence, and can't make peace with the apprehension.

I find myself gathering facts, as though arming myself with knowledge might somehow accomplish something in my struggles to reconcile what happened to that woman, with what happened on our farm, and with my ideal of a respectful cohabitation with the natural environment. I mull over the possibility that as I run along the back roads of our neighbourhood, a lone cougar could be perched on a limb high above, its thick heavy tail swaying as it eyes me moving along the ground below. I rehearse various responses to that possibility, discarding them one after another.

We live with a wariness now. Andrew asks questions every so often: Do cougars hibernate? Can they find enough food in the winter? Can they see in the dark? Mont and I keep better

269

track of the kids when they're playing. I'm especially prone to panic on the rare occasions when a silence becomes noticeable. Those times in the night when we hear Patsy barking, I strain to listen for sounds of predators and prey.

Jamie, all these months later, every now and then claims he wants to be a cougar hunter when he grows up—to drive a big black truck, carry a rifle, and have a couple of hounds. Once he said he wished *he* was a hound—called Windsock. And if he were, he'd smash that cougar's head in. He's planning on naming yet another new lamb Wayne Gretsky this spring, a big one this time. Meanwhile, we await lambing. The snow is deep yet and—though it seems such a distant prospect—spring will undoubtedly come.

And so the cycles turn, bringing new life and age-old fears.

# Back to the Button Box

Late last night I was digging, fist deep, in my button box, looking for a small brownish button to replace on a shirt. My button box is a can, really, not a box at all. But I've never called it that—probably because my mother's *was* a box. My aunt kept her buttons in gallon jars.

When I was a kid, I spent hours playing in the button box: I stirred and sorted, counted and classified, and built elaborate designs, even villages, from buttons.

To women, the button box represented thrift. But in the generation from my mother to me, the significance of the button box has shifted from thrift to ritual. Sewing on the button I had found, I kept thinking about thrift, and how far I have drifted from this value which consumed the women of my mother's generation.

Unlike my mother I do work outside of the home. Like her, I have a busy life. Our lives differ in almost every other way. But I have values I acquired from my mother, and standards I can neither uphold nor disregard. Mattresses should get turned, blankets aired, curtains washed, cutlery and cupboards wiped clean, bookshelves and bureaus organized, freezers defrosted, plants dusted, silver and shoes polished, rugs and dogs shampooed. Things kept clean reflect pride, maintain hygiene, and last longer.

Thrift. Get the most out of things. Stretch the dollar further.

Boil the flavour from the soup bones. It's a lost art, I'm afraid. It will go with the last of the women who know how to get three meals from a ham (first boiled dinner, then hash, then ham-bone soup); to "make-over" a hoop skirt into a little girl's jumper; to strip, wax, and buff a linoleum floor between lunch and the end of school.

Time has become more dear than money and the measures I take to live up to the standards I have inherited carry a value that hasn't kept up with inflation. I dutifully cut buttons from shirts too frayed even for the Salvation Army box, to save a dollar and thirty cents, should I ever actually make a shirt again, which is unlikely. Yet to throw five perfectly good buttons in the garbage goes against every value I was raised with. This, combined with the environmental values I've adopted along the way, is why I lie awake thinking about such things.

Environmentalism blends so naturally with frugality, yet it was distinctly *not* a value of my mother's time. She and my aunt considered TV dinners a marvel, with their individually foil-enclosed portions, so wholesome and convenient. Strong green garbage bags, Ziploc sandwich bags, disposable diapers: a marriage of frugality and hygiene that dazzled them. For me, not wasting has become the enduring value. Gone is the ideal of manic cleanliness. My furniture never shines, our cotton napkins are never crisp and always stained—but I do not waste. And I keep my button box. It's a challenge, to tread lightly upon the earth while shouldering the legacy of women before my time.

# At Armstrong, On Thursday

It is a lovely morning, with blue gaping through the overcast sky; a day full of promise. We are headed for Armstrong, driving along winding roads, through undulating valleys. It's been a long time since I've travelled in the farm truck, which is an old Chevy, the colour of Keene's hot mustard. It shudders on hills, the transmission whiffling in protest. Changing landscapes unfold across the broad, trembling expanse of its hood.

Armstrong is situated south and east of us, about eighty kilometres away, as the crow flies. But that crow would cover a fair bit of rugged mountain, lake, and dense bush. The drive takes us more than two hours. We travel east out of Kamloops, and then south on the Monte Creek Road. At Westwold, we turn east towards Falkland, then straight on to Armstrong.

It's a small town with dairy farms, a cheese factory, and the grassy, low rolling hills typical of dairy country. Along one of its back roads extend the auction grounds. On any Thursday, their parking lots are filled with vehicles. Clusters of farmers, hippies, ne'r-do-wells, and cowboys wander the grounds, searching for deals or satisfying idle curiosity. The atmosphere is unmistakably carnival, perfumed by smokies and grilled onions, coffee and dust.

We've come, this particular Thursday, for half a dozen weaner pigs, fair-sized, as it's already late fall. But the pens for small

273

livestock are only partially full this week. As luck would have it, this is a good week for goats.

Goats of every description buck at the wooden walls dividing the pens: a goat of midget proportions and another light grey one prance back and forth, unlikely pen-mates; a lanky, brown billy glares at us with malevolent yellowish eyes; four babies rough house in the second row; further down, a clean white billy fills the entire area with his baleful, bellowing wheeze.

Amid the goat-filled stalls, three dazed weaners scramble in their narrow enclosure, searching for just the right spot to nap. Two rows down from them sprawls an immense sow. She doesn't even lift her head as we wander around, looking. She's bound for sausage; not for her, the promise of this day.

People rove around, singly or in clusters, some with more apparent interest than others. The buyers eye one another, working hard at seeming so casual. At first, I can't tell who's bid, or what amount. The auctioneer's rumble, playful and musical, carries hints and messages I can't fathom. Gradually, it makes sense, and I can distinguish numbers from connective syllables, raised eyebrows from nods of assertion.

We watch an attractive man in a plaid flannel shirt bid out a few others on first one goat, then two others. His accent is thick and it takes some time for the auctioneer's assistant to get his name down in her notebook. He seems surprised at his success, but less so than his wife, who shakes her head at his apologetic grin, then backs away from him until she is standing a good five paces behind the action. After adding yet another two goats to their holdings, he searches her out with pleading eyes. He joins her then, and they watch the remaining small livestock sales from a safe distance.

Have we witnessed an early lesson in North American culture, or maybe the first steps toward an agrarian dream? Or is this man simply a sucker for cute goats and a struggling auctioneer?

I also watch a big gentle-looking man who has three long-haired blond girls and a small boy in tow. The kids appear to be between four and ten years old, and are dressed in an astonishing collection of fashions. The middle girl has a bold striped jersey over a billowing skirt of light cotton, its design faded. The tallest wears a black-and-white-checkered top over purple sweat-pants, which are half covered by a bright red skirt. The youngest, pretty like her sisters, wears a short fancy dress below which her skinny, bare legs poke out. Their dad looks like most of the other men, with his worn fleece jacket and runners. His son is similarly undistinguished. The father, only mildly engaged by the auctioneer and neither distracted nor perturbed by his own flock, holds whatever hand reaches out for his.

Later I see them again, in the bleachers above the cow sale, eating smokies and sharing an orange pop. I can't stop watching them. Something about their mild, colourful, pleasant ways impresses me. Why aren't the kids in school? What are they buying, or selling?

Across a parking lot from the small animal pens and in front of the main building, another auctioneer whines and wheedles his incantations to a small crowd of people who examine dusty machinery or prod a sack of potatoes or stand waiting for a certain fat rabbit to come up. I had hoped to bid on a twenty pound lot of carrots, but have missed it while waiting for the sow to be sold. Unlike the small animal bidding, the buyers here have numbers which they hold up to bid. I don't understand that difference: whether it's because of a preference of the auctioneer; or because the animal buyers already know one another; or perhaps due to the magnitude of the miscellany heaped around this area.

The cattle auction taking place inside the draughty main hall has its own mystique. This auctioneer's melody—somehow more distinguished, more professional than the others—blends statistics with low rolling stretches of sound. We watch from a back row, where I study the variety of ball-caps—from faded soft to brand new nylon—their bands adjusted tightly, tufting the white or grey or shaggy brown hair at the back. Cowboy hats in as many varieties and conditions—from felt to straw, new to ragged, ten gallon to pint-sized—bob and wag.

In here, cowboys hold court. They are clad in bright stiff jeans and shiny silver belt buckles, or faded white-blue jeans with quilted canvas vests above. The women demonstrate an exhilarating freedom of attire, from jeans, tooled leather belts, and hats, to flowing skirts, frilly blouses and ornately piled curls. Appearance provides no obvious clue to the seriousness of the bid, or the quality of calf acquired, or even, I suspect, to the prosperity of the couple.

Transactions roll along conforming to a protocol and etiquette all their own: Cow or calf is prodded in through one doorway by a cow handler as its weight is displayed in lit red digits; and then the animal is prodded out through the other doorway, by another handler. Sometimes the animal is gone long before the bidding has ceased. High in the back rows, we sit on the same bench as the father and four kids I'd been watching outside. Back here, we're all casual observers, sipping coffee, eating chips, chuckling or gaping or murmuring in awe, as the situation decrees.

Also indoors, but quite separate from the cattle sales, transpires the oddest of the auctions. This room has a high ceiling and is heaped with objects of every conceivable condition and purpose. The auctioneer exhorts the crowd to bid on first a yellow extension cord, then a heap of rope, and next a pair of table lamps, or a freezer, whose condition is wholly a mystery.

What profit would someone expect from selling a chunk of rope? Why ever would someone lay down ten dollars for a cord, length and condition unknown? Is this desperation, resourcefulness, or sport? And how on earth will the lanky man with the mike and his leisurely manner ever work through the accumulated clutter of this barn-sized room?

Yet, good humour and light-heartedness prevail here. In this room, no one looks at a watch. Typical of auctions, but intensified in here, is this suspension of time and of expectation: a continual gauging and reassessing of need and want, desire and whim, worth and means.

Before we leave Armstrong, I duck into this crowded room for one last look around, to see how things have progressed in the hour or so we have been watching the cattle sale. The auctioneer's cajoling and corn-ball humour hasn't flagged, and, amazingly, the heaps of stuff have dwindled.

"Help-me-here-would-ya-give-a-guy-a-hand-c'mon-help-me-please-good-ladies-and-gents-look-at-the-fine-frame-on-this-lovely-painting-give-me-two-do-I-hear-two-three . . ."

Three fifty for the portrait of somebody, and then on to—of all things—a toilet. He's having fun with this one. I watch, sure a toilet of undetermined age and condition will *never* move.

The next thing I know, the woman standing just in front of me stabs the air with her cardboard number. Her long, brown hair is drawn back in a simple braid and she stands holding up her number, alone and resolute. There are no other bids. For eight bucks, the toilet becomes hers. She can only hope it works. At an auction, you just never know.

# *Travels with Steinbeck*

For a long time, I've dreamed of taking a train trip through British Columbia. I've envisioned travelling alone, hoping to be good company for myself.

To prepare, I pulled down from a bookshelf that old classic, John Steinbeck's *Travels with Charley*. Steinbeck had set himself up for a trip far more ambitious than mine. But then, he claimed to suffer from wanderlust. I do not: I love staying put, sinking my roots in the rich depth of familiarity. My trip will spiral me just far enough away to displace me, and then loop me back home again.

That's my direction and destination: around and back home. I want to approach my home from an absence, and in solitude. Like Steinbeck's, my plan seems "clear, concise, and reasonable." The journey has been carefully designed, incorporating only one potentially faulty link where I could miss the connecting train from Jasper—which would mean several hours of waiting, till the midnight bus departed for Kamloops, and then hoping for a kindly driver to let me off partway, at Heffley Creek. Even without Steinbeck telling me, I know that "we do not take a trip; the trip takes us."

I will travel without Charley, and be sheltered by generic hotel rooms, not the charming trailer Rocinante of Steinbeck's clever design. I will not set off to the pummelling winds of a hurricane, only to the wracking coughs of our middle child.

I'll drive from Heffley Lake to Kamloops, and depart on a seven a.m. flight to Vancouver, where I will attend a day of work-related meetings: not exactly an auspicious beginning, but likely enough to convey me towards the feeling of desolation that Steinbeck anticipates. That's why he brings Charley. And that's why I'll bring Steinbeck.

The day after the meeting, I board Car #31 of the Cariboo Prospector. An ancient smoky smell, predating the no smoking days, permeates my seat.

Steinbeck claims to prefer a good photograph to even the most astounding view. At Cheakamus Canyon we see our train stretching out behind us, as we gaze back around the bend of a narrow bridge. Later, to our conductor's prompting, we all crowd to the right side of the car to peer down over the sheer three hundred foot drop of the Brandywine Falls.

I have stared dutifully at extraordinary views, feeling somehow inadequate, not quite up to the momentousness of the occasion. Steinbeck calls it the American way: to go not so much to see a place as to tell about it afterwards. Me, I go for reasons much more vague, though no more noble. I go, I think, to know I have gone. To check it off my list of dreams.

There's a rainbow later in the afternoon, to the east, as gleaming sunlight recedes beneath the spreading grey clouds which have risen to converge overhead. Textures change as red cedar and Douglas fir give way to birch, blue spruce, and larch. Atop homes along the tracks, chimneys spew their grey into the surrounding grey, of a different hue.

Throughout the day, lulled by the rocking of the train, I study the maps of my route, and read. Three meals, fourteen hours, and a couple of magazines later we pull into the yard at Prince George. On my bus ride across town to a hotel, it's too dark to see anything.

Before even settling into my room I call home, knowing it's

bedtime and my call will be expected. Steinbeck captures the emotional circuitry of our connection, in his description of the act of phoning his wife to reestablish his "identity in time and space." For a few minutes he has "a name, and the duties and joys and frustrations a man carries with him like a comet's tail." He describes this as "dodging back and forth from one dimension to another." My call home is a comfort, yet leaves me feeling more alone.

In the morning, beneath the stark, whitish morning light, Prince George takes on a different feel. This morning, it's a pleasant northerly place from which to turn southward.

Midway through *Travels*, Steinbeck digresses to explore a word from the Spanish language, "vacilando" for which he has a fondness. *Vacilando*, which has no good English equivalent, "does not mean vacillating at all. If one is vacilando, he is going somewhere, but doesn't care greatly whether or not he gets there, although he has direction."

That's me, on this day.

From my first few minutes on our east-bound VIA Rail car I know this ride will be different from my trip on the Cariboo Prospector. The VIA Rail car feels empty with hardly a dozen passengers on board. I speak to the conductor about the problem I expect in Jasper, where we are scheduled to miss, by fifteen minutes, the west-bound train which would take me home. He's sympathetic and confers with the woman who had issued my ticket. A couple of phone calls later, they have it all worked out.

I'm to get off in a town called Harvey, where a taxi will be waiting to take me to Valemount, where I'll intercept the west-bound train a few hours later. The woman at the ticket booth seems perplexed that I don't mind missing Jasper, the destination of this route. But I'm relieved not to have to wander through the streets of Jasper for seven hours, waiting for a Greyhound.

No one shows me a map, so I'm at a loss to picture Harvey, let alone its relation to Valemount. But I trust these people, and they're clearly satisfied by the plan, if perplexed by the spirit of *vacilando*—and no wonder, since they have no word for the thing.

Three hours along on our ride, my stomach is growling complaint, and I realize that no one will be bringing food. Nor will anyone direct us to move to the left side and look down at the salmon spawning, or hover to be sure we see the falls. We are left alone here, which I find agreeable, but for my hunger.

A restless young boy shows me, by example, that I am free to wander car to car: a wonderful freedom. I discover the joy of stepping into the cold air and the hissing wind between cars, and make my way to the deserted dome car. Outside, it's snowing, and the sky is pearly grey. Snow hits the windows around me, collapsing into water droplets that skitter off, forming patterns. It's an inversion of those shake-up Christmas bubbles: I am inside the bubble; the snow is sealed outside.

I travel this entire leg of my journey mapless. On the previous day's trip, we were issued maps with information (altitude, historical sketches, anecdotes) about the route. But solitude has its price; I'll adjust to the maplessness.

Steinbeck classifies people according to their reliance on maps: Ther are those "whose joy is to lavish more attention on the sheets of colored paper than on the colored land rolling by" and another kind who "requires to know in terms of maps exactly where he is pin-pointed every moment, as though there were some kind of safety in black and red lines, in dotted indications" and in "shadings that indicate mountains."

Steinbeck claims to have been "born lost," and wishes neither to be found, nor to establish identity "from shapes which symbolize continents and states." Once, he leaves Rocinante to rendezvous with his wife in a hotel, carrying a change of clothes wrapped inside of road maps—having brought along no suitcase.

Like Steinbeck, I was born lost, and for me orientation comes hard, when it comes at all. I don't form useful mental images in three dimensional space. My husband, on the other hand, seems able to merge map image with landscape, forming a seamless sense of place.

I do consult maps, but with different expectations—and certainly with different results. Before I left my hotel in Prince George, I ran my finger along the path we had followed, drinking in the names of places I had travelled to get there: Britannia Beach, Cheekeye River, Birken, Seton Portage, Shalalth, Ahbau Creek Bridge, 108 Ranch, Soda Creek. In my memory they will likely float free from their geographical axis, affixing themselves, instead, to a nuance of climate, a subtlety of mood.

On this day, we are travelling along the Fraser River. At every turn the river reveals some new aspect of itself—a steep bank, whitecaps frothing over a crop of rocks, a twist or bend, a tributary. The trees that line the river form tall, spare silhouettes of brown and grey-green. One tree has died and sunk, decaying, into the limbs of a neighbour tree. For how many decades has it kneeled in that embrace? One particular tree, a great sprawling conifer, has managed to take hold and grow on a barren ledge out over the river, from which it leans into the wind.

For hours I watch, expecting to see a bear, or a fox, or even elk. I know they inhabit this land, that they drink from the river and seek shelter from the winds. But I never do see one. On this whole trip, the only wildlife I've glimpsed have been five white mountain goats, occasional eagles, and three fat raccoons scurrying through an alley in North Vancouver.

As we bump along toward Jasper, the whine of the train over the rails, and the periodic clang and hiss, grow steadily more familiar. The side-to-side rocking combined with the steady hurtling forward mesmerize me. When we finally do pull into Harvey, I step off reluctantly. Despite a surge of relief that I'm moving closer to home, I already know that this will have been the finest instalment of my three-part rail journey.

The interior landscape, though less dramatic than the coast, is stirring and graceful. I love the river's inland swell. The yellow leaves of the aspens float on its surface, swirling into designs with the current. The Rockies first rise in the distant sky, then surround us, pulling us eastward.

It's cold in Harvey, and the sky is blue. There's snow in the mountains and in the air. My cab sits waiting. The driver has the rasping voice of a heavy smoker. In Valemount she shows me exactly where to catch the train, for which I don't have the sense to be grateful until, three and a half hours later, I notice the spot is unmarked. She collects her twenty dollars and leaves me at a hotel. I stand there missing her as much as one can miss an acquaintance of thirty minutes.

At the hotel they let me stash my bags at the back of the bar. I walk across the tracks and into town, which is three blocks of Main Street. In a Home Hardware I pick up gifts for our kids, and in a small grocery store I buy food. All the while, there's a strangeness I can't shake. From the glances thrown my way I get the distinct feeling that outsiders rarely venture into Valemount. Two teen-age girls just out of school hurry along the sidewalk in front of me, snickering. I slow down and slink off down a side street—wishing to stop noticing, or caring. "I'm not so strange," I'd like to tell them, "and not staying long."

But I just keep walking.

It's dark by 5:35 p.m., when I am waiting to intercept the train. Fifteen minutes before The VIA Line #1 is scheduled to appear, I stand exactly as directed by my cab-driver, on an unlit patch of gravel and weeds along the edge of the tracks a few feet from a wooden "Valemount" sign. For the briefest moment chill and boredom set in. Then the train approaches. I actually *feel* it first, a slight vibration which expands to become audible. As the vibration—punctuated by shrill whistle blasts—intensifies, so too does my heart rate, until the triangle of white lights hurls into view, flying straight towards me.

I jump back, then edge myself forward again, afraid alternately of being run over, or remaining unseen. With a hiss and whistle, the train lurches to a grinding stop. But instead of opening its doors to me, the train resumes its forward motion. I race along beside it, waving like a madwoman, desperate not to be left behind. Leaning out his window, the conductor waves me back, shouting something I can't decipher. The car for me to board turns out to be further down the line. A uniformed trainman reaches out to guide me up two metal steps, helping me up into the third of six cars full of sleepy passengers—many of whom have been together since Toronto, more than thirty hours earlier. Settling into my seat, I know that I have neither the luxury of wandering, nor of solitude.

Behind us a crisis erupts: A drunk young Japanese tourist is being thrown off; a quarrelsome Australian woman is taking up his cause (with more vigour and tenacity than even he seems inclined to exhibit); a lanky German student seems compelled to join the fray (limited though he is by immaturity and language). For the first hour the fracas is a welcome diversion, since the geographical drama unfolding outside is shrouded in darkness. But as the hours pass, pillows and blankets materialize, and one by one the wearied passengers drop off to sleep.

Resting my head on my pack, I also drift off—into a dream that I have missed my stop. Shaking myself awake, I stare out into the rushing, light-studded darkness.

"So much there is to see, but our morning eyes describe a

different world than do our afternoon eyes, and surely our wearied evening eyes can report only a weary evening world," admits Steinbeck.

All of those Vancouver-bound VIA-rail travellers will soon be hurtling along the western segment of the Fraser River—past some of the most glorious scenery imaginable—in the darkest hours of the night. Too bad they'll probably remember the interior of British Columbia as a vast, drowsy world. In Kamloops, I brush quietly past them, gather up my bags, and step off the train alone.

It will take a few days to dispel the effects of travel. No matter how brief the duration, when a family member goes away, the family seems to close in around that absence, adjusting to it, shifting their equilibrium. So a homecoming inevitably brings a measure of confusion and uneasiness. Often, too, a trip changes a person—perhaps so subtly that only a family could discern the changes. If, indeed, "the trip takes us," as Steinbeck claims, then it also seems to leave us transformed.

By the time I've dragged my bags across the dark, deserted parking lots of the train station and, with relief, located the car left there for me, I am at least accustomed to moving on solid ground again.

Against the driver's seat rests a sign that fairly shouts, "Welcome home, Mom!" in bold crayon lines of bright colour.

# Decentering the Core

Early one Monday, on a cold spring morning, the thirteen year old daughter of a colleague died. She had taken her own life, though for a week she'd survived the attempt—brain-dead, and tearing her family apart. I have tried not to think about it, but I can't release it, either.

A friend described the child's funeral as a traditional Christian affair all through which the mother wailed, sitting apart from her family for reasons which no one can explain. The girl lay in an open casket, looking tiny in her sari, and wearing pink lipstick.

This family lives astride two or even three cultures. My colleague is Indian, and her husband comes from Fiji. Their three children were born in Canada. I don't know much more about them, though I can imagine the stress of trying to raise a teenage daughter across chasms of value and idiom.

As for the harrowing turmoil of grief, guilt, or shame that could keep a mother separate from her loved ones through the funeral of a child: This I cannot even imagine.

Though our children were close in age, and we taught classes along the same hallways, we seldom talked. I felt distant from this woman. That troubled me. Maybe the distance was not personal, but rather cultural. I don't know. My own shyness, my longing for privacy, has troubled me for years. But this woman appeared shy also, certainly reserved. We share a social awkwardness which might have bound us together.

I was reading this morning, with half a sad heart, a book called *National Culture and the New Global System*, by Frederick Buell. I bought it months ago in one of those dark moods when I fear losing my intellectual rigour and so push myself, as a kind of penance, into a turgid study which will illuminate (or so I hope) something near and dear.

My study of Buell's hefty black book took me through his lengthy introduction, then the conclusion, then those middle chapters which hinted of promise. The book is about post-modernism, and, more specifically, the impact of cultural relativism. Midway, a section called "Decentering the Core" enticed me.

In it I found an image which did, in fact, shed some light upon issues of separation and of the rift from culture to culture. The image comes from Buell's deliberations upon the main character from a 1957 novel, *No No Boy*. This character is "torn by his alienation from his Japanese-American peers," after having refused to serve in the U.S. war effort.

> . . . He feels painfully that his fragmented identity is neither Japanese nor American. However, he experiences a small vision of hope, not by resolving his identity contradictions, but by generalizing the agony. He discovers that 'maybe the answer is that there is no in . . . that the outside could be the inside . . .'

On another page of the same chapter I found this sentence, which I set down here just to remind myself of the cost for extracting such a thought:

> In the preceding chapters, we have gradually shifted from analyzing the decentering of the culture of the core under

the interplay of two distinct and multifactorial narratives, one global and one national-local, to a perception that transformations in the core have been increasingly directly driven by, and interlock with, changes in the overall fabric of core-periphery relationships in the world system.

I consider myself a good reader, and if I run that sentence through my brain a few times, I come out, I think, with some inkling of what this man may wish to suggest. I think it might be this: Immigration is complex beyond any dimension that either the immigrants themselves, or the bureaucrats governing immigration ever even imagine. The impact plays out over generations, and reverberates endlessly in the surrounding culture and language and society.

Perhaps that isn't in the least what Buell meant to say, but it's a thought worth pondering, all the same.

Last week one of my students, an immigrant from Korea, waited at the doorway to catch me after class. She looked nervous and teary. Could I help her, she wanted to know.

She needed to withdraw from my course. Her ability in that class was more than adequate and I would miss having her—another mature woman, and a mother—in my literature class. But she couldn't balance the required class work with her work at home. She said she'd keep going in her other courses. This woman does not have academic goals, but needed, she explained, to learn English to raise her boys.

Relieved, I suspect, from the weight of her request, she talked on, words tumbling out and tripping over one another as though desperate for expression: It was so hard, she said, to raise boys who couldn't speak much Korean (or didn't want to), when her own English was so limited. While she could read English well, she became easily lost with listening, and could be difficult to understand. She was worried about her older child, who didn't seem to respect her. Her husband, also Korean, was raised in Canada and so didn't speak Korean any better than his boys did.

I tried to encourage this lovely, lonely woman to keep insisting upon clear communication and a modicum of respect for herself. But the tears she blinked back suggested that I was speaking of an interminable struggle which left her frail and weary. She would, I suspected, just keep plugging along; moving level by level through our academic ESL programme, surrounded by wealthy and unencumbered young international students.

Like the student who struggled, and that poor child who gave up the struggle, my mother was raised in a family dislocated—decentered—culturally and linguistically. She was born in Maine, in the new country, one of a pair of twins and last in a long line of children, in an Italian-American family.

I know from hushed family stories that my grandfather sang opera, that he was handsome and also given to violent outbursts. And from early memory I know Grandma was tiny, hard working, with long hair of which she was proud. They came by ship from the old country. They were young, filled with hope, carrying no more than their clothing and three small children.

Their older children grew up very Italian. All the children of my uncles and my oldest aunt speak Italian fluently, as do some of their children's children. And many of my aunt's offspring, both generations, are practising Catholics. One cousin is studying to become a priest.

At the other end of the family, my mother—child of worn-out parents, with siblings gone to college or war, and a fiercely individual woman in her own right—did not want her children speaking Italian. My oldest brother, who grew up surrounded by cousins and doting aunts, learned naturally, despite her intentions. He and my sisters all know nursery rhymes and songs, and the oft-heard curses. I know not a word.

My mother grew up, and remains, a proud and patriotic American. She follows the political situation in the U.S. closely, and argues with vigour and pleasure with my more conservative brother.

Yet, here I am, some hundred years after my grandparents arrived in their new country, an immigrant in Canada. It's my adopted country and my home. I'm more comfortable here than in the U.S. Last year I applied for dual citizenship, and this year I will be sworn in: a Canadian at last.

When Canadians make disparaging remarks about the U.S., as they commonly do, I get confused for a moment, at finding myself the subject of apologetic, or sometimes accusing, glances. It's an unsettling reminder of my invisible status as an American, which remains despite loyalty, or inclination to belong here.

My mother and I have never talked about my leaving home, my emigration. But I notice how she sends my children little gifts on Valentine's Day, or for Christmas: a ruler with pictures of all the American presidents; a replica of Plymouth Rock; a video of coastal Maine; a picture book about the Battle of 1812. She keeps reminding them of what I so often disregard: Their mother is an American.

And my husband and I keep waiting for her to remind them that their grandmother is Italian. She seldom does. I suspect that for my mother, there's so much about her heritage that she grew up trying to deny—the shame of an accent, the dark complexion and dated clothing, all that pasta they ate, day after day, through the years of financial strain.

My own children would eat pasta five days a week, if I'd make it that often. My husband would love to learn Italian and dreams of touring Tuscany. Me, I just want to become a good Canadian.

# Greek Salad Evades Me

Over the last decade, my cooking has taken a slow dive. Chicken canneloni, tarragon carrot bisque, *creme* caramels emerge from vague memory, prompted by the spattered recipe cards I leaf through in search of variations on Rice Krispy squares.

For me, the notion of a full-blown, many-course meal has become wed to Christmas and Thanksgiving. Roast turkey with all the trimmings is all the extravagance I can muster.

What I *have* managed to perfect in these years of frantic food preparation and guilt-laden nutritional awareness, is salad. Salad-making has become the prominent feature in my cuisine, the source of pride and basis of inventiveness.

Let me share a recipe, and a sad story. If you know these feelings of domestic despair, then accept my recipe as a small gift of commiseration.

Friends insist that this salad bears not the remotest relationship to *real* Greek salad. What I say to that is "Who cares?" My tone is not cheekiness, nor defiance, but rather a ragged disregard. It lacks the boldness and vitality of those other feelings.

The recipe goes like this:

Take half a head of cauliflower and break it into bite-sized pieces; pour boiling water over it and let it sit for two minutes or so. Red cabbage does fine, in its place. Whisk together half a cup of olive oil with the juice of a large lemon, a tablespoon of oregano, a pinch of dried mustard, lots of pepper, some salt, a chopped clove of garlic.

Drain the cauliflower, and pour the dressing over it. Chop half a cucumber, dice two Roma tomatoes, slice some green onions, and crumble a chunk of feta cheese. Add those things, plus one small avocado, chopped, and a handful of salty black olives; stir gently so as not to break up the feta and avocado. Chill.

Understand that a recipe, for me, is a generality. It's more important, I think, to appreciate how acid blends with oil, and to enjoy how a pinch of dried mustard or sugar binds them in a lemony suspension. There's artistry in how balsamic vinegar suffuses a salad with musty sweetness. A handful of currants can shift the direction of a salad, while the merest spoonful of capers will take it the other way entirely.

Besides texture and taste, pacing is critical. If a kid in tears or a phone call from the district zoning commissioner should come between the blanching and the draining of the cauliflower, put it in soup.

But *this* year, I've reached a new phase in my domestic maturation. Culinary confidence has come and gone, and returned, though diluted. The increasing maturity of our kids has freed some time; their bigger appetites have motivated production. But my memory loss—that inability to hold more than five thoughts at any given time—wreaks havoc with even the simplest plan!

For weeks I had Greek Salad in my week's meal plans. And on the grocery list I dutifully listed the necessary ingredients. But each day I pulled out vegetables from the drawer of the fridge, only to find one essential ingredient missing. Once, I'd used the avocado for tacos, an idea inspired by a plate of leftover chicken. Another time, the green onions went on sandwiches as our older son went through an onion-and-cheese phase. Then, no feta—only a container of milky, salted liquid kept, no doubt, as a reminder to buy more; refrigerated in a haze of distraction.

The day that I found myself out of lemons, I nearly wept. The following week I left the grocery store with no lemons, list in hand, lemons on list. That's when I felt the hand of fate pushing against my forehead. I put lemons on every list. Consequently, my husband assumed quantity was the issue and brought home a three pound bag. Alas, no cucumber.

I could end on an upbeat note: Last night we had a perfect Greek Salad. There's also a jar of bean salad marinating. I'm on top again. But I can't help wondering: How did it get this hard? And what's coming next?

# Journal Notes

## June 18, 1999

Two things on my mind.

One is popsicles, of all things. Mont brought them home for the kids yesterday. It's been so cold and rainy this May and June, that the first sunny day must have prompted him. Those popsicles were extravagant treats, bigger than they used to be, with wildly contrasting colours of ice spiralling up the edges, culminating in a twist.

I remember no such designer treats when we were kids. There were Popsicles: one brand, in five or six flavours, a nickel apiece. What's remarkable is how Mont and I, growing up in different countries, shared favourite popsicle flavours: rootbeer first; banana second. For third place, we differ. For me orange; him, chocolate.

Mont and I have tastes which diverge steadily as we get older, his moving toward pepper, chilies, hot mustard; mine, moderate to begin with, becoming bland. So it's a pleasant surprise, a small affirmation of our basic compatibility, that we share this remembered fondness for rootbeer popsicles. Presuming, of course, that half the population doesn't also share the preference (along with memories of Ed Sullivan, and hula hoops).

But what common connections of memory will our kids share, in their globe-trotting, choice-laden world?

◦

Also on my mind, thoughts about our neighbour Cameron's death, about the day of his wake at the Heffley Creek Hall, the funeral itself, and the bizarre tangle of logistics we negotiated to get there and home again (Nicole at Battle of the Bands at Sagebrush, where time stood still for me, sitting at the back watching band after band play, then waiting again, for adjudication; J home on bus with Bri, who babysat till Erin came; after which their mother returned from the funeral to take Erin to dance lessons, dropping J off at the hall, to get picked up by me, on way home from band thing, with N. . . ).

We escort friends to death just as we usher in our young—a crazy lifestyle, but not all together unsatisfying. That evening, for the first time, we talked about dying. Feeling both drained and also satisfied to have gracefully gotten through it all helped, I think.

We grieve despite ourselves, and shape our traditions to our own strange rhythms of living.

◦

Sept. 20<sup>th</sup>, '99

Just home from our Yakima Valley wine tour, our twentieth anniversary get-away. Good times, great drives, with the fragrance of grapes, apples, mint and wine. And five promising bottles of red, tucked in the wine cupboard.

Maybe it's a passing phase, but these days James brings me little gifts, disentangling them from pocket fuzz as he comes through the door from school, dropping packsack and jacket.

I have received, in this order: one rose hip, one mushroom, one dried seed pod, one acorn, three white rocks, and one pencil stub with small bear attached who holds aloft an Australian flag.

◦

## October 15th, 1999

Yesterday it snowed and I became a Canadian citizen. The snow was a surprise, coming this early in the fall, on the brightest of cornflower blue days. The flakes drifting down among falling yellow leaves seemed out of place.

The citizenship court ceremony took place in the gymnasium of John Peterson Secondary School, in town. Because we only got the notice last night, too late for arranging around work and school, I went there alone. The gym smelled of stale sweat, and bold posters shouted *BELIEVE, ACHIEVE, SUCCEED*. Seated on benches in one corner, band students chewed gum, squirmed, shot conspiratorial looks at one another, or gaped at nothing, eyes glazed with boredom. I had pictured a setting more regal, and my family around me.

The sixty-three of us who were becoming citizens sat in three rows of folding chairs. We had come here, to Canada, from twenty-three different countries. Facing us, up on a none-too-sturdy platform, stood a resplendent RCMP officer, whose booming voice called us to order before the judge strode in.

Two hours later, about ten minutes after the three o'clock bell had rung—causing the band members' restlessness to shoot up two notches—we had sworn our oath, sung our new anthem (once in English, with robust enthusiasm; again, in French, sounding rather more feeble): We were Canadians! Despite the setting, despite being alone, I was swept up by a current of emotion.

We shook hands and even embraced one another. Family members posed their newest Canadian relatives between judge and mountie for photographs. Children proceeded shyly toward a table of cookies and punch. One family of Lebanese was still hooting and hugging one another when I gathered up my certificate, small flag, and scrolled copy of the Canadian Charter of Rights, and made my way home.

# Snowloads and Landmarks

The most memorable stories will sometimes arise from the most ordinary circumstances. At morning coffee, while doing a renovation at the Seven-O Ranch, an hour's drive south of home, my husband was making small talk amongst men he'd never before met. Talk got around to locale, as it often does in the country. He was describing where we live.

Describing the location of a home in a rural area such as ours is not a matter of reeling off a street address, nor even a couple of prominent landmarks. Landmarks are cattle-guards (numbering four, to our place), bends in the road (which are many), or sign posts (which are few). My husband's description brought a flash of recognition from one old ranch hand, prompting this story, which belonged to his wife.

This woman had lived at a lumber mill situated on Little Heffley Lake, where the Urchit's place now stands. Back then, dances would sometimes be held in the community hall which we drive past now on our way to the farm where we pick up our Thanksgiving turkey each fall.

That little community hall—a tall, narrow wooden structure, with a pitched roof—still rises against the slopes about ten paces back along the west side of the Louis Creek Road.

On the day of a dance, all the young people along the Tod Mountain Road would pile in the back of an open truck to get there. Bumping along the long, cold ten miles they kept warm

297

by burying themselves in straw. They must have been quite a sight when they arrived: flecks of straw adhering to wool, chaff scattered on shining hair. Imagine their excitement, after the dark, quiet winter nights spent with family in rough hewn homes separated by long stretches of dark space.

The occasion of this particular story was not a dance at the hall, however. It was a Christmas party at the Whitecroft Ranch, which sprawls at the juncture of the two roads, in the flat valley bottom at the base of Tod Mountain.

Because the ranch was not too far, the party-goers were hiking there. Four of them—two couples—were trekking the seven miles between Little Heffley and Whitecroft. They started out in the early afternoon, planning to head back the next morning after staying the night.

They would have been travelling along the Shaw Road. Today that road sashays alongside the newer Tod Mountain Road. Sometimes the two run together for a ways. But where we live, the old road meanders off, providing one of my favourite running trails and giving way to the long steep driveways of our neighbours to the south. This was where the two couples were trudging, through deep snow, on a December afternoon like today, the last light of day having fallen off behind the ridge that juts up between the old road and the new one.

The fir trees along that stretch of land rise eighty to ninety feet from the ground, forming a thick, grey-green ceiling pierced at night only by the most persistent moonlight. The straight trunks of those trees are easy to walk between, since undergrowth is discouraged by their thick roots and dense overhead canopies.

Picture these four: for a while chattering, then singing perhaps; now silent, meditating on the rhythmic squeaking of boots settling in snow. Then, slicing through that blackness, a heart-stopping *whuump!* All four began to run—no time for the boys to be chivalrous, or the girls demure. From a distance they stopped to discover the source of terror: a hefty snow load released by one of those high fir limbs. Maybe the vibrations of their voices or the thudding of their heavy boots had triggered that release. Or maybe the temperature had risen a degree, shifting, ever so slightly, the finely balanced accumulation.

Imagine the nervous laughter, the warmth of cheeks blushing red, the prickly heat of fear chased by relief. How easily we can locate a memory of those sensations. And how reliably the sensation, remembered, triggers the story which caused it.

I have been on long silent runs along the same road, barely a path in some places, when the impact of a stone dislodged or mud flying off from the soles of my runners has frightened me to a stand-still. Paralysis yields to thumping pulse and heaving breath, as the recognition floods my stunned brain that the stalker amounts to no more than the momentum of my own stride.

Regardless of years of rural living, a comfortable familiarity with the landscape and a passing acquaintance with the neighbourhood brown bears, we do remain susceptible to the wildness around us, and to our own keen powers of imagination.

Thinking about these pathways and roadways, and the stretch of years in this lake region from the days of those young party-goers to now, leaves me thinking about the twists and turns into the next century. Landmarks distinguish those twists and turns, serving to keep us oriented. They designate boundaries, and also turning points. Sometimes, they mark time and distance for the inhabitants of a place. More often, though, landmarks serve to guide the unfamiliar into new territory.

One Christmas before we were married, as a landmark to

299

guide me to the Ontario farmhouse he and three friends were renting, my husband used a green mailbox at the end of the driveway. I must have driven back and forth past that yellow brick farmhouse six times before I stopped, on a hunch, to brush the thick white frost off from a mailbox, revealing its dark green undercoat.

Another time, also in December, I was on my first trip to this area we now call home. I had a sequence of detailed instructions to guide me through the last of twelve hours of driving, up to BC from Montana. But the "twelve miles from the turn-off" didn't help much, since both the speedometer and odometer of my 1950 Ford Coupe had long been defunct. Travel-lagged and wholly unused to unlit, winding, rural roads, I could not fathom twelve miles. The "four cattle-guards" should have helped. But I had no inkling of what a cattle-guard *was*, and I was so utterly weary that not even the jarring of tires passing over iron bars would yield its clue.

Embarrassed and in tears, I pulled over at one of the few homes visible from the road, hiked up the long driveway, knocked, and asked to use the phone. So much for self-reliance and figuring things out for myself. The voice at the other end of the phone told me to get back in my car and drive the remaining five miles, then turn at the BC Tel shack, just as the crumbled sheet of directions advised. I wondered if I'd know a BC Tel shack, when I saw the thing. (I did.)

Still, some twenty years later, I cringe when I drive past that home rising above the Knouff Lake turn-off, where I stopped to use the phone on that long drive. Knowing now how unusual it is, in these parts, to have a stranger knock at your door, I wonder what that family made of me—a weepy, lost American girl, going to visit her boyfriend.

In the midst of a wide expanse of grassy pasture—further up the road from the Knouff Lake turn-off—on a plateau not far from the cluster of homes which rise above Little Heffley, stood what we called The Chinaman's House. It was a significant landmark for those of us who drove the distance to Kamloops daily. To me it always felt like half-way, though it was actually closer to home than that: something about feeling that you were beyond the reach of town, or maybe the way that house drew your eyes up toward the northern bluffs, just as you turned the corner and dipped gently downward before the long ascent.

The old man who had lived there came from China, probably to find work on the railway, along with so many others. But he'd ended up working for the local ranchers and squatting on that lovely bit of land, in a carefully tended, greying wooden home. Then, in the early 1980's, a new owner ripped down that house, taking with it all traces of the landmark—but not the memory of it standing there. One neighbour has a painting of The Chinaman's House above the fireplace in his living room.

Landmarks occupy my mind during long runs, in the meditative stages where effort gives way to aimless reflection. What will become the landmarks for the next generations who take up residence on this land? In the way that the rise of a particular bluff, or a stand of firs or a sharp bend in the road can trigger that lovely memory of the teens hiking to a party, will this area conjure up stories which will attach themselves to the landscape when our children's children come back to this place?

I imagine a young dark-haired granddaughter casting her eyes at the meadow where our sheep pens now stand, and telling a friend how her grandparents once lost five sheep to a cougar in that very place. And that once her father, when he was a scrawny five-year-old, tried to catch a chick, got chased by an irate banty hen, and took refuge on the roof of the doghouse.

I can conjure up a round-eyed grandson who likes to tell the story of how his mother got knocked face first into the manure pile when the sheep stampeded through to pasture one mucky spring morning. Or how she'd been knocked off a toboggan, driven by her brother, as she was coming down the rocky, tree-studded hill that spilled below their home.

But by then, our homestead might have vanished entirely from view—like the Chinaman's House—perhaps mentioned only in the stories that neighbours tell to one another.

# Acknowledgments and Credits

Versions of the following essays have appeared in the publications noted, to which I am grateful:

"The Chaos Theory," in *High Plains Literary Review*, Spring 1992 (cited by Robert Atwan in *Best American Essays, 1992*)

"The Rhythms That Bind Us," also in *High Plains*, Fall 1995

"Between Outlook and Appearance," in the *Washington English Journal*, Spring 1992

"Inside the Lions," (as "I Wish I Were a Star") in *Mothering*, Winter 1993

"The Gifts We Give," in *North Dakota Quarterly*, Spring 1994

"The Stuff of Life, in the *Christmas Blues Anthology*, published by Amador, in 1995

"Montana Nights," in *Grand Tour* (sadly, no longer), Summer 1996

"High Notes," in *Harpweaver*, Fall 1996

"Finding the Canadian Side," in *The River Review/la Revue Riviere*, Fall 1997

"Studies in Silence," as part of "A Few Simple Stories, One Tough Question," in *Wordworks* (the B.C. Writers' Federation Publication), Fall 1998

"Potluck," in *Canadian Women Studies*, Spring 1998

"Things That Fall from the Sky" as "Twenty-five Years with *War and Peace*," in *Missouri Review*, Vol. 23, no. 1, 2000

I also wish to acknowledge the University College of the Cariboo for generously approving a semester's assisted leave of absence in the fall of 1997, and for generally and variously supporting my writing habit.